The
John Donne
Treasury

Dr. Erwin P. Rudolph, Editor

While this book is designed for the reader's personal enjoyment and profit, it is also intended for group study. A leader's guide is available from your local bookstore or from the publisher at $.75.

VICTOR BOOKS

a division of SP Publications, Inc., Wheaton, Illinois
Offices also in Fullerton, California • Whitby, Ontario, Canada • London, England

Library of Congress Catalog Number:
ISBN: 0-88207-514-4

© 1978 by SP Publications, Inc.
    World rights reserved
    Printed in the United States of America

VICTOR BOOKS
A division of SP Publications, Inc.
P.O. Box 1825 Wheaton, Ill. 60187

CONTENTS

John Donne, The Man

John Donne was a brilliant master of verse and prose; he also had something substantive to convey. His works are charged with a vital energy, and certain passages are unforgettable: "Our life is a warfare; God would not choose cowards." "And therefore never send to know for whom the bell tolls; it tolls for thee." "No man is an island, entire of itself; every man is a piece of the continent, and part of the main . . . Any man's death diminishes me because I am involved in mankind." "Batter my heart, three-personed God." "On a huge hill / cragged and steep, truth stands."

Contemporary interest in Donne may be accounted for in part by such significant studies as Sir Edmund Gosse's *Life and Letters of John Donne* and Sir Herbert Grierson's two-volume edition of the *Poems;* also, John Sparrow's edition of the *Devotions* and the more recent 10-volume edition of the *Sermons* by George Potter and Evelyn Simpson. T.S. Eliot, W. B. Yeats, and C. S. Lewis have also helped stimulate renewed interest in Donne's abounding vitality and penetrating thought.

The details of Donne's early life are not well-known. He was born in London in 1572. His father, a prosperous tradesman, died when Donne was about five years old, and he was left to the care of his distinguished mother, who made every effort to "improve his knowledge."

He entered Oxford in 1584 and studied law at Lincoln's Inn in 1591. Between these two dates he is thought to have studied for a time at Cambridge.

Although his family was Roman Catholic, Donne began early to reject the dogmas of that church. He was by nature bold, restless, and impatient of convention. His early poems display a reaction against the smooth lyricism of the Petrarchan convention, and reveal a daring to flout the gods of regularity in both form and subject matter. He could be cynical of platonic love and yet he could extol it. As Herbert Grierson reminds us, "A spirit of skepticism and paradox plays through and disturbs everything he wrote."

After a privateering trip with the Earl of Essex to the Azores, Donne returned to England. He became secretary to Sir Thomas Egerton, Lord Keeper of the Great Seal, and was subsequently sent on responsible missions abroad. This promising start to his diplomatic career miscarried when he met and secretly married Anne More, niece of Lady Egerton. Anne was 17, and under age. When her father discovered their marriage, he had Donne thrown into prison for a time, on the charge of breaking the civil and canon law of marrying a girl without her father's consent.

The ideal love Donne felt for his wife lasted to the end of his life and was a stabilizing force. However, years of financial insecurity followed. Poverty, sickness, a growing family, and delayed preferment proved very discouraging. During this period Donne wrote *Biathanatos,* a pamphlet justifying suicide under certain circumstances. For a time he thought of coming to

America. The mother of the poet, George Herbert, aided and sustained him during part of this crisis.

Donne's background and his knowledge of divinity enabled him to assist Bishop Morton in his controversy with the Catholics. Morton was so impressed with Donne that he offered him a position in the Anglican church. Donne felt unsuited for such a calling, even though he was financially pressed; he chose rather to wait for a political or courtly appointment.

Later, there came a reconciliation with Anne's father, who agreed to furnish a regular allowance as Anne's dowry. Donne also won the patronage of Sir Robert Drury for writing an elegy on the death of his younger daughter, Elizabeth. Life became more comfortable and happy as he met with friends at Drury House or with those gathered around Lucy, Countess of Bedford, at Twickenham Garden.

Donne's continued effort to win court preferment was unsucessful, as the King was determined to secure his services for the Church. After further study of divinity and a personal struggle with his conscience, Donne finally entered the Anglican church in 1615. Quick advancement followed. He became chaplain of James I, and at the King's request, was granted an honorary degree from Cambridge. He was made divinity reader at Lincoln's Inn and in 1621 was appointed Dean of St. Paul's.

Anne lived only two years after Donne's decision to enter the Anglican church. This accentuated his interest in the subject of death. His *Devotions Upon Emergent Occasions*, composed during an illness in 1623, reveal his delight in analyzing the complicated emotions that filled him as he traced the steps of the disease and faced the prospect of death. Izaak Walton, his contemporary biographer, tells how he even posed for his portrait wrapped in a shroud. He preached frequently on death, and "Death's Duel" was really his own funeral sermon. Death is also treated in such poems as "Death Be Not Proud."

Donne did not leave a record of his experience leading up to his conversion, but the deep repentance he felt for the sins committed in his youth comes up repeatedly in his prose and poetry.

As a theologian, Donne's views differed little from those of Andrewes or Laud. His assistance of Bishop Morton reveals his dislike for papal interference in English affairs. He defended the Reformation as essential, although his tone was usually conciliatory. He held to the fundamental doctrines expressed in the Apostles' and Nicene Creeds, as well as those of the Orthodox Anglican Church. His sermons stressed the birth, death, and resurrection of Christ.

Composed during a serious illness, thought to be spotted fever, in the winter of 1623, *Devotions Upon Emergent Occasions* describe the stages of the disease and even more the power of sin, the miseries of human life, mercy, and the judgment of God. Although very introspective, they are most sincere and reveal the intense spiritual conflict that helps make them instructive devotional reading. While not as eloquent as the sermons, the *Devotions* reveal the metaphysical wit, immense learning, and delight in paradox so characteristic of Donne's mind. He is full of contradictions—a genuine mixture of sinner and saint. Keenly aware of his human mistakes, he was quick to admit them.

Donne was by training and inclination a man of letters. (On his mother's side he came from a family known for its devotion and learning.) His library was well-stocked with Latin classical writers; he was strongly influenced by Virgil, Horace, Ovid, and Cicero, and he knew Greek writers through Latin translation. As a typical Renaissance scholar he had traveled in Spain, France, and Italy and knew something of the language and literature of those countries.

Donne's poems were composed at different times and in different moods. Frequently he is startling and abrupt in his opening lines: "Go and catch a falling star" or "Spit in my face, you Jews, and pierce my side." Both before and after his conversion to Christianity his poems reflect the conflicts and tensions of a mind battling for a solution to conflicts that beset him; his conversion did not change the habit of his mind to strive for truth and clarity of vision. His metaphysical manner was still evident, with images drawn from widely disparate sources. His sonnets, because of their concentration, intensity, and sincerity, are among the best religious verse in the English lanugage.

Perhaps Donne's creative powers as a prose writer are best displayed in his sermons. He was easily the most famous preacher in an age of great preachers. The sermons are not only intense and eloquent, but they reveal a keen knowledge of the Scriptures (in the Latin Vulgate, as well as the English of the Geneva Bible and Authorized Version), the Church Fathers, and the Schoolmen. He also reveals an interest in many fields, such as law, medicine, and science. The parishioner at times may have been repelled by the many Latin quotations from unfamiliar authors and the frequent Latin phrases. However, his aim was not so much to impress as it was, in Walton's words, to carry "some to Heaven in holy rapture and enticing others by a sacred art and courtship to amend their lives."

Stylistically, Donne knew how to use the long paragraph, marshalling his clauses for cumulative effect. Sometimes he used the homely phrase or image to convey his meaning. He knew the Ciceronian manner of juxtaposing a short, pithy sentence against a long one. His sermons were saturated with the language of Hebrew poetry as found in the Psalms and Prophets, with the musical devices of balance, parallelism, and antithesis. He used alliteration and repetition of key words from clause to clause without overdoing it. When he chose, he could be terse like Bunyan or rhetorical like Milton.

Donne's eloquence and personality enhanced the effect of his sermons upon the audience. Walton said, "He was a preacher in earnest, weeping sometimes for his auditory, sometimes with them, always preaching to himself like an angel from a cloud." Behind the rhetoric was the voice of a human soul agonizing over his past sins and the power of temptation, entreating his hearers to prevail upon the mercy of God. Although not popular with the extreme Puritan, Donne was a preacher of great influence who drew large crowds and who was much beloved by the more educated Londoner.

Paradoxical and startling by turns, Donne shook his readers out of complacency. Knowing well both joy and sorrow, he perceived life's ironies and understood the diversity of the human predicament. He revealed a tension and soul-searching with which people of any age may easily identify. His vision, however, remains undimmed, and his works continue to inspire new life in the Spirit.

The writer of a Christian devotion has for his controlling purpose the aiding of the reader in his quest for the "godly" life. In his preaching, and to a marked extent in his writings, Donne strove to raise the intellectual and spiritual level of his hearers; his achievement has earned for him a place in the tradition of great devotional literature.

Part 1

Devotions upon Emergent Occasions

The *Devotions* were divided into 23 sections, each representing a stage of the disease from which he suffered in the winter of 1623, thought to be spotted fever, and each consisting of Meditation, Expostulation, and Prayer. The fever ran its course in about three weeks and left Donne very weak. However, after a protracted convalescence he was able to resume his usual duties.

The *Devotions* reveal Donne's delight in minute introspection; he found a spiritual parallel for each stage of the disease. The passionate sincerity and intensity of the sonnets are evident here in prose. The author writhed "under a sense of God's infinite purity and stern justice," but he took courage as he remembered the death of Christ, and entreated for divine mercy.

1
Man's Condition

Man's Miserable State

Variable, and therefore miserable condition of man! This minute I was well, and am ill, this minute. I am surprised with a sudden change, and alteration to worse, and can impute it to no cause, nor call it by any name. We study health, and we deliberate upon our meats and drink and air and exercises; and so our health is a long and regular work: but in a minute a cannon batters all, overthrows all, demolishes all; a sickness unprevented for all our diligence, unsuspected for all our curiosity, summons us, seizes us, possesses us, destroys us in an instant.

O miserable condition of man! which was not imprinted by God, who, as He is immortal Himself, had put a coal of immorality into us, which we might have blown into a flame, but blew it out by our first sin. We beggared ourselves by hearkening after false riches, and infatuated ourselves by hearkening after false knowledge. Hence, now, we not only die, but die upon the rack by the torment of sickness. Not only that, but we are pre-afflicted, super-afflicted with suspicions, and apprehensions of sickness before we can call it that: we are not sure we are ill.

If I were but mere dust and ashes, I might speak unto the Lord, for the Lord's hand made me of this dust, and the Lord's hand shall re-collect these ashes; the Lord's hand was the wheel upon which this vessel of clay was framed, and the Lord's hand is the urn in which these ashes shall be preserved. I am the dust and ashes of the temple of the Holy Ghost, and what marble is so precious?

But I am more then dust and ashes; I am my best part; I am my soul. And being so, I may breathe back these pious expostulations to my God: My God, my God, why is not my soul as sensible as my body? Why has not my soul these apprehensions, these presages, these suspicions of a sin as well as my body of a sickness? Why is not there always a pulse in my soul to beat at the approach of a temptation to sin? Why is there not always water in my eyes to testify to my spiritual sickness?

I stand in the way of temptations naturally; all men do, for there is a snake in every path, temptations in every vocation. But I run, I fly into the ways of temptation which I might shun; nay, I break into houses where the plague is. I press into places of temptation, and tempt the devil himself. I fall sick of sin and am bedded and buried in the practice of sin, and all the while have no pulse or sense of my sickness. But O my God, You have imprinted a pulse in our soul, but we do not examine it, and a voice in our conscience, but we do not hearken unto it. We talk it out, we jest it out, we sleep it out; and when we wake, we do not say with Jacob, "Surely the Lord is in this place, and I knew it not." Though we might know it, we will not.

But will God pretend to make a watch and leave out the spring? Will He make so many wheels in the faculties of the soul and in the organs of the body and leave out grace that should move them? Or will God make a spring and not wind it up? Or infuse His first grace and not second it with more, without which we can no more use His first grace when we have it than we could dispose ourselves readily by nature to have it?

Alas, that is not our case. We are all prodigal sons, and not disinherited. We have received our portions and misspent them. We are God's tenants here, and yet here, He, our landlord, pays us rents, not yearly, nor quarterly, nor hourly, but every minute He renews His mercy, but we "will not understand, lest that we should be converted, and He should heal us."[1]

Man's State a Paradox

We attribute one privilege and advantage to man's body above other moving creatures: he is not, as others, groveling, but of an erect and upright form, naturally built and disposed to the contemplation of heaven. Indeed, it is a form that carries the soul so many feet higher toward heaven. Other creatures look to the earth, and even that is no unfit object, no unfit contemplation for man. But man is not to stay there, as other

---

[1]Matt. 13:15

creatures; man in his natural form is carried to the contemplation of that place which is his home, heaven.

This is man's prerogative. But what state has he in this dignity? A fever can hurl him down or depose him. A fever can bring that head, which yesterday carried a crown of gold five feet toward a crown of glory, as low as his foot today. When God came to breathe into man the breath of life, He found him flat on the ground. When He comes to withdraw that breath from him again, He prepares him to it by laying him flat on his bed. A sick bed is a grave, and all that the patient says there is but a varying of his own epitaph. Miserable, and (though common to all) inhuman posture, where I must practice my lying in the grave by lying still, and not practice my resurrection by rising anymore.

O Lord, whither shall I come to Thee? To this bed? I cannot sit up, and yet am loathe to go to bed. Shall I find Thee in bed? The bed is not ordinarily Thy scene. Lord, dost Thou not accuse me, dost Thou not reproach me for my former sins when Thou layest my upon this bed? Is not this to hang a man at his own door to lay him sick in his own bed of wantonness? How shall they come to Thee whom Thou hast nailed to their bed?

Thou art in the congregation, and I in a solitude. When Peter's wife's mother lay sick of a fever, Christ came to her; she could not come to Him.[2] My friends may carry me home to Thee in their prayers in the congregation, but Thou must

[2]Matt. 8:14

come home to me in the visitation of Thy Spirit and in the seal of Thy sacrament.

When I am cast into this bed, my slack sinews are iron fetters and those thin sheets iron doors upon me. But Lord, Thou art Lord of hosts and lovest action. Why callest Thou me from my calling? "In the grave no man shall praise Thee." In the door of the grave, this sick bed, no man shall hear me praise Thee. Thou hast not opened my lips that my mouth might show Thee Thy praise. Thou couldst take me by the head, as Thou didst Habakkuk, or by a chariot, as Thou didst Elijah, and carry me forth. But Thou carriest me in Thine own private way by which Thou carriedst Thy Son.

Thy hand strikes me into this bed; therefore, if I rise again, You will be my recompense all the days of my life in making this sickness beneficial to me. And if my body fall yet lower, You will take my soul out of this bath and present it to Your Father, washed again and again in Your own sweat, in Your own tears, in Your own blood.

It is too little to call a man a little world. Excepting God, man is a diminutive to nothing. Man consists of more parts than the world. If those parts were extended and stretched out in man as they are in the world, man would be the giant and the world the dwarf. If all the veins of our bodies were extended to rivers, and all the sinews to veins of mines, and all the muscles that lie upon one another to hills, and all the bones to quarries of stones, and all the other parts to the proportion of those which correspond to them in the world, the air would be too little for the orb of this man to move in.

Enlarge this meditation upon this great world, man, to consider the immensity of the creatures this world produces. Inexplicable mystery! I, their creator, am in a close prison in a sickbed. My thoughts are with the sun and beyond, but as the world produces serpents and vipers and venomous creatures to devour the world which produced them, so this world, ourselves, produces in us venomous and infectious diseases of all sorts. O miserable abundance, O beggarly riches! We have the physician, but we are not the physician. Here we sink in our dignity below the very mean creatures who are physicians to themselves. The hart that is pursued and wounded, they say, knows an herb which, when eaten, throws off the arrow. The dog that pursues it, though he be subject to sickness, knows the grass that makes him recover. But what has become of man's great extent and proportion when he is consumed to a handful of dust? What has become of his soaring thoughts when he must bring himself to thoughts of the grave?

I have not the righteousness of Job, but I have the desire of Job: "I would speak to the Almighty, and I would reason with God."[3] My God, how soon would You have me to go to the physician and how far would You have me go with the physician? I know You have made the matter and the man and the hart and that I go not from You when I go to the physician. But reveal to me Your method, O Lord, and see whether I have followed it, that You may have glory if I have, and pardon if I have not.

---

[3] Job 13:3

I know that even my weakness is a reason, a motive to induce Thy mercy, and my sickness an occasion for Thy sending health. I send for the physician, but I will hear him enter with those words of Peter, "Jesus Christ maketh thee whole."[4] I long for His presence, but I look "that the power of the Lord should be present to heal me."[5]

The Plague of Solitude

As sickness is the greatest misery, so the greatest misery of sickness is solitude—when the infectiousness of the disease deters them who would assist you from coming; even the physician scarcely dares to come. Solitude is a torment which is not threatened in hell itself. When I am dead, and my body might infect, they have a remedy: they bury me. But when I am sick, they have no remedy but their absence and my solitude. It is an excuse for them that are great who are loathe to come; it is an inhibition to those who would truly come because they would be helpful instruments, but might infect others because of their coming.

A long sickness will weary friends at last, but a pestilential sickness averts them from the beginning. God, who saw that all that He made was good, came not so near seeing a defect in any of His works as when He saw that it was not good for man to be alone; therefore, He made him a helper—one that should help him to increase the number, and give him her own and more society. Angels, who do not propagate nor multiply, were

---

[4]Acts 9:34   [5]Luke 5:17

made at first in an abundant number; so were the stars. But for the things of this world, their blessing was *increase*. God, nature, and reason concur against solitude. The height of an infectious disease of the body is solitude—to be left alone. This makes an infectious bed worse than the grave.

Take it not ill, O my God, that I say You have ordained it for a blessing and for a dignity for Your people to dwell alone "and not be reckoned among the nations"[6] and that they should "dwell in safety alone,"[7] and yet You have also said that "two are better than one" and "woe be unto him that is alone when he falleth."[8] I know that Thy Son refused not many solitary times; but at all times He was able to command "more than twelve legions of angels"[9] to His service. When He did not, He was far from being alone. He said, "I am not alone, but I, and the Father that sent Me."[10]

I am not able to pass this agony alone without You. If You or mine abandon me, I am alone, and woe unto me if I be alone. Elias fainted under the apprehension, "Lo, I am left alone,"[11] and Martha murmured, and said to Christ, "Lord, do You not care that my sister has left me to serve alone?"[12] O my God, it is the leper that You have condemned to live alone. Have I such leprosy in my soul that I must die alone without You? May I not remember that though God came not to Jacob till He found him alone, yet when He found him alone, He wrestled with him and lamed him.[13]

---

[6]Num. 23:9   [7]Deut. 33:28   [8]Ecc. 4:10   [9]Matt. 26:53
[10]John 8:16   [11]1 Kings 19:10   [12]Luke 10:40   [13]Gen. 32:24-25

When a man is left alone with God, may his conscience be dealt with faithfully by Him.

Fear Considered

I observe the physician with the same diligence as he the disease. I see he fears, and I fear with him. I overtake him, I overrun him in his fear. I fear the more because he disguises his fear. I know not what fear is: I know not what it is that I fear now. I fear not the hastening of my death, and yet I do fear the increase of the disease. I should belie nature if I should deny that I feared this; and if I should say that I feared death, I should belie God. My weakness is from nature, who has but her measure; my strength is from God, who possesses and distributes infinitely.

My God, I find in Thy Book that fear is a stifling spirit, a spirit of suffocation. It was so in the case of your servant Job who said, "Let Him take His rod away from me, and let not His fear terrify me; then would I speak and not fear Him."[14] Shall a fear of You take away my devotion to You? Do You command me to speak to You and command me to fear You? And do these destroy one another? There is no perplexity in Thee, my God. You are my light—my sun and my moon that direct me in the night of adversity and fear, as well as in my day of prosperity and confidence.

When one prays at midnight, God does not say, "I will hear thee on Sunday at church; God is no dilatory God; prayer is never unseasonable; God is never asleep, nor absent. But O my God, can I do this and fear Thee? Can I speak to Thee in all

---

[14]Job 9:34

places, in all hours, and fear Thee? O my abundant God, how gently dost Thou unentangle me in any scruple arising out of consideration of Thy fear.

Is not this that which You intend when You say, "The secret of the Lord is with them that fear Him"?[15]—have it and benefit by it; have it, and be directed by it rather than dejected with it. And do You not propose the church for our example when You say, the church of Judea "walked not in the fear of God"?[16] They had it, but did not sit down lazily, nor fall down weakly, nor sink under it. There is a fear that weakens men in the service of God. But in Thy fear, my God, is hope and love and confidence and peace. They joy in Thee, O Lord, that fear Thee, and fear Thee only who feel joy in Thee. Thy fear and love are inseparable.

Though I pretend to no other degree of wisdom, I am abundantly rich in this—that I lie here possessed with that fear which is Thy fear, for it is a fearful thing to fall into Thy hands. Yet this fear preserves me from inordinate fear arising out of the infirmity of nature, because Thy hand being upon me will never let me fall out of the infirmity of nature, because Thy hand being upon me will never let me fall out of Thy hand.

As the Heart Inclines

O how little a thing is all the greatness of man, and through how false glasses does he make shift to multiply it and magnify it to himself! He thinks he treads upon the earth with all things under his feet. But the brain that thinks so is but earth. How

---

[15]Ps. 25:14   [16]Acts 9:31

little of man is the heart, and yet it is all that man has or is.

O God of light, I know that You know all and do declare what is in man's heart. I could not know how ill my heart was. You have declared unto me in Your Word that for all this deluge of evil, You sought and found a man after Your own heart.[17] And I can gather out of Your Word good testimony of the hearts of men: docile, straight, clean, perfect hearts. But I find stony hearts, too, and I have made mine such. I have found hearts that are snares, and have conversed with such—hearts that burn like ovens, that fuel on envy, lust, and ambition. I have found these and worse—hearts into which the devil himself has entered. What shall I do?

I humbly beseech Thee to manifest always a more effectual presence in my heart than in the other offices. Into the house of Thy anointed, disloyal persons, traitors, will come; into Thy house, the church, hypocrites and idolaters will come; into some rooms of this house, my body, temptations will come, infections will come; but be my heart Thy bedchamber, O my God, and thither let them not enter.

As Thou has not delivered us, Thine adopted sons, from these infectious temptations, so neither hast Thou delivered us over to them, nor withheld Thy cordials from us. I was baptized in Thy cordial, water, against original sin; and I have drunk of Thy cordial, blood, for my recovery from actual and habitual sin, in the other sacrament . . . I see Thy hand upon me now, O Lord,

---

[17] 1 Sam. 13:14

and I ask not why it comes, what it intends—whether Thou wilt bid it stay still in this body for some time or bid it meet Thee this day in Paradise ... A silent and absolute obedience to Thy will, even before I know it, is my cordial. Preserve that to me, O my God, and that will preserve me to Thee—that when Thou hast catechised me with affliction here, I may take a greater degree and serve Thee in a higher place in Thy kingdom of joy and glory. Amen.

Misery and Happiness: Malignity of Spots

We say that the world is made of sea and land as though they were equal. But we know that there is more sea in the Western than in the Eastern hemisphere. We say the elements of man are misery and happiness, as though he had an equal proportion of both. But it is far from that. He drinks misery, and he tastes happiness; he mows misery and he gleans happiness; he journeys in misery, he does but walk in happiness. And what is worse, his misery is positive and dogmatical, his happiness is but disputable and prob-lematical: all men call misery "misery," but happiness changes the name by the taste of every man.

It is a faint comfort to know the worst when the worst is remediless. A woman is comforted with the birth of her son; her body is eased of a burden. But if she could prophetically read his history, how ill perchance a son would prove, she would receive a greater burden into her mind. There is scarce any purchase that is not clogged with secret encumbrances; there is scarce any happiness that has not in it so much of the nature of false and base money as that the alloy is more than the metal. Is it not so even in the exercise of virtues? I must be poor and wanting before I can exercise the virtue of gratitude; miserable and in torment before I can exercise the virtue of patience. How deep do we dig, and for how coarse gold! And what other touchstone have we of our gold but comparison—whether we be as happy as others?

My God, You have made this sickbed Your altar, and I have no other sacrifice to offer but myself. Will You accept no spotted sacrifice? Does Your Son dwell bodily in this flesh that You should look for an unspottedness here? Or is the Holy Ghost the soul of this body, as He is of Your spouse, who is therefore all "fair, and no spot in her"? Or had your Son Himself no spots, who has all our stains and deformities in Him? Or has Your spouse, Your church, no spots when every particular limb of that fair and spotless body, every particular soul in that church is full of stains and spots?

You bid us "hate the garment that is spotted with the flesh."[18] The flesh itself is the garment, and it spots itself with itself. Lord, if You look for a spotlessness, whom will You look upon? Your mercy may go a great way in my soul and yet not leave me without spots. Your corrections may go far and burn deep, and yet not leave me spotless. You do rain upon us, and yet do not always mollify all our hardness; You kindle Your fires in us, and yet do not always burn up all our dross. You heal our wounds and yet leave scars. You purge

---

[18]Jude 23

the blood, and yet leave spots. But the spots that You hate are the spots that we hide. When we hide our spots, we become idolators of our own stains and foulness. But if my spots come forth by the strength of nature, or by voluntary confession (for grace is the nature of a regenerate man, and the power of grace is the strength of nature), You are pleased.

Even my spots belong to Your Son's body and are part of that which He came down to earth to fetch and challenge and assume for Himself. When I open my spots, I do but present Him with that which is His; and till I do so I detain and withold His right. When, therefore, You see them upon me as His, and see them by the way of confession, they shall not appear as the pinches of death, but these spots upon my breast and soul shall appear to me as the constellations of the firmament to direct my contemplation to that place where Thy Son resides.

Reflections on Time

I would not make man worse than he is, nor his condition more miserable than it is. But could I, if I would? As a man cannot flatter God, nor overpraise Him, so a man cannot injure man, nor undervalue him. Those false happinesses that man has in the world have their times and seasons and their critical days, and they are judged and denominated according to the times when they befall us.

What poor elements are our happinesses made of if time be an essential part of our happiness! All things are done in some place, but if we consider place to be no more but the hollow superficies of the air, alas! How thin and fluid a thing air is. All things are done in time, too, but if we consider time to be but the measure of motion, and though it seems to have three stations—past, present, and future, yet the first and last of these are not (one is not now and the other is not yet), and that which you call present is not the same as it was when you began to call it so.

If this imaginary, half-nothing time be of the essence of our happinesses, how can they be thought durable? Time is not so; how can they be thought to be? If we consider eternity into that time never entered, eternity is not an everlasting flux of time, but time is a short parenthesis in a long period, and eternity had been the same as it is though time had never been.

If we consider, not eternity, but perpetuity— not that which had no time to begin in, but which shall outlive time and be when time shall be no more, what a minute is the most durable creature compared to that! And what a minute is man's life in comparison with the sun's. And yet, how little of our life is occasion or opportunity to receive good and how little of the occasion do we lay hold of? How busy and perplexed a cobweb is the happiness of man here that he must watch for and lay hold of occasion which is but a little piece of that which is nothing—time? And yet, the best things are nothing without that.

Honors and pleasures are presented to us in time. Youth is their critical day that judges them and informs them and makes them honors and pleasures; when they come to unapprehensive age, they come as a cordial when the bell rings out, as a pardon when the head is off. We rejoice in the comfort of a fire, but does any man cleave to it in midsummer? Or are the pleasures of the spring acceptable in autumn? If happiness be in the season, or in the climate, how much happier are the birds than men who can change the climate and enjoy the same season forever.

My God, my God, would You call Yourself the Ancient of days[19] if we were not to call ourselves to an account for our days? Would You chide us for "standing idle here all the day"[20] if we were sure to have more days to make up our harvest? When You bid us "take no thought for tomorrow, for sufficient to the day is the evil thereof"[21] is this truly, absolutely to put off all that concerns the present life? When You reprimand the Galations by saying that they "observed days, and months, and years,"[22] and when You forbid the Colossians all critical days, "Let no man judge you in respect of a holy day, or a new moon, or of a Sabbath,"[23] do You take away all consideration, all distinction of days?

Though You remove them from being of the essence of our salvation, You leave them for assistance, for exaltation of our devotion, to fix ourselves at certain periodical, stationary times for consideration of those things which You have done for us, and the crisis, the trial, the judgment of how those things have wrought upon us and disposed us to a spiritual recovery. For there is to every man a day of salvation. "Now is the accepted time, now is the day of salvation."[24]

---

[19]Dan. 7:22   [20]Matt. 20:6   [21]Matt. 6:34   [22]Gal. 4:10
[23]Col. 2:16   [24]2 Cor. 6:2

Children of the Day

We, who have not only the day of the prophets, the first days, but the last days in which You have spoken unto us by Your Son[25]—we are the children of the day,[26] for You have shined in as full noon. And shall we who are in the day, not of the prophets, but the Son, stone those prophets again, and crucify the Son again, for all the evident light afforded us?

O Lord, let a day be as a week to me; and in this one, let me consider seven critical days and judge myself that I be not judged by You. First, this is the day of Your visitation. Your coming to me. Would I look to be welcome to You and not entertain You in Your coming to me? We measure not the visitations of great persons by their apparel, by their equipage, by the solemnity of their coming, but by their very coming. Therefore, however You come, it is a crisis to me.

This leads me from my first day, Your visitation by sickness, to a second, to the light and testimony of my conscience. From this day breaks out my third day, my day of preparing and fitting myself for a more special receiving of Your Son in His institution of the sacrament. Having walked with You these three days, O my God, the day of Your visitation, the day of my conscience, the day of preparing for this seal of reconciliation, I am less afraid of the clouds or storms of my fourth day, the day of my dissolution and transmigration from hence. Nothing deserves the name of happiness that makes the remembrance of death bitter. Therefore, You have, O my God, made this

---

[25]Heb. 1:2   [26]1 Thes. 5:8

sickness in which I am not able to receive meat, my fasting day, my eve to the great festival, my dissolution.

This day of death shall deliver me over to my fifth day, the day of my resurrection. However long a day You make that day in the grave, yet there is no day between that and the resurrection. Then we shall be reapparelled in our own bodies that have been superinvested with glory. This day of awaking me and reinvesting my soul in my body, and my body in the body of Christ, shall present me to my sixth day, the day of judgment, which is truly the most critical day. All judgment shall be manifested to me then, and I shall assist in judging the world, and that judgment shall declare to me and possess me of my seventh day, my everlasting Sabbath in Thy rest, Thy glory, Thy joy, Thy sight, Thyself. Here I shall live as long without reckoning any more days, as Thy Son and Thy Holy Spirit lived with You before You three made any days in the Creation.

Sleep and Death

Natural men have conceived a twofold use of sleep: that it is a refreshing of the body in this life and that it is a preparing of the soul for the next; that it is a feast, and it is the grace at the feast; that it is our recreation and cheers us, and it is our catechism and instructs us. We lie down in a hope that we shall rise the stronger, and we lie down in the knowledge that we may rise no more. Sleep is an opiate which gives us rest, but such an opiate, as perchance, being under it we shall wake no more.

However, though natural man, who induced

secondary and figurative considerations, found out this second emblematical use of sleep, that is, of death, God, who wrought and perfected His work before nature began, intended sleep only for refreshing man by bodily rest, and not for a figure of death, for He intended not death itself then. But man having induced death upon himself, God took man's creature, death, into His hand and mended it. Whereas it has in itself a fearful form and aspect so that man is afraid of his own creature, God presents it to him in an agreeable and acceptable form in sleep.

As we then need sleep to live out our three-score and ten years, so we need death to live that life which we cannot outlive. And as death being our enemy, God allows us to defend ourselves against it as often as we eat, so God having so sweetened death unto us as He has in sleep, we put ourselves into our enemy's hands once every day so far as sleep is death. And sleep is as much death as meat is life.

This then is the misery of my sickness—that death, as it is produced from me is my own creation, is now before my eyes, but in that form in which God has mollified it to us and made it acceptable. In sleep I cannot see it.

He that has seen his friend die today or knows he shall see it tomorrow, yet will sink into a sleep between. If I be entering into eternity where there shall be no more distinction of hours, why is it all my business now to tell clocks? And why being entered into that presence where I shall wake continually and never sleep more, do I interpret my continual waking here to be a preparation to that?

My God, I know that "he that keepeth Israel shall neither slumber nor sleep";[27] but shall not that Israel, over whom Thou watchest, sleep? Jonah slept in one dangerous storm and Thy blessed Son in another.[28] Shall I not have benefit of those examples? Let me not, O my God, take this too precisely or literally: "There is that neither day nor night seeth sleep with his eyes,"[29] says that truly wise servant Solomon. Whether he speaks that of worldly men, or of men that seek wisdom, whether in justification or condemnation of their watchfulness we cannot tell. My eyes fix themselves upon Thy peace and joy and glory above. Almost as soon as Thy apostle had said, "Let us not sleep"[30] lest we should be too much discomforted if we did, he says again, "Whether we wake or sleep, let us live together with Him."[31]

Though then this absence of sleep may argue the presence of death, yet this gentle sleep and rest of my soul betroths me to Thee, to whom I shall be married indissolubly, though by this way of dissolution.

[27]Ps. 121:4
[29]Ecc. 8:16
[31]1 Thes. 5:10

[28]Jonah 1:5; Matt. 8:24
[30]1 Thes. 5:6

2
Death and Dying

For Whom the Bell Tolls

Perchance he for whom this bell tolls may be so ill that he knows not it tolls for him, and perchance I may think myself so much better than I am as that they who are about me and see my state may have caused it to toll for me, and I know it not. The church is Catholic universal so are all her actions; all that she does belongs to all. When she baptizes a child, that action concerns me, for the child is thereby connected with that body which is my head too and ingrafted into that body whereof I am a member. And when she buries a man, that action concerns me. All mankind is of one author, and is one volume. When one man dies, one chapter is not torn out of the book, but translated into a better language; and every chapter must be so translated.

God employs several translators. Some pieces are translated by age, some by sickness, some by war; but God's hand is in every translation, and His hand shall bind up all the scattered leaves again for that library where every book shall lie open to one another. As, therefore, the bell that rings to a sermon calls not upon the preacher only, but upon the congregation to come, so this bell calls us all; but how much more me, who am brought so near the door by this sickness.

The bell does toll for him that thinks it does; and though it intermit again, yet from that minute that the occasion wrought upon him he is united with God. Who casts not his eyes toward the sun when it rises? Or who takes his eyes off a comet that breaks forth? Who bends not his ear to any bell which rings upon any occasion? And who can keep that bell from passing a piece of himself out of this world?

No man is an island unto himself; every man is a piece of the continent, a part of the main. If a clod be washed away by the sea, Europe is the less, as well as if a promontory were, as well as if a manor of thy friend's or of thine own were: any man's death diminishes me, because I am involved in mankind, and therefore never send to know for whom the bell tolls; it tolls for thee.

No man has affliction enough that is not matured and ripened by it and made fit for God by that affliction. If a man carry treasure in bullion, or in a wedge of gold, and have none coined into current money, his treasure will not defray him as he travels. Tribulation is treasure, but it is not current money except we be nearer and nearer to our home, Heaven. Another man may be sick unto death, too, and the affliction may lie in his bowels, as gold in a mine, and be of no use to him. But this bell that tells me of his affliction digs out and applies that gold to me: if by this consideration of another's danger I take my own into contemplation, and so secure myself by making my recourse to my God, who is our only security.

My God, my God, is this one of Your ways of drawing light out of darkness to make him for whom this bell tolls to become an overseer, a bishop to as many as hear his voice in this bell? Is this one of Your ways to raise strength out of weakness to make him who cannot rise from his bed come home to me and in this sound give me the strength of healthy and vigorous instruction?

O my God, what thunder is not a well-tuned cymbal, what hoarseness, what harshness is not a clear organ if You be pleased to set Your voice to it? And what organ is not well played if Your hand is upon it? Your voice, Your hand is in this sound, and in this sound I hear this whole concert. I hear Thy Moses telling me, and all within the compass of this sound, "This is the blessing wherewith I bless you before my death."[1] I hear Thy prophet saying to Hezekiah, "Set thy house in order, for thou shalt die, and not live."[2] He makes use of his family, and calls this a setting of his house in order to compose us to the meditation of death. I hear Thy apostle saying, "I think it meet to put you in remembrance, knowing that shortly I must go out of this tabernacle."[3] This is the publishing of his will, and this bell is our legacy, the applying of his present condition to our use.

I hear that which makes all sounds music, and all music perfect. I hear Thy Son Himself saying, "Let not your heart be troubled,"[4] only I hear this

---

[1]Deut. 33:1   [2]2 Kings 20:1   [3]2 Peter 1:13   [4]John 14:1

change, that whereas Your Son says there, "I go to prepare a place for you," this man in this sound says, "I send to prepare you for a place—for a grave."

O my God, since heaven is glory and joy, why do not glorious and joyful things lead us, induce us to heaven? Thy legacies in Thy first will, in the Old Testament, were plenty and victory, wine and oil, milk and honey, alliances of friends, ruin of enemies, peaceful hearts, and cheerful countenances, and by these galleries You brought them into Your bedchamber to the joys and glories of heaven. Why have You changed your old way and carried us by the ways of discipline and mortification, by the ways of mourning and lamentation? Is the joy of heaven no perfecter in itself but that it needs the sourness of this life to give it a taste?

I know, my God, it is far, far otherwise. Pardon, O God, this unthankful rashness. I that ask why You do not find even now in me what You do must conclude that they find not joys in their sorrows, glory in their dejections in this world, are in a fearful danger of missing both in the next.

The Soul's Departure

If I will ask, not only philosophers, but divines, how the soul, being a separate substance, enters into man, I shall find some that will tell me that it is by generation and procreation from parents, because they think it hard to charge the soul with the guilt of original sin if the soul were infused into a body in which it must necessarily grow foul and contract original sin; and I shall find some that will tell me that it is by immediate infusion from God, because they think it hard to maintain an immortality in such a soul as should be begotten and derived with the body from a mortal person.

If I will ask many what becomes of the souls of the righteous at the departing from the body, I shall be told by some that they attend an expiation, a purification in a place of torment; by some, that they attend the fruition of the sight of God in a place of rest and expectation; some say that they pass to an immediate possession of the presence of God.

But it is the going out more than the coming in that concerns us. This soul this bell tells me is gone out, whither? Who shall tell me that? I know not who it is, much less what he was, the condition of the man, and the course of his life. I was not there at his sickness, nor at his death. But my charity tells me he is gone to everlasting rest, and joy, and glory. I owe him a good opinion, because I have received benefit and instruction from him when his bell is tolled. Assisted by the occasion, I pray for him, not without faith, charitably, and do faithfully believe that his soul is gone to everlasting rest, and joy, and glory.

If he who, as this bell tells me, is gone now, were some excellent artificer, who comes to him for a cloak or for a garment now? Man, before he has his immortal soul, has a soul of sense and a soul of vegetation before that. This immortal soul did not forbid other souls to be in us before, but when this soul departs, it carries all with it; no more vegetation, no more sense. Such a mother-in-law is the earth, in respect of our natural mother; in her womb we grew, and when she was delivered of us, we were planted in some place, in some calling in the world. In the womb of the earth we diminish, and when she is delivered of us, our grave opened for another, we are not transplanted, but transported, our dust blown away with every wind.

The Metaphor of Water

We cannot awake the flowers in January, nor retard the flowers of the spring to autumn. We cannot bid the fruits come in May, nor the leaves to stick on in December. A woman that is weak cannot put off her ninth month to a tenth for her delivery, nor can a queen hasten it to a seventh that she may be ready for some other pleasure.

Nature will not admit obligations upon her, for she will be left to her liberty. Nature would not be forced to mend her pace. Some tree bears no fruit, except much dung he laid about it. Some trees require much visiting, much watering, much labor; some require incision, pruning, and lopping. Some trees require the early and the often access of the sun. Reward is the season of one man, and importunity of another; friendship is the season of one man, and natural affection of another. He that knows not their seasons must lose the fruits.

Thou art not figurative, metaphorical in Thy Word only, but in Thy works, too. The style of Your works, and the phrase of Your actions is metaphorical. The institution of Your whole worship in the old Law was a continuous allegory; types and figures overspread all, and figures flowed into figures. Circumcision carried a figure of baptism, and baptism carries a figure of that purity which we shall have in the perfection of the New Jerusalem.

How much more often does Christ call Himself a way and a light and a gate and a vine and bread than the Son of God. How much more often does He exhibit a metaphorical Christ than a literal one. Wherefore, O my God, have You presented to us the afflictions and calamities of this life in the name of waters? Must we look to be drowned by them? Are they boundless?

That is not the dialect of Your language. You have given a remedy against the deepest water, against the inundation of sin by baptism. The first life that You gave to any creatures was in waters; therefore, You do not threaten us with irremediableness when our affliction is the sea. You called the Mediterranean the great sea because the inhabitants saw no other sea. But that is truly great that overflows the channel, that is really a great affliction which is above my strength. But thou, O my God, art my strength, and what can be above it? "Mountains shake with the swelling of Thy sea."[5] But "Thou givest the sea Thy decree, that the waters should not pass Thy commandment."[6] All our waters shall run into Jordan, and thy servants passed Jordan dry foot.

You can save without means, but You have told no man that You will. You gave St. Paul the lives of all them that sailed with him.[7] If they had not been in the ship with him, the gift had not extended to them. "As soon as thy Son was come out of the ship, immediately there met with Him out of the tombs, a man with an unclean spirit,

[5]Ps. 46:3   [6]Prov. 8:29   [7]Acts 27:24

and no man could hold him, no, not with chains."[8] Your Son needed no use of means; yet there we apprehend the danger to use if we leave the ship, the means, in this case the physician.

Man's Place and God's Call

If man had been left alone in the world at first, shall I think that he would not have fallen? If there had been no woman, would not man have served to have been his own tempter? When I see him now subject to infinite weaknesses, fall into infinite sin without any foreign temptations, shall I think he would have had none if he had been alone?

God saw that man needed a helper if he should be well, but to make woman ill, the devil saw that there needed no third. When God and we were alone in Adam, that was not enough; when the devil and we were alone in Eve, it was enough. O what a giant is man when he fights against himself, and what a dwarf when he needs or exercises his own assistance for himself. I cannot rise out of my bed till the physician enable me. I do nothing, I know nothing by myself; how little and how impotent a piece of the world is any man alone? He can sin alone and suffer alone, but not repent, nor be absolved without another.

Someone tells me I may rise, and I do so. But I am more ready to fall to the earth when I am up than when I lie in bed. O perverse way, irregular motion of man; even rising itself is the way to ruin! How many men are raised, and then do not fill the place they are raised to? No corner of any

[8]Mark 5:2-3

place can be empty; if that man does not fill the place, other men will; complaints of his insufficiency will fill it.

A man rises sometimes and stands not because he does not fill his place; and sometimes he stands not because he overfills his place. Man has no center but misery; there, and only there, he is fixed and sure to find himself. However little he be raised, he moves in a circle giddily. And as in the heavens there are few circles that go about the whole world, so of those men who are raised and put into circles. Everything serves to exemplify, to illustrate man's misery. But I need go no farther than myself: for a long time I was not able to rise; at last I must be raised by others; and now I am up, I am ready to sink lower than before.

O my God, I have a bed of sin; delight in sin is a bed. I have a grave of sin; senselessness of sin is a grave. And where Lazarus had been for four days, I have been 50 years in this putrefaction. Why do you not call me as you did him, "with a loud voice,"[9] since my soul is as dead as his body was? I need Thy thunder, O my God; Thy music will not serve me.

When your Son concurred with You to the making of man, there was but a speaking. There was none to hear but You three, O blessed and glorious Trinity. And You easily hear one another because You say the same things. But when Your Son came to the work of redemption, You spoke[10] and they that heard it took it for thunder. Thy Son Himself cried with a loud voice upon the cross

---

[9]John 11:43   [10]John 12:28

twice.[11] Your voice is a mighty voice, not only mighty in power, and mighty in obligation, but mighty in operation. It is such a voice as Thy Son says, "the dead shall hear it";[12] and that is my state. Why, O God, do You not speak to me in that effectual loudness?

O my God, speak more loudly that though I do not hear Thee now, then I may hear nothing but Thee. My sins cry aloud; my afflictions cry aloud; "the floods have lifted up their voice, but thou, O Lord, art mightier than the voice of many waters."[13] Why do You not speak to me in that voice?

When will You speak to me in your loud voice? When will You bid me "take up thy bed and walk"?[14] As my bed is my afflictions, when shall I bear them so as not to murmur at them? When shall I take up my bed and walk and not lie down upon it, nor sink under it?

O God, the God of all flesh and spirit, let me be content in my fainting spirit, that as this body is content to sit still, it may learn to stand, and to learn by standing to walk, and by walking to travel so that my soul by hearing Your voice of rising may grow farther in Your grace and be so established as may remove all suspicions, all jealousies between Thee and me, that I may be acceptable to Thee and satisfied from Thee.

Purging the Leaven

How ruinous a farm has man taken in himself! How ready is the house every day to fall down, and how is all the ground overspread with weeds, all the body with diseases, where not only turf,

---

[11]Matt. 27:46, 50   [12]John 5:25   [13]Ps. 93:3-4
[14]Matt. 9:6

but every stone bears weeds; not only every muscle of the flesh, but every bone of the body has some infirmity. Every little flint upon the face of this soil has some infectious weed. How dear a rent does man pay for this farm!

What reparations and subsidies and contributions he is put to besides his rent! What medicines besides his diet. The whole ground is of an ill nature, the whole soil ill-disposed. There are inclinations to diseases in the body out of which diseases will grow, and so we are put to a continual labor upon this farm, to a continual study of the whole complexion of the body.

I have taken a farm at this hard rent; to cure the sharp accidents of diseases is a great work; to cure the disease itself is greater; but to cure the body, the root, the occasion of diseases is a work reserved for the Great Physician, which He does never in any other way but by glorifying these bodies in the next world.

The root and fuel of my sickness is my sin, my actual sin, but even that sin has another root, another fuel—original sin. Can I divest that? Will you bid me to separate the leaven that a lump of dough has received or the salt that the water has contracted from the sea? Should I so look to the fuel or embers of sin that I never take fire? The whole world is a pile of fagots upon which we are laid, and we are the bellows. Ignorance blows the fire, but knowledge much more.

Our fathers have imprinted the seed, infused a spring of sin in us. We are open to infinite temptations, and yet we are tempted of our own lusts.[15]

---

[15]James 1:14

When You bid be "to put off the old man,"[16] do You mean not only my old habits of actual sin, but the oldest of all, original sin? When You bid me "to purge out the leaven,"[17] do You mean not only the sourness of my own ill-contracted customs, but the innate tincture of sin imprinted by nature?

Avoiding Relapse

My God, Thou mighty Father, who has been my physician, shall I alone be able to overthrow all Your work and relapse into those spiritual sicknesses from which Your infinite mercies have withdrawn me? Where is my assurance? How slippery a way is murmuring! Today's murmuring is tomorrow's idolatry. I have found it in myself, O God, and seeing it has made me afraid of relapsing, too.

Why, O my God, is a relapse so odious to Thee? Not so much their murmurings and their idolatry as relapsing into those sins seems to affect Thee in Thy disobedient people. "They limited the holy One of Israel,"[18] You complained of them; that was for murmuring, but before You charged them with the fault itself, You charged them with redoubling of that fault before the fault was named: "How oft did they provoke Me in the wilderness, and grieve Me in the desert." What brings You to exasperation against them was that "they had tempted Thee ten times."[19]

No tongue but Yours, O my God, can express Your indignation against a nation relapsing into idolatry. Idolatry in any nation is deadly, but

---

[16]Eph. 4:22   [17]1 Cor. 5:7   [18]Ps. 78:41
[19]Num. 14:22-23

when the disease is complicated with a relapse, it is desperate, and Your anger works, not only where the evidence is pregnant, but where there is even rumor or suspicion of such relapse Your anger is awakened and Your indignation stirred.

Why is relapse such an odious sin? It must be that he who has sinned and then repented has weighed God and the devil in a balance; he has heard God and the devil plead, and after hearing, given judgment on that side to which he adheres by his subsequent practice. If he returns to sin, he decrees for Satan, he prefers sin before grace, and Satan before God. In contempt of God he declares precedence for His adversary, and contempt wounds deeper than an injury; a relapse is deeper than a blasphemy.

My sickness brought me to You in repentance, and my relapse has cast me farther from You. "The end of that man shall be worse than the beginning"[20] says Thy Word, Thy Son; my beginning was sickness, punishment for sin; but a worse thing may follow if I sin again; not only death, which is an end worse than sickness, but hell, which is a beginning worse than that end.

If I relapse, must not my case be desperate? Not so! For as Thy majesty, so is Thy mercy: both are infinite. You who have commanded me to pardon my brother 70 times seven have limited Yourself to no number. If Your mercy in pardoning did so far aggravate a relapse that there were no mercy after it, our case would be the worse for that former mercy, for who is not under a necessity of sinning while he is here if we place this

---

[20]Matt. 12:45

necessity in our own infirmity, and not in your decree? I speak this, O my God, not as preparing a way for my relapse out of presumption, but to preclude all access of desperation, though out of infirmity I should relapse.

Part II
Divine Poems

Donne's *Divine Poems* reveal the same intellec-
tual strength and range of feeling found in his
other poetry. One notes the conflicting moods
and startling analogies that led to his style being
termed "metaphysical." Often he is abrupt or
colloquial or paradoxical, but always his manner
is forceful and intense.

The numberings and captions of the sonnets
are editorial and are not meant to correspond to
the sequence followed by Helen Gardner or Her-
bert Grierson.

3
God's Grace

1. Knowing Christ's Bride

Show me, dear Christ, Thy spouse so bright and
    clear.
What! is it she which on the other shore
Goes richly painted?[1] or which, robbed and tore,
Laments and mourns in Germany and here?[2]
Sleeps she a thousand, then peeps up one year?
Is she self-truth, and errs? now new, now out-
    wore?
Doth she, and did she, and shall she evermore
On one, on seven, or on no hill appear?[3]
Dwells she with us, or like adventuring knights
First travel we to seek, and then make love?
Betray, kind husband, Thy spouse to our sights,
And let mine amorous soul court Thy mild dove,
Who is most true and pleasing to Thee then
When she is embraced and open to most men.

---

[1]The Church of Rome   [2]The Protestant Church
[3]Mt. Moriah, where Solomon's temple stood; the seven hills of
Rome; the Genevan Church stood on no hill.

2. Saved by Grace

Thou hast made me, and shall Thy work decay?
Repair me now, for now mine end doth haste;
I run to death, and death meets me as fast,
And all my pleasures are like yesterday.
I dare not move my dim eyes any way,
Despair behind, and death before doth cast
Such terror, and my feeble flesh doth waste
By sin in it, which it towards hell doth weigh.
Only Thou art above, and when towards Thee
By Thy leave I can look, I rise again;
But our old subtle foe so tempteth me
That not one hour myself I can sustain.
Thy grace may wing me to prevent[4] his art,
And Thou like adamant[5] draw mine iron heart.

3. Death Be Not Proud

Death, be not proud, though some have called
    thee
Mighty and dreadful, for thou art not so;
For those whom thou think'st thou dost
    overthrow
Die not, poor Death, nor yet canst thou kill me.
From rest and sleep, which but thy pictures be,
Much pleasure; then from thee much more must
    flow,
And soonest our best men with thee do go,
Rest of their bones, and souls' delivery.[6]
Thou art slave to fate, chance, kings, and
    desperate men,
And dost with poison, war, and sickness dwell,

---

[4]Strengthen me to frustrate   [5]A magnet
[6]Rescue, also birth of a soul

And poppy or charms can make us sleep as well
And better than thy stroke; why swell'st[7] thou,
    then?
One ·short sleep past, we wake eternally,
And Death shall be no more; Death, thou shalt
    die.

4. Mourning for Sin

At the round earth's imagined corners,[8] blow
Your trumpets, angels; and arise, arise
From death, you numberless infinities
Of souls, and to your scattered bodies go;
All whom the flood did, and fire shall, o'erthrow,
All whom war, dearth, age, agues, tyrannies,
Despair, law, chance hath slain, and you whose
    eyes
Shall behold God, and never taste death's woe.[9]
But let them sleep, Lord, and me mourn a space;
For, if above all these, my sins abound,
'Tis late to ask abundance of Thy grace
When we are there. Here on this lowly ground,
Teach me how to repent; for that's as good
As if Thou hadst sealed my pardon with Thy
    blood.

5. Resigning to God

As due by many titles I resign
Myself to Thee, O God: first I was made
By Thee, and for Thee, and when I was decayed,
Thy blood bought that, the which before was
    Thine;
I am Thy son, made with Thyself to shine;
Thy servant, whose pains Thou hast still repaid;

---

[7]Puff up with pride   [8]Rev. 7:1   [9]Luke 9:27

Thy sheep, Thine image, and till I betrayed
Myself, a temple of Thy Spirit divine.
Why doth the devil then usurp on[10] me?
Why doth he steal, nay ravish that's Thy right?
Except Thou rise and for Thine own work fight,
Oh, I shall soon despair, when I do see
That Thou lovest mankind well, yet wilt not
   choose me,
And Satan hates me, yet is loth to lose me.

6. Consumed by Zeal

I am a little world made cunningly
Of elements, and an angelic sprite;
But black sin hath betrayed to endless night
My world's both parts, and oh, both parts must
   die.
You which beyond that heaven which was most
   high
Have found new spheres, and of new lands can
   write,[11]
Pour new seas in mine eyes, that so I might
Drown my world with my weeping earnestly,
Or wash it if it must be drowned no more.[12]
But oh, it must be burnt![13] Alas, the fire
Of lust and envy have burnt it heretofore,
And made it fouler; let their flames retire,
And burn me, O Lord, with a fiery zeal
Of Thee and Thy house, which doth in eating
   heal.[14]

---

[10]Claim unjustly; appropriate wrongfully
[11]Donne addresses astronomers and explorers who had made
new discoveries.
[12]God's promise to Noah in Gen. 9:11
[13]By the fire which would end the world.
[14]Ps. 69:9

7. Imputed Righteousness

This is my play's last scene; here heavens
    appoint
My pilgrimage's last mile; and my race
Idly, yet quickly run, hath this last pace;
My span's last inch, my minutes' latest point,
And gluttonous death will instantly unjoint
My body and soul, and I shall sleep a space;
But my ever-waking part shall see that face,
Whose fear[15] already shakes my every joint.
Then as my soul to heaven, her first seat, takes
    flight,
And earth-born body in the earth shall dwell,
So fall my sins, that all may have their right,
To where they are bred, and would press me, to
    hell.
Impute me righteous, thus purged of evil,
For thus I leave the world, the flesh, the devil.

8. Christ Clothed in Flesh

Spit in my face, you Jews, and pierce my side,
Buffet, and scoff, scourge, and crucify me,
For I have sinned, and sinned, and only He,
Who could do no iniquity, hath died:
But by my death cannot be satisfied[16]
My sins, which pass the Jews' impiety;
They killed once an inglorious man, but I
Crucify Him daily, being now glorified.
Oh, let me then, His strange love still admire;
Kings pardon, but He bore our punishment.
And Jacob came clothed in vile harsh attire
But to supplant, and with gainful intent;[17]

---

[15]The fear of whom   [16]Atoned for
[17]Jacob's deception of his father, Gen. 27

God clothed Himself in vile man's flesh, that so
He might be weak enough to suffer woe.

9. Ravished by God

Batter my heart, three-personed God; for You
As yet but knock, breathe, shine, and seek to
    mend;
That I may rise, and stand, o'erthrow me, and
    bend
Your force, to break, blow, burn, and make me
    new.
I, like an usurped town to another due,
Labor to admit You, but oh! to no end;
Reason, Your viceroy in me, me should defend,
But is captived and proves weak or untrue.
Yet dearly I love You, and would be loved fain,
But am betrothed unto Your enemy.
Divorce me, untie, or break that knot again,
Take me to You, imprison me, for I
Except You enthrall me, never shall be free;
Nor ever chaste, except You ravish me.

10. Human Inconstancy

Oh, to vex me, contraries meet in one:
Inconstancy unnaturally hath begot
A constant habit; that when I would not,
I change in vows and in devotion.
As humorous[18] is my contrition
As my profane love, and as soon forgot;
As riddling distempered, cold and hot;
As praying, as mute; as infinite, as none.
I durst not view heaven yesterday; and to-day
In prayers and flattering speeches I court God.

[18]Changeable

To-morrow I quake with true fear of His rod.
So my devout fits come and go away
Like a fantastic ague:[19] save that here
Those are my best days, when I shake with fear.

Hymn to God, My God, in My Sickness[20]

Since I am coming to that holy room
   Where, with Thy choir of saints for evermore,
I shall be made Thy music, as I come
   I tune the instrument here at the door,
   And what I must do then, think here before.
Whilst my physicians by their love are grown
   Cosmographers, and I their map,[21] who lie
Flat on this bed, that by them may be shown
   That this is my southwest discovery,
   Per fretum febris, by these straits to die,[22]
I joy, that in these straits I see my west;
   For though their currents yield return
   to none,
What shall my west hurt me? As west and east[23]
   In all flat maps, and I am one, are one,
   So death doth touch the resurrection.
Is the Pacific sea my home? or are
   The eastern riches? Is Jerusalem?
Anyan[24] and Magellan and Gibraltar,
   All straits, and none but straits, are ways
   to them,

---

[19]A fever, with hot and cold spells and shaking or shivering.
[20]Possibly refers to Donne's illness in 1623
[21]It was believed that every man was a "little world."
[22]As Magellan made a south-west journey through the Straits of Magellan and later died in the Philippines, so Donne will make his last journey "through the straits of fever" *(per fretum febris)*; south connotes heat, and west, where the sun sets, connotes death.
[23]The east, where the sun (Son) rises, suggests life, rebirth.
[24]Bering Strait.

Whether where Japhet dwelt, or Ham, or
Shem.[25]
We think that Paradise and Calvary,
    Christ's cross and Adam's tree, stood in one
place;
Look, Lord, and find both Adams met in me:
    As the first Adam's sweat surrounds my face,
    May the last Adam's[26] blood my soul embrace.
So, in His purple[27] wrapped, receive me, Lord:
    By these, His thorns, give me His other
    crown;
And as to others' souls I preached Thy Word,
    Be this my text, my sermon to mine own:
    Therefore that He may raise, the Lord throws
    down.

A Hymn to God the Father[28]

Wilt Thou forgive that sin where I begun,
    Which is my sin, though it were done before?
Wilt Thou forgive those sins, through which
    I run,
    And do run still, though still I do deplore?
    When Thou hast done, Thou hast not done,
    For I have more.

Wilt Thou forgive that sin which I have won
    Others to sin? and made my sin their door?
Wilt Thou forgive that sin which I did shun
    A year or two, but wallowed in a score?

---

[25]Noah's sons, whose decendants were said to inhabit, respectively, Europe, Africa, Asia.

[26]Christ's.

[27]Christ's blood; also the color of royal robes and of the garments the soldiers put on Christ (Mark 15:17).

[28]Donne puns on his name throughout the poem, which Walton says Donne wrote in his illness in 1623.

When Thou hast done, Thou hast not done,
For I have more.

I have a sin of fear, that when I have spun
My last thread, I shall perish on the shore;
But swear by Thyself, that at my death Thy Son
Shall shine as He shines now, and heretofore;
And, having done that, Thou hast done,
I fear no more.

Part III

Selections from the Sermons

Very few of Donne's sermons were published during his lifetime. The chief collections were prepared by his son and issued in 1640, 1649, and 1660-1661. Donne did not read his sermons but carefully prepared the heads of his discourse, with voluminous notes, trusting his memory for the detailed meditations. They represent his wide reading and the multiple cares and emotions that possessed him. The note of intense, personal religious experience is evident; his consciousness of God leads him continually to a love for the souls of men. However, he seldom introduces himself personally.

Donne saw all material things as symbols of an inner reality. Rather than replacing the literal, however, the symbolic interpreted and enriched it.

4

Our Whole Service to God

Man

"Man is," says the prophet Isaiah, "as a drop of a bucket."[1] And what is a drop upon the bucket to a river or sea or to the waters above the firmament? Man to God? "Man is," says the same prophet, "as small dust upon the balance." Man is not all that small grain of dust, but some little thing towards it. And what can a grain of dust work in governing the balance? What is man that God should be mindful of him?

Vanity seems to be the lightest thing that the Holy Ghost could name; and when He had named that, He says very often, "All is vanity." But when He comes to weigh man with vanity itself, He finds man lighter than vanity. When the great apostle says of himself that he was in "nothing behind the very chiefest of the apostles" he says he was nothing.[2] Who can make himself anything? How poor and inconsiderable a rag of this world is man. If all men were together, they

---

[1] Isaiah 40:15   [2] 2 Cor. 12:11

would not have the power of one angel, whereas all the angels (who are conceived to be more in number, not only of the species, but of all the individuals of this lower world) have not in them all the power of one finger of God's hand: man, of whom David had said, (as the lowest diminution that He could put upon him) "I am a worm and no man."[3] He might have gone lower and said, "I am a man and no worm"; for man is so much less than a worm that the worms of his own production shall feed upon his dead body in the grave, and an immortal worm gnaw his conscience in the torments of hell.

Afflictions

All our life is a continual burden, yet we must not groan. As in the tenderness of our childhood, we suffer and yet are whipped if we cry, so we are made delinquents if we call the times ill. And that which adds weight to weight and multiplies the sadness of this consideration, is that the best men have had most laid upon them.

As soon as I hear God say that He has found "an upright man, one that fears God and eschews evil," in the next lines I find a commission to Satan to bring fire and tempest upon His children. As soon as I hear God say that He has found a "man according to His own heart" I see His sons ravish His daughters and murder one another and rebel against the Father. As soon as I hear God testify of Christ at baptism, "This is My Son in whom I am well pleased," I find that Son deserted, abandoned, and given over to Scribes and Pharisees and Judges and executioners, and He that was called the beloved Son of God made

---

[3]Ps. 22:6

partaker of the glory of heaven, is now made the sower of all the corruption of all the sins of the world as no Son of God, but as mere man—a contemptible worm.

As though the greatest weakness in this world were man, and the greatest fault in man were to be good, man is more miserable than other creatures, and good men more miserable than other men. But then there is "An exceeding weight of glory" that turns the scale, for as it makes all worldly prosperity as dung, so it makes all worldly adversity as feathers.

The World Is a Sea

As the sea is subject to storms and tempests, so is every man in the world. The sea is never shallower for its calmness; there is as much water in the sea in a calm as in a storm. We may be drowned in a calm and flattering fortune or prosperity as irrecoverably as in a wrought sea of adversity.

As the sea is bottomless to any line and endless to any discovery we can make of it, so the purposes and ways of the world exceed our consideration. Yet we are sure the sea has a bottom and limits it cannot overpass. The power of the greatest in the world, the life of the happiest in the world cannot exceed those bounds which God has placed for them. So the world is a sea.

It is a sea in that it has ebbs and floods and no man knows the true reason for those floods and ebbs. It is a sea in that it affords water enough for all the world to drink, but such water as will not quench the thirst. The world affords conveniences enough to satisfy nature, but these increase our thirst with drinking, and our desire grows and enlarges itself with our abundance, and though we sail in a full sea, yet we lack water.

The world is a sea if we consider the inhabitants. In the sea the greater fish devour the less, and so do the men of this world. And as fish, when they mud themselves, have no hands to make themselves clean, and the currents of the water must work it, so the men of the world have no means to cleanse themselves from those sins which they have contracted in the world of themselves till a new flood, waters of repentance, drawn up and sanctified by the Holy Ghost, work that blessed effect in them.

Especially is the world a sea in that the sea is no place of habitation, but a passage to our habitations. As the Apostle expresses of the world, "Here we have no continuing city, but we seek one to come"[4] so we do not seek one here. The two great works which we are to do in the world are first, to know that this world is not our home, and then to provide ourselves with another home while we are in this world. Therefore the prophet says, "Arise, and depart, for this is not your rest."[5] Worldly men that have no further prospect promise themselves some rest in this world, ("Soul, thou hast much goods laid up for many years; take thine ease, eat, drink, and be merry," says the rich man) but this is not your rest. You must depart by death before you come to that rest. But you must arise before you depart, for except you have a resurrection to grace here before you de-

---

[4]Heb. 13:14   [5]Micah 2:10

part, you shall have no resurrection to glory in the life to come.

Now is this sea, every ship that sails must have some part of the ship under water. Every man that lives in this world must likewise have some of his thoughts and labors spent upon this world. But that part of the ship by which he sails is above water. Those meditations and endeavors which must bring us to heaven are removed from this world and fixed entirely upon God. And in this sea we are made fishers of men—of all men. And for this fishing in this sea the Gospel is our net.

Eloquence is not our net; nor is tradition; only the Gospel is. The devil angles with hooks and baits; he deceives and wounds in the catching. But the Gospel of Jesus Christ has power to lay flat any stubborn and rebellious heart. And it has . . . the power of absolution and application of the mercies of God that swim above all His works to erect a humble and contrite spirit above all the waters of tribulation and affliction. . . .

Reason and Faith

He that comes to a natural, uncatechised, uninstructed man and says, "Believe all, or you burn in hell" would find that the latter would find an obvious way to escape all, that is, not to believe in hell itself. The reason of man must first be satisfied to make him see that this world, a frame of so much harmony, must necessarily have had a workman, for nothing can make itself; that no such workman would deliver such a frame and work of so much majesty to be governed by fortune casually, but would retain the administration thereof in his own hands; that if He made the world and sustains it by His watchful providence, there belongs a worship and service to Him for doing so; that He has certainly revealed to man what kind of worship and service shall be acceptable to Him; that this manifestation of His will must be permanent and written; it must be a Scripture, which is His Word and His will. From that Word of God all articles of our beliefs are to be drawn.

If man's reason confesses all this, ask further proof of how he knows that these Scriptures accepted by the Christian church are the true Scriptures. Let him bring any other book which pretends to be the Word of God to compare with these. It is true we cannot demonstrate such evidence that these Scriptures are the Word of God, as that one and two are three. God has not proceeded in this manner to drive our reason into a pound and force it to accept this for Scriptures, without the exercise of our will. But yet, these Scriptures have so orderly, sweet, and powerful a working upon the reason and understanding that he would be drawn to such an historical, grammatical, and logical belief of our Bible as to prefer it before any other. He would believe it and he would know why he did so.

Knowledge cannot save us, but we cannot be saved without knowledge. Faith is not on this side of knowledge, but beyond it. We must necessarily come to knowledge first; a regenerate Christian, being now *a new creature*, has also a *new faculty of reason*, and so believes the mysteries of religion out of another reason than as a mere natural man who believes natural and moral things. He believes them for their own sake by faith, though he takes knowledge of them before by that common reason and by those human arguments which work upon other men in natural and moral things.

So the common light of reason illumines us all, but one employs this light upon the searching of impertinent vanities, another by a better use of the same light finds out the mysteries of religion; and when he has found them he loves them, not for the light's sake, but for the natural and true worth of the thing itself.

Some men by the benefit of the light of reason have found out things profitable and useful to the whole world. For instance, in *printing* the learning of the whole world is communicable to one another, and our minds and our inventions and our wits and compositions may trade and have commerce together. By the benefit of this light men have seen through the darkest and most impervious places—*in courts of princes;* and the greatest *officers* in courts can submit themselves to advance the humors of men in great place.

All the ways of *wisdom* and *craft* lie open to the light of natural reason, but when they have gone all these ways by the benefit of this light, they have gone no further than to have walked by a tempestuous sea and to have gathered pebbles and speckled cockleshells. Their light seems to be great for the same reason that a torch on a misty night seems greater than in a clear one because it has kindled an admiration or an applause in airy flatterers, not because it is so indeed.

But if you can take this light of reason that is in you, this poor snuff that is almost out in you, the

faint and dim knowledge of God that rises out of
the light of nature; if you can in those embers,
those cold ashes find one small coal and will take
pains to kneel down and blow that coal with your
devout *prayers,* and light you a *little candle* (a
desire to read the Scriptures); if with that candle
you can creep humbly into low and poor places;
if you can find your Savior in a *manger* and in His
humiliation, and bless God for that beginning . . .
and if according to His example you can with this
little poor light, these *first degrees of knowledge
and faith* follow Him into the *garden* and gather
up some of the drops of His precious blood and
sweat which He shed for your soul; if you can
follow Him to *Jerusalem* and pick up some of
those *tears* that were shed upon that city and
upon your own soul; and if you can follow Him to
the place of scourging and to His crucifying and
provide yourself some of the balm which must
cure your soul; if after all this you can turn your
little light inward and discern where your
wounds and diseases and corruptions are, and
can apply those tears and blood and balm to
them, you will never envy the luster and glory of
the great lights of worldly men. You will find that
however they magnify their lights, their wit, their
learning, their industry, their fortune, you will
see that you by your small light have gathered
pearl and *amber,* and they by their great lights
nothing but shells and pebbles. They have de-
termined the light of nature upon the book of
nature and you have carried the light of nature
higher to that *love* that God has set to the seal of
faith.

Before the sun was made there was a *light*

which did that office of distinguishing night and day; but when the sun was created, it did all the offices of the former light, and more. *Reason* is the first light of natural man; but in a man regenerated by faith, that light does all that reason did, and more. All his moral and civil and domestic actions have a deeper tincture, a heavenly nature, a relation to God in them.

Prayer

Prayer is our whole service to God. Earnest prayer has the nature of importunity. We press, we importune God in prayer. Yet that puts not God to a morosity or frowardness; He does not withdraw from that. God suffers that importunity and more. Prayer has the nature of impudency. We threaten God in prayer.

Prayers have the nature of violence. In the public prayers of the congregation we besiege God, says Tertullian, "and we take God prisoner and bring God to our conditions, and God is glad to be straitened by us in that siege."

How blessed is the state of the soul that reaches God by prayer. This means prayer that is more than every sudden uttering of "Lord, Lord" or occasional holy interjection, but serious prayer. This is not those fixed hours in the Roman Church where men are bound to certain prayer at certain hours. Not that it is inconvenient for men to bind themselves to certain fixed times of prayer in their private exercises so that it shall be an impiety to break it. I have known the greatest Christian prince, even at the audience of an ambassador, at the sound of a bell to kneel down in our presence and pray. God forbid he should be blamed for doing so. But to understand the merit in observing those times as they do is not a right understanding of prayer. Nor are those transitory and interlocutory prayers which out of custom and fashion we make and still proceed in our sin when we pretend to speak to God, but like a comedian upon a stage, turn over our shoulder and whisper to the devil.

The manifestation of the Gospel, that is, the helps which God offers us in the ministry of the Gospel and the ordinances of His church, is the time of finding God. And woe unto us if we seek Him not while He affords us these helps. And then the time of affliction, when God threatens to hide His face, but has not yet hidden it, but awakens us by some calamity, is a time of finding God.

But the best and clearest time is in the sunshine, when He appears to us in the warm and cheerful splendor of temporal blessings upon us: then when you have a good estate and good children to let it descend upon and good health and a good profession in which to exercise your strength and labor; then when the dishes upon your table are doubled and your cup overflows and the hungry and thirsty souls of the poor do not feed only upon the crumbs under your table and lick up the overflowings of your cup, but divide dishes with you and enter into the midst of your bowls.

Then when you have temporal blessings (that is God's silver) and His grace to use those blessings well (that is God's gold), then is the best time for finding the Lord, for then He looks upon you in the sunshine, and then your thankful acknowledgment of former blessings is the most effectual prayer you can make for the continuance and enlargement of them.

Prayer at the Table and Bed

Beloved, since every master of a family who is a *bishop in his house* should call his family together to humbly pour out their souls to God, let him consider that when he comes to kneel at the *side of his table* to pray, he comes to build a church there. Therefore he should sanctify that place with a due and penitent consideration of how voluptuously he has formerly abused God's blessings at that place and how idolatrously he had humored some great guests invited by him and how expensively he has served his own ostentation and vainglory by excessive feasts at that place, while *Lazarus* has lain panting and gasping at the gate. Let him consider what a dangerous mockery to Christ Jesus it is if he pretends to build for Christ a church by a solemnity at the table-side and then crucify Christ again by these sins when he is at the table.

When you kneel down at your bedside to close the day or to begin it in the morning with your children and little flock around you, there you build a church too. Therefore, sanctify that place; wash it with your tears and with a repentant consideration that you have made the bed which God gave you for rest and reparation of your weary body a place of idleness and licentiousness.

Unconscious Prayer

That soul that is accustomed to direct herself to God upon every occasion, that as a flower at sun-rising conceives a since of God in every beam of His and spreads and dilates itself towards Him in a thankfulness in every small blessing that He sheds upon her.

That soul that as a flower at the sun's declining contracts and gathers in and shuts up herself as though she had received a blow when she hears her Saviour wounded by an oath or blasphemy; that soul who, whatever string be struck in her, whether bass or treble, her high or low estate, is ever turned towards God—that soul prays sometimes when it does not know that it prays.

God's Mirror

There is no creature so poor but that it may be a glass to see God in. The greatest flat glass that can be made cannot represent anything greater than it is. If every gnat that flies were an archangel, all that could tell me is that there is a God. And the poorest worm that creeps tells me that. If I should ask the slow worm how he come to be without eyes, he would tell me that God made him so.

The cedar is no better a glass to see God in than the hyssop upon the wall. All things that are are equally removed from being nothing. And whatsoever has any being is by that very being a glass in which we see God, who is the root and the fountain of all being. The whole frame of nature is the theater, and the whole volume of creatures is the glass, and the light of nature, reason, is our light.

God a Circle

One of the most convenient hieroglyphics of God

is a circle. A circle is endless. Whom God loves, He loves to the end: and not only their own end, death, but to His end, and His end is that He might love them still.

His hailstones and thunderbolts (instruments of His judgment) fall down in a direct line and strike some one person or place. His sun, moon, and stars (instruments of His blessing), move circularly and communicate themselves to all. His church is His chariot; in that He moves more gloriously than in the sun, as much more as His begotten Son exceeds His created sun, and His Son of glory at His right hand the run of His firmament.

This church, His chariot, moves in that communicable motion, circularly. It began in the east, it came to us and is passing now, shining out now in the farthest west.

5

The Wages of Sin

God's Mercies

"I will sing of Thy mercy and judgment,"[1] says
David. When we fix ourselves upon meditation of
the mercy of God, even His judgments cannot put
us out of tune; we shall sing and be cheerful even
in them. As God made grass for beasts before He
made beasts, and beasts for man before He made
man, so in the regeneration, our recreation, He
begins with that which was necessary for that
which follows: mercy before judgment.

To say that mercy was first is but to post-date
mercy and to diminish it. His mercy has no rela-
tion to time, no limitation in time. It is not first,
nor last, but eternal and everlasting. Let the devil
make me so far desperate as to conceive a time
when there was no mercy, and he has made me so
far an atheist as to conceive a time when there
was no God.

The true root of the word "mercy" through all
the prophets is to love. As long as there has been

[1]Ps. 101:1

73

love (and God *is love*) there has been mercy. And mercy began not at the helping of man when he was fallen and miserable, but at the making of man, when he was nothing. We consider here mercy, not as it is radically in God, and an essential attribute of His, but productively in us, as it is an action, a working upon us as God takes all occasions to exercise that action and to shed that mercy upon us.

If I should inquire upon what occasion God elected me and wrote my name in the Book of Life, I should sooner be afraid it were not so than find a reason why it should be so. God made sun and moon to distinguish the seasons, and day, and night, and we cannot have the fruits of the earth but in their seasons. But God has made no decree to distinguish the seasons of His mercies. In paradise the fruits were ripe the first minute, and in heaven it is always autumn; His mercies are ever in their maturity.

We ask our daily bread, and God never says you should have come yesterday or you must come tomorrow, but *today, if you will hear His voice*, today He will hear you. He brought light out of darkness, not out of a lesser light. He can bring your summer out of winter though you have no spring. Though in the ways of fortune or conscience you have been benighted until now, God comes to you, not as in the dawning of the day, not in the bud of the spring, but as the sun at noon to illustrate all shadows, as the sheaves in harvest, to fill all penuries.

The Image of God in Man

No image but the image of God can fit our soul;

every other seal is too narrow, too shallow for it. The magistrate is sealed with the *lion;* the *wolf* will not fit that seal. Princes are sealed with the *crown;* the *miter* will not fit that seal. Powerfully and graciously they protect the church and are supreme heads of the church, but they minister not the sacraments of the church. They give preferments, but they give not the capacity of preferments. They give orders who shall have, but they have not orders by which they are enabled to have what they have.

Men of inferior and laborious callings in the world are sealed with the *cross;* a *rose* or a *bunch of grapes* will not answer that seal. Ease and plenty must not be looked for without crosses and labor and industry in youth. All men, prince and people, clergy and magistrate are sealed with the image of God with a conformity to Him; and worldly seals will not answer that, nor fill up that seal.

We should wonder to see a man whose chambers and galleries were full of curious masterpieces thrust into a village fair to look upon sixpenny prints. We all have the image of God at home. The masterpiece is our own, in our own bosom, and we thrust in country fairs. We endure the guiltiness and reproach of having decieved the trust which a confident friend reposes in us, and solicit his wife or daughter. We endure the decay of fortune of body and soul and honor to possess lovers' pictures—pictures that are not originals, not made by that hand of God, nature, but artificial beauties. And for that body we give a soul, and for that drug which might have been bought for a shilling, we give an estate. The image of God is worth more than all substances, and we give it for colors, for dreams, for shadows.

The Creation

There is but one God; but yet was that one God ever *alone?* Was there not always a *Father* and a *Son* and a *Holy Ghost?* And had not they always an acquiescence in one another, an exercise of *affection,* a love, and a delight towards one another, so that the Father could not be without the Son and Holy Ghost; neither could the Son and the Holy Ghost be without the Father. God was from all eternity collected into *one God;* yet from all eternity He was three persons. God could not be so alone that there has been one God.

Had God company enough of Himself? Was He satisfied in *three persons?* We see He proceeded further; He made a *creation.* And as soon as He made light, He took pleasure in it; He said it was good. He was glad for it—glad for the *sea,* the *earth,* the *sun,* the *moon,* and the *stars.* He said of every one, "It is *good.*" But when He had made all; when He had peopled the whole world and brought all creatures together, then He was *very glad.* Then He said, not only that it was *good,* but that it was *very good.* God was so far from being alone He found not the fulness of being till *all* was made, till all creatures met together in a *host,* as Moses calls it.

Did God satisfy Himself with this *visible* world? Let every star in the firmament be a world. Was all this enough? We see that God drew persons nearer to Him than sun or moon or stars or any other thing visible. He created angels. How many? Arithmetic lacks numbers to express them. So far was God from being alone.

And yet God had not shed Himself far enough. He had the whale in the sea, the elephant upon the land, all these heavenly bodies in the way, and angels in their countless numbers and manifold offices in heaven. But because angels could not propagate nor make more angels, He enlarged His love in making *man* that He might enjoy all natures at once and have the nature of angels and the nature of *earthly creatures* in one person.

God would not be without man, nor would He come alone to the making of man. But God, in His whole counsel, in His whole society, in the whole Trinity, made man in whom the whole nature of the world should meet.

A Harmonious World

God made this world in such a uniformity, with such a correspondence of parts that it was an instrument perfectly in tune. We may say the trebles, the highest strings, were disordered first. Angels and men put this instrument out of tune. God rectified all again by putting in a new string, the seed of the woman, the *Messias*. Any only by sounding that string in your ears do we become true music, true harmony, true peace.

If we shall say that God's first string in this instrument was reprobation, that God's first intention was, for His glory, to damn man and that He put in another string of creating man that He might have somebody to damn and then another of enforcing him to sin and then another of disabling him to lay hold upon any means of recovery, then there is no music nor harmony in all of this. But if we take this instrument when God's hand tuned it the second time in the promise of a *Messias* and offer of the love and mercy of God to all that will receive Him, then we are truly *musicum carmen*, as a love song when we present the love of God to you and raise you to the love of God in Jesus Christ.

We cannot hear the music of the spheres. For the decrees of God in heaven, we cannot say we have seen them. Our music is only that salvation which is declared in the Gospel to all them who take God by the right hand, as He delivers Himself in Christ.

Original Sin

Hardly any man considers the weight of original sin. And yet as the strongest temptations fall upon us when we are weakest, in our *deathbed*, so the heaviest sin seizes us when are weakest.

As soon as we are anything we are sinners. In our mother's womb when no world, nor flesh, nor devil could present a provocation to use to sin, yet there in that weakness we are under the weight of original sin. If at this time God would vouchsafe to me my choice whether He should pardon me all those actual and habitual sins which I have committed in my life, or extinguish original sin in me, I should choose to be delivered from original sin, because, though I be delivered from the *imputation* thereof by baptism so that I shall not fall under a condemnation for original sin only, yet it still remains in me, and practices upon me and occasions all the other sins that I commit.

For all my actual and habitual sins I know God has instituted means in the church—the Word and the sacraments—for my reparation. But with what holy alacrity, with what heavenly joy, with what cheerful peace should I come to the participation in these means and seals of my reconciliation and pardon of all my sins if I knew myself to be delivered from original sin—from that snake in my bosom, from that poison in my blood that casts me into relapses of those sins which I have repented?

What a cloud upon the serenity of my conscience that though I have washed myself in the tears of repentance and in the blood of my Saviour, and though I have no guilt of my former sin upon me at the present, yet I have a sense of *root* of sin, of original sin that will cast me back again.

Hardly any man considers the weight and oppression of original sin. No man can say that an acorn weighs as much as an oak. Yet, in truth, there is an oak in that acorn. No man considers that original sin weighs as much as an actual or habitual sin, yet in truth all our actual and habitual sins are in the original. Therefore, Saint Paul's vehement prayer to God to deliver him from original sin, that provocation of the flesh, that *messenger of Satan,* that God would give him sufficient grace for it not to work to his destruction.

The infinite merit of Jesus Christ Himself, that works upon all actual and habitual sin, even after that merit has been applied so that those sins are no sins, does not do away with original sin. Though I am eased in the dominion and imputation thereof, yet the same original sin is in me still, and though God delivers me from eternal death due to my actual and habitual sins, yet from the temporal death, due to original sin, He delivers not His dearest saints.

Delight in Evil

What is this *setting of the heart upon evil?* What is this *fulness* that leaves little room for a cure?

When a man receives figures and images of sin into his fancy and imagination and leads them on to his understanding and discourse, to his will and consent and his heart by a delightful dwelling upon the meditation upon that sin, yet this is not a *setting of the heart upon doing evil.* To be suprised or overthrown or held down by it for a time is not it. It is not when the devil looks in at the window of the heart and presents occasions of temptation to the eye, nor when he comes in at the door of our heart or the ear, either in lascivious discourse or satirical or libelous defamation of other men. It is not when the devil is put to his circuit to *seek whom he may devour* or how he may corrupt the soul by the senses.

It is when by a habitual custom in sin the sin rises immediately from myself. It is when the heart is able and apt to sin of itself, even if there were no devil or no outward objects of temptation; it is when our own heart has become such a willful madness and such a voluntary and natural devil to itself that we would be ambitious and licentious though we were in a wilderness. This man begins at a delight in the sin and comes instantly to a defense of it and to an obdurateness and impenitence in it. This is the evil of the heart by the misuse of God's grace to lose all tenderness and remorse in sin.

The Burden of Sin

"For mine iniquities are gone over my head, as a heavy burden, they are too heavy for me."[2] Our sin wearies us and we cannot divest ourselves of it. We would leave that sin, and yet there is *one talent* more to be added, *one child* more to be provided for, *one office* or *one title* more to be compassed or *one temptation* more to be satisfied. Though we grumble, it is not out of a remorse of conscience, but out of a bodily weariness of the sin. Yet we proceed in it. How often men go to Westminster or to the Exchange to attend unjust suits or answer the call to unjust bargains when their ease or health prompts them to stay at home.

We have wearied ourselves in the way of wickedness in doing as other wicked men have done—ways that have been beaten out to us by the frequent practices of other men. *We have gone through deserts where there lay no way;* that is, through sins in which we had no example, no precedent.

Hilly ways are wearisome ways and tire the ambitious man. Carnal pleasures are *dirty ways* and tire the licentious man. Desires for gain are *thorny ways* and tire the covetous man. Emulations of higher men are *dark and blind ways* and tire the envious man. Every way that is out of the way wearies us. *We labor and have no rest.* When

2Ps. 38:4

we have done, we are wearied with our sins and have no satisfaction in them.

We go to bed at night weary of our sinful labors, and we will rise fresh tomorrow to the same sinful labors again. And when a sinner does so little remember *yesterday*, how little does he consider *tomorrow?* He that forgets what he has done foresees not what he shall suffer. So sin is a burden; it crookens and wearies us. Those are the first two inconveniences.

All Must Die

Does not man die even in his birth? The breaking of prison is death, and what is our birth but a breaking of prison?

As soon as we were clothed by God our very apparel was an emblem of death. In the skins of dead beasts He covered the skins of dying men. As soon as God set us to work, our very occupation was an emblem of death. It was to dig the earth—even graves for ourselves.

Has any man here forgotten today that yesterday is dead? And the bell tolls for today and will ring out anon for as much of every one of us as appertains to this day. We die every day, and we die all the day long. Because we are not absolutely dead, we call that an eternity of dying. And is there comfort in that state? Is that not the state of hell itself—eternally dying and yet never dead?

To this the moral man says that this death is merely natural; you were born under the Law and condition to die and it is a rebellious thing not to be content to die. It is an imposition which nature, the queen of this world, lays upon us. It comes equally to us all and makes us all equal when it comes.

The ashes of an oak in the chimney are no epitaph of that oak to tell me how high or how large it was. It tells me not what flocks it sheltered while it stood or what men it hurt when it fell. The dust of great persons' graves is speechless, too; it says nothing, it distinguishes nothing.

Death is the last, and in that respect the worst enemy. The enemy that reserves himself unto the last and attends our weak estate offers more danger. If my enemy meets me in the times of my youth through temptation, if I do not dwell upon a delightful meditation of that sin or assist and encourage that sin, I shall have reason on my side as well as grace; also, I shall have the history of a thousand that have perished by that sin on my side. But when I lie under the hands of that enemy that has reserved himself unto the last—to my last bed when I shall not be able to stir a limb more than a fever or palsy shall shake them; when the last enemy shall watch my remediless body and my disconsolate soul where neither the physician nor priest shall be able to give assistance; and when he shall shift the scene and throw me from that bed into the grave and there triumph over me, God knows how many generations till the Redeemer, my Redeemer, the Redeemer of body as well as soul, come again.

As death is the enemy which watches me at my last weakness, and shall hold me when I shall be no more till that angel come who shall swear that time shall be no more, in that consideration he is the most powerful and fearful enemy. Yet this enemy shall be destroyed.

Death Inevitable

Adam might have lived, if he would, but I cannot. God has placed a mark of my death upon every living thing that I can set my eyes upon. Everything is a remembrance, a judge upon me and pronounces, I must die.

The whole frame of the world is mortal; heaven and earth pass away.[3] Upon us there is an irrecoverable decree that it is appointed unto all men that they shall once die. But when? Quickly!

If you look up into the air, remember that your life is but a wind.[4] If you see a cloud in the air, ask Saint James his question, "What is your life?" He answers, "It is a vapor that appears and vanishes away."[5] If you behold a tree, then Job gives you a comparison of yourself. A tree is an emblem of your self; in fact, it is the original and you are but the copy of it. There is hope for a tree, for if the roots wax old and the stock be dead and if it be cut down, by the action of the waters, it will bud forth again. But when man is sick and dies, where is he? He shall not awaken again till heaven shall be no more.

Look at the earth. We are not like that, but we are earth itself. God has made many testimonies of our death in the walls and windows, and He only knows whether He will not make another testimony of our mortality of the youngest among us before we part and make the *very place of our burial* and *deathbed*.

The Resurrection of the Body

There are so many evidences of the immortality

---

[3]Heb. 9:27   [4]Job 7:7   [5]James 4:14

of the soul, even to natural man's reason, that it required not an article of the Creed to fix the notion in man's mind.

But the resurrection of the *body* is discernible by no other light but that of *faith*, and could be fixed by no less assurance than by an article of the Creed.

Where are all the atoms of the flesh which corrosion or consumption has eaten away? In what furrow or bowel of the earth lie all the ashes of a body burned a thousand years since? In what corner of the sea lies all the jelly of a body drowned in the general *flood?* What coherence, what sympathy, what dependence maintain any relation or correspondence between that arm that was lost in Europe and that leg that was lost in Africa or Asia with scores of years between?

One humor of our dead body produces worms and those worms exhaust all other humor and then all dies and dries and molders into dust, and that dust is blown into the river and that water tumbles into the sea, which ebbs and flows in infinite revolutions.

Still, God knows in what *cabinet* every *seed-pearl* lies and in what part of the world every grain of every man's dust lies, and (as His prophet speaks in another case[6]) He beckons for the bodies of His saints, and in the twinkling of an eye that body that was scattered over all the elements has sat down at the right of God in a glorious resurrection.

---

[6]Zech. 10:8

6

A More
Glorious Light

Joy

As God has cast upon the unrepentant sinner two
deaths—a temporal and a spiritual—so has He
breathed into us two lives. Though our natural
life were but a continual dying, yet we have two
lives besides that—an eternal life reserved for
heaven and a heavenly, spiritual life even in this
world.

As God does thus inflict two deaths and infuse
two lives, so does He pass two judgments upon
man, or rather repeats the same judgment twice.
For that which Christ shall say at the last Judg-
ment, "Enter into thy Master's joy,"[1] He says to
your conscience now, "Enter into Thy Master's
joy." The blessedness of the next life is afforded
here. . . .

Howling is the noise of hell; singing the voice
of heaven. Sadness is the damp of hell; rejoicing
the serenity of heaven. He who has not this joy
here lacks one of the best pieces of evidence for

[1]Matt. 25:23

86

the joys of heaven and has neglected or refused that earnest by which God binds His bargain—that true joy in this world that shall flow into the joy of heaven as a river flows into the sea. As my soul as soon as it is out of my body is in heaven, so that soul that goes to heaven meets heaven here.

As my soul goes by heaven to heaven, so the true joy of a good soul in this world is the very joy of heaven. And we go thither not without joy that we might have joy infused into us, but as Christ says, "Our joy might be full"[2]—perfected, sealed with an everlastingness.

As in the face of death I shall see the face of God, so in the agonies of death . . . I shall have a joy that shall no more evaporate than my soul shall evaporate—a joy that shall rise and put on a more glorious garment above and be joy superinvested in glory.

The Joy of Heaven

Humiliation is the beginning of sanctification. As without holiness no man shall see God, though he pore whole nights upon the Bible, so without humility no man shall hear God speak though he hear three two-hour sermons every day.

If God brings you to that humiliation of soul and body here, He will improve and advance your sanctification more abundantly, and when He has brought it to the best perfection that this life is capable of, He will provide another manner of abundance in the life to come.

There was never joy like unto the joy which

---

[2]John 16:24

our Lord had set before Him when He endured the cross. If I had the joy of all the martyrs, yet I shall have a joy more abundant, even superlative joy, in the world to come.

What a dim vespers of a glorious festival, what a poor half-holyday is Methuselah's 900 years to eternity? If I could believe the transmigration of souls and think what my soul had been successively since the creation, what a yesterday is that?

Whatever a man has in this world of temporal abundance, I have life more abundantly than that, for I have the spiritual life of grace, and what measure I have of this spiritual grace in this world, I shall have more abundantly in heaven. There my term shall be a term for three lives; for those three are that as long as the Father and the Son and the Holy Ghost live I shall not die.

Seeing God

All the world is but a glass in which we see God. The church itself, and even faith, are but a dark representation of God to us till we come to that state to "see God face to face and to know as we are also known."

As for the sight of God here, our theater was the world, our *medium* and *glass* was the creature and our light was reason. For our knowledge of God here, our academy was the church, our *medium* the ordinances of the church, and our light the light of faith.

The sphere in which we shall see God is heaven. He who asks me what heaven is, means not to hear me but to silence me. He knows I cannot tell him. When I meet him there I shall be able to tell him, and then he will be able to tell me; then we shall be but able to tell one another. What we enjoy is heaven, but the tongues of angels and glorified saints shall not be able to express what that heaven is, for even in heaven our faculties shall be finite.

Heaven is not a place that was created, for all that was created shall be dissolved. God did not plant a Paradise for Himself and remove to that, as He planted a paradise for Adam and removed him to that. But God is still where He was before the world was made. And in that place where there are more suns than there are stars in the firmament and more light in another Sun, the Sun of righteousness, than in all of them, in that illustration, that effusion of beams of glory, which began to shine not 6,000 years ago, but 6,000 millions before that, in those eternal, in those uncreated heavens shall we see our Omniscient God. . . .

God made light first, and three days afterward that light became a sun, a more glorious light. God gave me the light of nature when I was quickened in my mother's womb to receive a reasonable soul. God gave me the light of faith when I received my baptism. But in my third day, when my mortality shall put on immortality, He shall give me the light of glory by which I shall see Himself.

To this light of glory the light of honor is but a glow-worm and majesty itself but a twilight. The cherubim and seraphims are but candles. The Gospel itself, which the apostles call the glorious Gospel, is but a star of the least magnitude. If I cannot tell what to call this light by which I shall see it, what shall I call that which I shall see by it—the essence of God Himself?

Joy in Heaven

When we shall love everyone as well as ourselves, and so have that joy of our own salvation multiplied by that number, we shall have that joy so many times over as there are souls saved. Because we love them as ourselves, how infinitely shall this joy be enlarged in loving God so far above ourselves.

We have but this to add: heaven is called by many pretentious names. *Life:* simply and absolutely there is no life but that. And *kingdom:* simply, absolutely there is no kingdom that is not subordinate to that. And *Sabbath:* a perpetual Sabbath. But the name that should enamour us most is that it is fulness of *joy*—fulness that needs no addition, that admits no leak.

Though we place blessedness in the sight of God, yet the first thing that this sight of God shall produce in us is joy. The measure of our seeing of God is the measure of joy. See Him here in His blessings, and you shall joy in those blessings here. And when you come to see Him in His essence, then you shall have this joy in essence and in fulness, of which God in His goodness gives us an earnest here. Such an earnest may bind us to that inheritance hereafter, which His Son, our Saviour, has purchased for us with the inestimable price of His incorruptible blood.

Death's Duel: Donne's Last Sermon

All our *periods* and *transitions* in this life are so many passages from *death* to *death*. Our very birth and entrance into this life is an *issue from death*, for in our mother's womb we are dead, for we do not know we live even as much as we do in our sleep; neither is there any grace so close a prison as the womb would be if we stayed in it beyond our time or died there before our time. In the womb we have eyes and see not, ears and hear not; there in the womb we are fitted for the works of darkness; all the while we are deprived of light.

This whole world is but a universal church-yard, our common grave, and the life and motion that the greatest persons have in it are but the shaking of buried bodies in their grave by an earthquake. That which we call life is but a week of death—seven days spent in dying, and there is an end. Our birth dies in infancy, and our infancy dies in youth, and youth and the rest die in age, and age also dies and determines all.

Nor do these arise as a phoenix out of the ashes of another phoenix formerly dead. Our youth is worse than our infancy and our age worse than our youth. Our youth is hungry and thirsty after those sins which our infancy knew not. And our age is angry that it cannot pursue those sins which our youth did. And besides, all the way so many deadly calamities accompany every condition and period of this life that death itself would be an ease to them that suffer them.

But for us that die now, we must all pass this death after death, this dissolution after dissolution, when these bodies must say, "Corruption, you are my father" and to the worm, "You are my mother and sister." Miserable riddle when the same worm must be my mother and my sister and myself.

When my mouth shall be filled with dust and the worm shall feed sweetly upon me; when the ambitious man shall have no satisfaction if the poorest alive tread upon him, nor the poorest receive any contentment in being made equal with princes, they all shall be equal but in dust. This is the most inglorious and contemptible vilification, the most deadly and peremptory nullification of man that we can consider.

Selected Bibliography

Donne, John. *Devotions Upon Emergent Occasions*. Ann Arbor: The University of Michigan Press, 1959. Contains the complete text of the *Devotions*, together with the engaging *Life of John Donne* by Izaak Walton.

Gardner, Helen, ed., *The Divine Poems*. Oxford: The Clarendon Press, 1959. Contains an introduction and a helpful discussion of the dating, ordering, and interpretation of the Holy Sonnets.

Gardner, Helen, ed., *John Donne: A Collection of Critical Essays*. Englewood Cliffs (N. J.): Prentice Hall, 1962. These essays help to clarify various attitudes toward Donne.

Grierson, Herbert, ed., *The Poems of John Donne*. London: Oxford University Press, 1912. Volume 1 gives the text of the poems, with appendices. Volume 2 contains an introduction and commentary.

Potter, George and Simpson, Evelyn eds., *The Sermons of John Donne*. 10 Vol. Berkeley: University of California Press, 1953. This monumental work furnishes reliable texts of Donne's known sermons, listing variant readings in seventeenth-century manuscripts and editions and treating biographical, historical, and literary concerns in the introduction.

Simpson, Evelyn. *A Study of the Prose Works of John Donne.* Oxford: The Clarendon Press, 1948. A very useful survey of Donne's life and achievement as man of letters, theologian, and child of the Renaissance. It also comments on the wide range of Donne's prose, including the sermons, essays, letters, and the *Devotions.*

Smith, Logan Pearsall, ed., *Donne's Sermons.* Selected Passages. Oxford: The Clarendon Press, 1932. Although this collection is no match for the newer edition of the sermons by Potter and Simpson, it has value for the general reader who desires to sample the "purple passages." This work provides the major basis for the present study.

WATCH THE COMPANY YOU KEEP.
IT CAN GET YOU KILLED.

Her blood turned to ice and her heart almost stopped.

She looked up at Tyler, her jaw slack. Her heart had resumed a frantic pace, and moisture coated her palms. "He was watching us. He saw us leave for Home Depot together." She took a step back, shaking her head. "You have to stay away from me."

He moved closer until he was standing at the threshold. "Do you really think I'm intimidated by this creep, who's too much of a coward to show his face?"

"Maybe *you're* not intimidated, but *I* am. I'm not willing to risk you getting hurt. This is my battle, not yours." Although she had no idea what she'd done to get drawn into it.

He took a step closer and put both hands on her shoulders. "It's *our* battle. Friends stick together. Or have you forgotten that?"

Carol J. Post writes fun and fast-paced inspirational romantic suspense stories and lives in sunshiny central Florida. She sings and plays the piano for her church and also enjoys sailing, hiking, camping—almost anything outdoors. Her daughters and grandkids live too far away for her liking, so she now pours all that nurturing into taking care of two fat and sassy cats and one highly spoiled dachshund.

Books by Carol J. Post

Love Inspired Suspense

Midnight Shadows
Motive for Murder
Out for Justice
Shattered Haven
Hidden Identity
Mistletoe Justice
Buried Memories

BURIED MEMORIES

CAROL J. POST

HARLEQUIN® LOVE INSPIRED® SUSPENSE

Recycling programs
for this product may
not exist in your area.

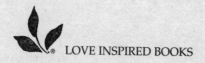

LOVE INSPIRED BOOKS

ISBN-13: 978-0-373-45683-3

Buried Memories

He heals the brokenhearted and binds up their wounds.
—Psalms 147:3

Acknowledgments

A huge thank you to my friend Chaplain (Major) Andrew Ropp, US Army (retired). I appreciate your willingness to share your experiences. Your help on this project has been invaluable.

Thank you to my critique partners, Karen Fleming and Sabrina Jarema. Your sharp eyes and creative minds always make my writing better.

Thank you to my editor, Giselle Regus, and my agent, Nalini Akolekar. I'm thrilled to be working with both of you.

And thank you to my husband, Chris. I might be able to do this without your love and support...but I wouldn't want to.

ONE

Nicki Jackson wheeled her bulging carry-on through the carport, the rumble of the plastic wheels against the concrete breaking the silence of the dark night. The golden retriever prancing behind her had enough energy for both of them. Of course, the dog hadn't spent the past eight hours trapped in the car, battling traffic.

Nicki sighed. The last of her single friends was now married. But at less than a year from thirty, what did she expect? In fact, she'd almost made it to the altar herself. Instead, she was free and single, and her former intended was facing a hefty jail term.

She hesitated in the glow of the Ram's headlights to finger through her keys, then dragged her bag the final few feet to the kitchen door. Bed was only a few minutes away. Unpacking could wait till morning. So could a shower.

She raised the key and stopped short. The door wasn't shut tightly, and the jamb was chipped and scratched.

The headlights clicked off automatically, casting her in darkness, and the hair rose on the back of her neck. Someone had broken in to her house. Heart pounding in her chest, she pulled her phone from her purse and dialed 911.

"Come, Callie." With a small tug on the leash, she moved to the truck and opened the door. The dog stared at her, a question in her big brown eyes. After a moment's hesitation, she jumped onto the seat, and Nicki slid in after her. Uneasiness crawled along her skin, the sense someone was nearby, watching. Why hadn't that call gone through yet?

She lowered the phone and stared at the screen. Half a bar. More like a dot. In several places on Cedar Key, her cell service was sketchy. Under her metal carport, it was nonexistent. Sitting inside the truck wasn't helping, either.

Leaving the driver's side door open, she moved out into the moonlight, pulling Callie with her. Two bars. It was better than nothing.

The dispatcher answered, and Nicki's hand tightened on the phone. Perspiration coated her palms, and all the strength seemed to have left her limbs. "Someone broke in to my house." She quickly provided the address.

"Is anyone there now?"

"I don't know. I haven't been inside." Her gaze darted across the front of the house, and she backed toward the road, putting as much distance between herself and the house as she could. But nowhere felt safe.

A shadow fell over her, and she lifted her gaze. Clouds rolled across the sky, obscuring the three-quarter moon. Thunder rumbled in the distance, a far-off storm that might or might not reach Cedar Key.

After finishing with the dispatcher, she slid her phone back into its pouch. The police would be there soon. Meanwhile, Callie was with her. Of course, Callie was a big pussycat.

She turned to head back toward the truck, the sense of vulnerability too strong to ignore. She was used to living out of sight of the neighbors. She'd grown up in the country, at least from age nine onward. That was when she'd moved to Crystal River and found out what a real family was. The dozen or so foster homes before that didn't count. Neither did the time she'd spent with her birth mother.

But now, looking at the trees shielding her house on three sides, the privacy she'd cherished when she bought the place felt more like isolation. And not in a good way.

A rustle sounded nearby and grew rapidly closer. Her heart leaped into her throat. Callie stiffened, a low growl rumbling in her chest. Something was barreling toward them through the strip of woods separating her yard from the one next door. Something large. She jerked Callie's leash, ready to run for the truck, but Callie wasn't budging.

A male voice cut through the noise. "Sasha, heel."

Sasha? The breath she'd been holding spilled out in a rush. Sasha was the German shepherd next door, her neighbor Andy's dog.

A fraction of a second later, sixty pounds of quivering excitement broke from the trees and charged across the yard toward them. Both dogs' tails waved back and forth at a frantic pace. By the time Sasha's human counterpart appeared, the two dogs were busy exchanging sniffs.

She watched him retrieve the leash and loop it around his hand. The other end was attached to Andy's dog, but the man standing in her driveway wasn't Andy. In fact, he looked sort of like... No way. She squinted in the bit of moonlight leaking through the clouds.

"Tyler?"

He hesitated for two beats. Then recognition flashed across his face. "Nicki." He wrapped her in a hug, then held her away from him, his hands on her shoulders. "Wow, you look good." The recognition turned to confusion. "What are you doing here?"

"I live here." The hesitation in her tone proclaimed her own bewilderment.

Long ago, they'd been friends—close friends—until his mom got sick and moved him to Atlanta, where his aunt could care for them both. He'd been a scrawny fifteen-year-old at the time. She'd been a year younger and pretty skinny herself.

Now he was anything but. Her three-inch heels, added to her own five feet nine inches, put her almost eye to eye with him. But he outweighed her by a good seventy pounds, all of it muscle.

She shook her head, trying to clear it. "What are you doing here with Andy's dog?"

"Andy's my brother. I'm going to help him renovate that run-down inn he bought."

The confusion cleared. Andy's kid brother. The soldier. Andy and his wife Joan had told her he was coming and had given her a bit of his history, how two years ago, he'd been finishing his third tour in Afghanistan and had come under attack during a recon mission and how he almost didn't make it out alive. Andy had just failed to mention his kid brother was Tyler Brant.

"He told me you were coming, but I didn't make the

connection." With different fathers, they didn't have the same last name. And during the two years she and Tyler had hung out, Andy was already out of the house and married.

"I just arrived this afternoon, and we had a lot of catching up to do. Since I'd kept them up way past their bedtime, I told Andy I'd take Sasha out. I didn't realize she was going to bolt as soon as I stepped out the door, or I'd have kept a death grip on the leash."

The teasing grin he flashed her carried her back fifteen years. When she was a cranky adolescent, he'd had a knack for sending the dark clouds scurrying with his quirky sense of humor. Of course, she'd done her share of warding off his storms, too.

She returned his smile. "Sasha probably picked up Callie's scent. They're best buds."

He nodded down at the golden retriever. "She must like late night walks, too."

"Actually, I'm just getting home."

He had the *late* part right. It was three hours later than she'd planned. After the Saturday wedding in Miami, she'd stayed a second night and enjoyed a long lunch with friends. The northerly drive from Miami to the Gulf town of Cedar Key wasn't a lot of fun anytime. Independence Day weekend, it was the pits. The truck that had overturned and strewn produce all over the turnpike hadn't helped, either.

Sirens sounded in the distance and moved closer. When the glow of red-and-blue lights shone from the end of the road, Tyler raised his brows. "I've only been here a few hours, but when I used to come here as a kid, it was a pretty quiet place. I wonder what's going on."

"That would be me. Someone broke in to my house while I was gone."

He frowned, the concern on his face obvious in the light of the moon, which had once again made an appearance. "Is anything missing?"

"I haven't been inside yet." But considering the creep had had all weekend to clean her out, the possibilities weren't looking good.

"That's probably smart. I hope it isn't too bad."

"Yeah, me, too."

A cruiser pulled into the driveway, and the siren stopped midsqueal. The door swung open, and Amber Kingston stepped out. Amber was the newest member of the Cedar Key Police Department and among the group of people who'd taken Nicki under their wings from the moment she'd arrived in town.

"You had a break-in?"

Nicki nodded. "I left midafternoon on Friday and just got home, so no one's been here all weekend." Andy had agreed to collect Saturday's mail, and her friends Allison and Blake had kept Callie. She hadn't seen a need to have anyone keep an eye on the house.

Amber's attention shifted to Tyler. "And you are?"

"Tyler Brant." He jammed a thumb toward the house next door. "Andy's brother."

Amber gave a sharp nod before moving up the drive. "Let's see what we have inside."

Nicki started to follow, but Tyler's hand on her shoulder stopped her.

"Are you okay? I can go in with you if you'd like."

She hesitated, then shook her head. She didn't need anyone to prop her up. She was just overtired. She'd made the harrowing drive home on too little sleep.

But all the excuses in the world couldn't stave off the sense of vulnerability that had swept over her the instant she realized someone had come into her house. There were things inside those four walls that couldn't be replaced at any price, because they'd belonged to the two people she'd cared for more than anyone in the world. Two people who'd taken a foster kid with a chip on her shoulder the size of Texas and shown her a love that wouldn't quit.

She squared her shoulders and forced a smile. If there was one thing life had taught her to do well, it was to stand on her own two feet. "Thanks, but I'm sure I'll be fine."

He opened his mouth as if ready to argue, then reached up to jam his fingers through his hair. No longer in the military buzz cut she would have expected, it rested in soft layers, light brown or dark blond—it was hard to tell in the moonlight. "Let me know if you need anything."

She watched him lead the dog toward the road, a sudden sense of nostalgia sweeping over her. She had friends, close ones, but Tyler knew things about her no one else did. There'd been no pretense for either of them. Could they pick up where they left off and renew the friendship they'd had so many years ago? She wasn't the same person she'd been then, and after the horrors he'd lived through, he probably wasn't, either.

She turned and, with Callie trotting beside her, led Amber toward the carport. She might as well get it over with.

"This is where he got in." She pointed at the door. "Looks like I'm going to need some work done on the doorjamb."

Amber removed her pistol from its holster. "I'm going to go in and clear the place, make sure no one's hiding inside. You might want to wait in the truck."

Nicki coaxed Callie up into the seat for the third time that evening. A few minutes later, Amber stepped back into the carport, her expression somber.

"You've got a little bit of a mess." She held up a hand. "Nothing major."

Nicki followed her into the house, her insides settling into a cold, hard lump. She reached to unhook the leash from Callie's collar, then changed her mind.

"I'd better close her up." Her house had become a crime scene. She didn't need the dog traipsing through and destroying evidence.

She opened the door leading into the laundry room, then filled a bowl with dry food. Callie dove in right away. That would keep her occupied for a few minutes. After a couple of pats on the dog's back, Nicki pulled the door shut and stepped into the kitchen.

It was the same as she'd left it two days earlier. The living room, too, appeared untouched. Two curios held thousands of dollars of figurines—Swarovski, Lenox and Armani—all undisturbed. A sliver of the tension eased. The intruder apparently wasn't interested in electronics, either, because the big-screen TV and pieces of accompanying equipment still occupied their cubbyholes in the entertainment center.

Which meant the mess Amber had referred to was in her bedrooms. The guest room she'd chosen for herself, leaving the large master bedroom to function as a combination hobby room and office.

As soon as she stepped into the hall, she gasped. The

open door at the end revealed her wooden work table covered with papers and files. She closed the distance at a half run.

All of her tools and materials for making stained glass were where she'd left them, but both file drawers were all the way open, the majority of the contents removed and strewn across her work area. Her bulletin board hung above the table, her to-do list pinned in the center. The first three items were crossed through. The remaining four, she'd assigned time frames for completion. Organization in the midst of chaos. But the sense of control it usually gave her had evaporated the moment she stepped into the room.

She reached for one of the files on the table. Amber's voice stopped her.

"Don't touch anything. I'm going to try to lift prints."

Nicki let her hand fall to her side but scanned the items. Lots of papers lay on top, pulled from their folders. One stack was the paperwork from the sale of the Crystal River house, an hour from Cedar Key. It had belonged to her parents. Seven months ago, they'd taken early retirement to see the country and reward themselves for all the years of hard work.

Some reward. They'd been headed toward a picturesque small town in North Carolina when a tired trucker had crossed the center line. And she'd been left with a three-bedroom house on five acres and a great big hole in her heart.

Next to the Crystal River sale documents was the paperwork from the purchase of the Cedar Key house. And beside that was the file from opening her account at Drummond Community Bank upon first moving to

Cedar Key. Her income tax forms were also there, along with some credit card statements.

All of her personal information was right out in the open—her name, address, Social Security number, date of birth—everything needed to steal her identity.

"You'd better file fraud alerts with the credit reporting agencies." Amber's voice was soft but filled with worry.

She nodded and followed Amber from the room, an emptiness weaving through her. She'd come to Cedar Key to regain her footing after life had kicked out one too many of her foundation blocks. The quaint town's peace and tranquility had gone a long way toward mending the tattered pieces of her soul. And she wasn't going to let this break-in take that away.

She squared her shoulders and started down the hall. Before she'd gotten very far, Amber stopped her with a raised hand.

"The intruder did some damage in this room, too. I'm hoping you can shed some light on what's going on."

During her mad rush to her work room, she'd hurried right past her bedroom without even looking inside. Now something in Amber's tone sent dread showering down on her. Could anything be worse than what she'd already witnessed?

Amber stepped aside and Nicki closed the remaining distance to her room.

Then froze in the open doorway. Her old plush rabbit was hanging from the ceiling fan with a noose around its neck. Stuffing protruded from a slash that ran from throat to tail and littered the carpet beneath.

Her knees started to buckle, and she gripped the doorjamb for support. Lavender wasn't just an old, scruffy stuffed animal. She was her childhood friend who'd gotten her through nights of terror while her mother was being beaten by her men in the next room. She'd been Nicki's constant companion through one foster home after another when the parents couldn't cope anymore with a disturbed, destructive child, and through weeks of uncertainty as she waited for her adoptive family to give up and throw in the towel. Lavender had been hugged and kissed and cried on. And had been there for a lonely, terrified little girl when no one else had.

Why Lavender? Houses got burglarized all the time. Maybe not in Cedar Key, but plenty of other places. Even going through her paperwork made sense. But why destroy a stuffed toy?

Nicki dragged her gaze from the rabbit to take in the rest of the room. Several dresser drawers were open, the contents hanging over the sides. The closet doors were open, too. Other than that, and the empty spot on the shelf Lavender had occupied, it looked undisturbed.

A soft hand on her shoulder reminded her she wasn't alone. Nicki dropped her hand from the jamb and faced Amber. "I'm guessing the intruder was ticked about not finding any money and figured he'd do a little vandalism before he left."

Amber shook her head, eyes now back on the stuffed rabbit. "That doesn't look like vandalism to me. It looks like a threat."

Tyler stepped out the door behind Sasha and drew in an earth-scented breath. Early morning sunlight slanted over the landscape, and the final remnants of pink still stained the eastern sky. The rain that had passed through during the night had left behind glistening droplets that clung to the shrubbery lining Andy's front walk.

Cedar Key was a nice change from the city. Maybe he'd even stay awhile. He was committed to two months, anyway. Andy had bought an old inn and needed help with renovations. So he'd offered his services. He might as well put to good use those long-ago afternoons and weekends he'd spent working in his best friend's dad's construction business. Besides, after all the care packages that had traveled from Andy and Joan's doorstep to Afghanistan, it was the least he could do. How long he stayed after the work was completed would depend on how quickly the nightmares caught up with him.

In the months following the attack, they'd been relentless. He'd been stationed at Fort Sam Houston, Texas, undergoing treatment, both physical and mental. After a year, the Army cut him loose with a monthly disability check.

Now another year had passed, and the nightmares were still pursuing him. Strenuous activity helped. So did starting fresh. That was how he'd lived ever since his discharge—move, find a temporary job, get semi-settled, repeat. So far it was working. Sort of.

Halfway down the drive, Sasha stopped walking, head angled toward the strip of woods and undergrowth separating Andy's yard from Nicki's. A few seconds later, a soft rustle sounded about twenty feet away.

The German shepherd lunged, and Tyler tightened his grip on the leash. "Oh, no, you don't." Callie would be inside, and he didn't need to be led on a chase after some poor opossum or armadillo. He gave the leash a tug and continued down the drive.

Nicki's in Cedar Key. The realization was still sinking in. He'd thought he'd never see her again. They'd promised to stay in touch. For a while they had. Then life got in the way and they'd each moved on. He'd had a terrible crush on her, something he kept secret throughout their entire two-year friendship.

When he reached the end of the driveway, he turned left and cast a glance toward Nicki's house. It was dark except for the single light burning by the front door, apparently turned on after he'd gone home.

Since she'd had such a late night, she was probably still asleep. The same place he should be. But he'd woken up in the darkness after his usual four or five hours. And once he was awake, he was done. Sleep invited nightmares.

He continued down Hodges Avenue at an easy jog, Sasha as far in front of him as the leash allowed. The dog would have preferred a full-out run. But he wasn't giving her the choice. Running long distances was one of several things he couldn't do anymore.

Just past Gulf Boulevard, he turned Sasha around and headed toward Andy's. Maybe by the time he got back, Nicki would be out and about. Last night, when he'd offered her his help, she'd stood straight and tall, projecting confidence. But her eyes had given her away. They'd held a fear and vulnerability even the nighttime shadows couldn't hide. And his protective instincts had kicked into overdrive. He should have insisted on going in the house with her. But if there was one thing he remembered about Nicki, it was that once her mind was made up, there was no changing it.

He slowed to a brisk walk and struggled to catch his

breath. It was barely six-thirty, and already the humidity was getting to him. It had never bothered him before. But neither had running. That last mission had changed a lot of things. Even more for his men.

He pushed the thought from his mind. He wasn't going there. He had no say over where his thoughts traveled while sleeping, but he could control them when he was awake.

Today would be the first day on his new job, temporary though it was. He was looking forward to it. Over the next few weeks, he'd work hard. And when he and Andy finished, they'd have something beautiful. It was an appealing thought. He'd seen enough destruction to last a lifetime.

He'd almost reached Nicki's driveway when she stepped off her porch, holding Callie's leash. She looked up and raised a hand in greeting.

"Good morning."

As soon as Sasha saw Callie, she shot off in that direction, pulling him with her. He didn't resist. It gave him the perfect excuse to approach Nicki.

"How did everything go last night?"

She nodded, but there was something stiff about the action. "Okay. It doesn't look like he took anything. I'm guessing he was hoping for some quick cash."

"Good." He studied her. There was more to it than that. "And no damage was done?"

"The doorjamb where he pried the lock is pretty messed up. The lock itself is kind of iffy, too. I'm having it replaced, but I'm getting one with a dead bolt this time."

Callie led her down the driveway toward the road, and he fell in beside her.

"Can I install the lock for you? I brought power tools, and I'm sure Andy has a mortising kit I can borrow."

She waved aside his offer. "That's okay. There's a handyman in town who has done some work for a friend of mine."

"I want to help you out. Andy can tell you I know what I'm doing." He paused. "I like to stay busy." He *had* to stay busy. It was how he stayed sane.

She hesitated but finally nodded. "All right. But I'm going to pay you."

He grinned. Stubborn as always. Of course, he hadn't expected any different.

When they reached the road, Callie turned to go in the same direction he and Sasha had gone, but Sasha didn't seem to mind repeating their route. She pranced along next to Callie, ears erect, head held high, which left him to walk beside Nicki, something he didn't mind, either.

He'd thought she was pretty years before, but she was gorgeous now. Her features had matured, erasing the last traces of childish softness, and her green eyes held a determined sparkle, confidence replacing the scrappiness that had been there earlier. Her hair fell in soft waves around her face and brushed her shoulders. Previously a light brown color, it was now a shade of auburn too bright to be natural, but somehow perfect.

"I've got to be at work in an hour, so I won't be able to get the lock to you until this evening. We don't have a Lowe's or Home Depot here. I guess I need to find a hardware store." She glanced up at him. "I've lived here only a month."

"No problem. Andy and I will be hitting Home Depot

in Crystal River to pick up some materials for the inn. I'll get your locks while we're there."

She released a relieved sigh. "I appreciate it. I was trying to figure out how to fit everything in today. I took off an hour early Friday to get a jump on my trip to Miami, so I hated to have to beg off again today, being the new kid on the block."

"You won't have to. I'll make sure we have everything you need, and by bedtime tonight, I'll have you secure."

She frowned. "As secure as I can be with my personal data out there."

He raised his brows.

"The intruder went through my files. Seemed to be especially interested in my financial information."

"Not good." No wonder she was ill at ease. "Have you filed fraud alerts?"

"I will in a few minutes. That's going to be my entertainment over breakfast." She gave him a wry smile, then tugged Callie's leash to turn her around. Sasha eagerly followed.

"Anything else disturbed?"

She hesitated, her lower lip pulled between her teeth. It was something she used to do whenever she was perturbed or confused or any number of other emotions. Apparently she still did. "Lavender."

"Lavender?" The purple rabbit? He'd once asked her why she was hanging on to an ugly, ragged-out stuffed animal, and she'd gotten rather…defensive. The bruises on his arm had lasted several days. "You still have Lavender?"

"Until this weekend, I did." She frowned again. "Someone was apparently not happy about finding no money in the house and decided to string her up to the ceiling fan and slice her belly open."

His gut clenched, and a cold wave of unease washed through him. "That doesn't sound like your regular, run-of-the-mill burglar."

She pursed her lips. "Amber took it as a threat."

"I'd tend to agree."

"But I don't have any enemies."

Maybe she didn't have any she knew of. "How about saving my contact info in your phone?"

She pulled it from her pocket and her thumbs slid over the screen. When she was ready, he gave her his number.

"If anything happens or you feel at all unsafe, call me. I'm right next door. I can be here a lot faster than the police can."

She slid the phone back into her pocket. "Thanks, but I think you're worrying over nothing. I'm sure it was a simple act of vandalism." She stopped at the end of her driveway. "I'll see you tonight. Meanwhile, Callie will stand guard."

"Let me walk you to your door." He would make sure she was locked safely inside, then cut through the woods.

Halfway up the drive, his gaze stopped on her porch. Something was attached to her front door. She saw it at the same time he did and picked up her pace.

It was a single sheet of paper, folded in half, secured with a piece of tape. As she removed it, he cast an uneasy glance toward the woods. When he'd first stepped out of the house, he'd heard a rustle. He'd assumed it was an animal. Was it possible...

When he looked at Nicki again, she was staring at

the unfolded paper, brow creased. Before he could ask, she angled the page toward him. It was blank except for three words written in all caps—THE PARTY'S OVER.

She gave him a sudden dry laugh. It held no humor, just a lot of desperation. "Trust me, these past few months, my life has been anything but a party."

"Someone apparently disagrees and is planning to make sure things get unpleasant fast." He put a hand on her shoulder. "You need to call the police."

"I will. But it'll have to wait till tonight. I've got to get to work. I can't be late."

She pushed the key into the lock and turned it, then opened the door. Her hands shook, something she was trying hard to hide.

"Where do you work?"

"City hall."

"How about if I take you?"

"Thanks, but I'll be fine. No one is going to bother me here with Callie around, and I don't think anyone would dare approach me at work." She stepped over the threshold and raised a hand in farewell. "Later."

He watched her close the door, then moved toward the woods with Sasha. Nicki wasn't the only one who needed to get to work. Andy would be ready to start soon, too.

He'd just reached the driveway on the other side of the trees when the front door swung open. Andy stepped onto the porch holding up a cell phone. Tyler patted his pocket. He'd left the phone on the table after finishing his coffee.

"It's Bridgett."

Their older sister. He cringed. He'd forgotten to call her when he'd arrived yesterday. Of course, Andy could have assured her he was alive and well. But he knew Bridgett, and she wouldn't be satisfied until she'd heard it from him. She'd worried about him as much in the past two years that he'd lived stateside as she had during his tours in Afghanistan. Maybe more. His mom would have been right there with Bridgett. But the day before his eighteenth birthday, the cancer she'd fought since the summer he turned fifteen had finally won. His dad wasn't doing any worrying, either. He'd walked out years earlier.

He stepped onto the porch and took his phone from Andy. Once he'd convinced his sister that he was all in one piece, he headed to the back to dress for work. Tonight he'd get Nicki's lock replaced. While he was at it, he'd check the ones on her other doors and windows. Any he wasn't happy with, he'd replace the following day.

The fact was, he'd cared for her all those years ago, and he felt no less for her now. As young teenagers, they'd been drawn together by a mutual toughness. He'd had a chip on his shoulder from his dad walking out, and she'd still had an attitude from her years in foster care.

But things had been simple then compared to now. In the fifteen years since he'd left Crystal River, he'd faced too many battles. He bore the scars, both physical and emotional. Nicki probably had enough of her own issues to fight without having to deal with his. Besides, he couldn't stay in one place long enough to pursue anything more serious than friendship with anyone. He had to keep moving to hold the memories at bay.

But that wasn't going to stop him from doing everything he could to protect her while he was here. Someone was threatening his longtime friend, and he was going to get to the bottom of it. He wouldn't leave until he made sure she was safe.

Maybe, if he was successful, it would help make up for the other times he'd tried to protect someone but failed.

TWO

Nicki picked up the porcelain bowl in the corner and crossed the kitchen. The painted paw prints lining the bottom shone clean and clear, licked to a glossy shine. As she placed the empty dish in the sink, Callie watched her every move, tail wagging, eyes filled with doggy eagerness. She never gave up hope that maybe, just this once, there would be seconds.

Nicki strolled toward the side door and cast a glance back at the golden retriever staying right on her heels. "You behave yourself."

She would be out all evening for the midweek church service. But she hoped the admonition wouldn't be necessary. A year ago, yeah. When she'd first brought Callie home from the Humane Society, she'd been well past the energetic puppy stage, but past abuse had made her terrified of everything that moved and a whirlwind of destruction when left alone.

Now she didn't even need crating. Finding a forever home where she was showered with love had made a world of difference. Nicki bent to scratch the dog's neck. She could relate.

After stepping into the carport and closing the door,

she fished for the key. Two nights ago Tyler had installed a new lock, complete with a deadbolt, and made repairs to the jamb. And he'd done a great job. So much so she might see if she could hire him to do some other projects. She would love to have the pedestal sink in the hall bath replaced with a vanity, and some shelves added to the two closets in her hobby room.

She hadn't seen him since he'd made the repairs. Their times for taking the dogs out hadn't coincided, and they'd both been busy. She was almost disappointed. It had been fun having someone to talk to on her morning walk.

She inserted the key into the deadbolt and turned it. The lock slid home with a satisfying click. She'd regained a little of her sense of control, thanks to Tyler. He'd even checked the locks on all her windows to make sure they were secure.

Fifteen years ago, they'd been the best of friends, spending hours hanging out at the park or high on a branch of the huge oak overshadowing most of her backyard. As he'd opened up about his anger with his father, she'd let down some of her own walls. Back then, he'd just been Tyler, her friend and confidante, the one person in the world she'd been able to connect with, because he was as lost as she was.

He was still Tyler. But now he was Tyler all grown up. It was hard not to notice how well he filled out those T-shirts he wore, or how his golden-brown eyes filled with warmth every time he smiled. But with her track record, she didn't have any business contemplating anything that smacked of romance. She was still trying to ward off the repercussions of the last disaster.

She pressed a button on her key fob, and the Ram's

locks popped up. Tonight she would be occupied, with or without Tyler. She was going to church, something her friend Darci had talked her into. She'd been surprised to find she enjoyed attending. It was almost like belonging to a family again—a loving heavenly Father and lots of brothers and sisters.

That wasn't all she'd been talked into. After the crash that killed Nicki's parents, Darci was the one who'd suggested she sell out and come to Cedar Key. When her ex had dropped the second bombshell on her, she'd finally agreed. One month had passed since the move. She still missed her parents terribly, but she hoped the call from Peter a week ago was the final one. He claimed that everything he'd done was for her. So what? It was over.

She swung open the driver's door of her truck, but before she could get in, a dark sedan pulled into her driveway. As she watched a man and woman exit, tension crept across her shoulders. Both visitors were strangers.

"Can I help you?"

The man showed her his badge. "I'm Detective Granger, and this is Detective Mulling. We're with the Jacksonville Sheriff's Office."

As he spoke, her mind whirled. Maybe they'd learned something about her break-in. But Jacksonville? That was where she'd spent her early years. In a run-down shack with peeling plaster, grime-encrusted windows and puke-green shag carpet.

"Can we have a few minutes of your time? We need to talk to you about your mother's murder."

She nodded, a weight pressing in on her chest. She'd worked hard to leave those memories behind. The steady stream of creepy men who'd paraded in and out of the house. The way some of them had leered at her, making her hair stand on end. The nights she'd spent curled into a ball with her pillow over her head, trying to shut out the thud of angry fists and her mother's muffled pleas.

She swallowed hard and led them toward the house. "It's been twenty-two years. Why now?" If they hadn't solved it then, with fresh evidence, how would they uncover anything leading them to the killer over two decades later?

"We're investigating an incident that happened two weeks ago, also in Jacksonville. There are some similarities, and we think they might be connected."

"I don't know how much help I'll be. I wasn't there." She unlocked the door and ushered them inside. After a few quick sniffs, Callie apparently decided the visitors were okay and plopped down in front of the entertainment center, dark eyes alert.

Nicki motioned toward the sectional sofa. "Have a seat."

Once they'd settled onto the couch, Mulling turned back the cover on a notebook.

Granger clasped his hands loosely in his lap. "Thank you for talking to us." Although the female detective was sitting closer to Nicki, it looked as if Granger would be the one asking the questions. "I'm sure it's going to be difficult, but I need you to tell me everything you can remember about that night."

She drew in a deep breath. Yeah, it would be difficult. Not because she still grieved for her mother. She'd come to terms with her death years ago. In fact, if events hadn't gone the way they had, Nicki's life would have turned out quite differently. Ending up in the Jackson home was the best thing that had ever happened to her. No, this was going to be difficult because she didn't want to remember.

She leaned back against the padded leather. "I was spending the night with a friend, Lizzie. She lived next door."

"Do you remember Lizzie's last name?"

"McDonald. Elizabeth McDonald."

"What about her parents' names?"

She shook her head. "I never met her dad, and I just called her mom Mrs. McDonald."

Granger continued while his partner filled up the first small page. "Was anyone there when you left to go to your friend's house?"

"My mom and my sister. I don't remember anyone else."

"When was the first time you learned about your mother's murder?"

"The next morning. Mrs. McDonald said something awful had happened. She was crying. And she wouldn't let me go home." In fact, Nicki never set foot inside her house again. By lunchtime, the authorities had gathered up her belongings and whisked her away to the first of many foster families.

"Did you know of anyone who'd have wanted to hurt your mother?"

Hurt or *kill*? "A lot of them hurt her."

"How?"

"Slapping her, punching her, throwing her against the wall, pushing her to the floor." Fights were a regular occurrence, especially after a night of heavy drinking and shooting up.

Granger leaned forward, sympathy filling his eyes. Or was it pity?

She drew in a deep breath and lifted her chin. She didn't need sympathy. She'd put her past behind her a long time ago. And she didn't want pity.

"These men who used to hit your mother, did you ever see any of them with a knife?"

She shook her head.

With a signal from Granger, Mulling removed a picture from the back of the notebook and handed it to her.

"Does this man look familiar?"

She looked down at what she held. Cords of steel wrapped around her chest and throat, squeezing the air from her lungs. It was a booking photo. Wicked tattoos reached out from beneath the wife beater shirt, and eyes as black as sin glared back at the camera with a lethal hatred. To a seven-year-old child, the man had seemed huge. Judging by the thick neck and monster pecs, her perception hadn't been far off.

All the men had scared her. But this one had frightened her the most.

She shook off the fear. He had no reason to hurt her. And her mother was beyond his reach.

"Uncle Louie." She handed the photo back to Mulling.

"No blood relation, I take it."

"No, same as all the others. I had more uncles than any girl alive."

Granger gave her a soft smile. It held the same hint of sympathy she'd noticed earlier. "What can you tell us about Louie?"

"He was there a lot the last few weeks before my

mom was killed. I think he was mostly living there." A shudder passed through her. "I didn't like him."

"Why not?"

"I was afraid of him. He had an awful temper. Whenever I was home, I'd stay in my room and sneak to the kitchen to get something to eat once he and my mom were passed out."

She closed her eyes, events she'd tried hard to forget bombarding her. "Once I made the mistake of taking the peanut butter to my room. He grabbed me by the hair and slammed me into the wall. When my mom tried to stick up for me, he turned on her and beat her to a bloody pulp."

She suppressed another shudder. At the time, she'd thought it was her fault. Now she knew better.

"You haven't heard from him since that night, right?"

"No."

"He was picked up near Ocala the morning after your mother was found and jailed on drug charges. Ended up doing fifteen years. But he was never charged with the murder. He had an alibi, albeit a shaky one, and although he was a suspect, we were never able to find enough evidence to convict him. Two weeks ago, another woman was stabbed to death. She'd recently ended a rocky relationship...with Louis Harmel."

Nicki nodded, a cold numbness spreading inside her. Maybe her mother's killer would finally pay for his crime. But how long would it take? And what would she go through in the meantime? How many memories would have to be dredged up before it was all over?

"Do you have any contact with your sister?" Granger's words cut across her thoughts.

"No. We were separated after our mother was killed."

And even before that, they hadn't been close. They'd shared a room—a dinky space hardly big enough for the two twin beds and single chest of drawers. But Nicki hadn't taken much comfort in her sister's presence. No matter how terrifying the sounds coming from the next room, Jenny had never let her share her bed.

"Six months ago, I hired a private investigator to find her," Nicki said. Although the dysfunctional home and five-year age difference had kept them from being close, she'd thought of Jenny often over the years. Now Jenny was the only family Nicki had left.

"Are they making any progress locating her?"

"Yes and no. Three different times, the investigator has gotten leads, but every time he gets close, she disappears. It's as if she doesn't want to be found."

There was probably a good reason. A criminal background check had turned up a hefty list of arrests. Nothing too serious. Just a bunch of petty stuff—forged checks, shoplifting, possession of marijuana, disorderly conduct. And likely plenty of other stuff waiting to catch up with her. No wonder she kept running.

"We've had the same experience. We haven't been able to get close enough to explain what we want with her."

"My guy is going to keep trying." As long as she had the money. Her inheritance had allowed her to start the search and would enable her to keep it going for some time. "He's making it clear to everyone he talks to that it's her half sister looking for her, not law enforcement."

Nicki hoped the message would eventually reach her. At least she was pretty sure that was what she wanted. Twice the investigator had asked her if she wished to continue, his tone heavy with doubt both times. Jenny's life was a mess. She'd stayed in the foster care system until she aged out and had never known the love of a real family. Nicki didn't even try to deny what she might be getting herself into seeking a relationship with her long-lost sister.

But she couldn't turn her back on her. Yes, Jenny was messed up. But Nicki had been pretty messed up herself when Chuck and Doris Jackson chose to look past her faults and love her anyway. She could do no less for Jenny.

Granger stood, and his partner closed the notebook and followed suit. He extended a hand to shake Nicki's, then handed her his business card. "We'll be back in touch. Meanwhile, if there's anything you remember that you haven't told us, please give us a call. It doesn't matter how insignificant it seems."

She walked them to the door. "I will. And if you happen to find her, you'll let me know?"

"We will."

She watched them walk toward the sedan, then closed and locked the door. It was too late to go to church. Wednesday night services started at seven, and it was already seven-twenty. She crossed the room to sit on the couch, the same spot she'd vacated earlier. Callie approached and rested her head in Nicki's lap.

Was Louie the one who'd killed her mother? Any number of men could have done it. But from everything she remembered, he seemed the most likely. He had the worst temper. And it wasn't just that. He seemed to radiate evil.

She shuddered again and reached for the remote. An evening of brainless television held a lot of appeal, the opportunity to lose herself in someone else's life for a short time. She let her head fall against the padded back of the couch and closed her eyes.

She'd spent the last two decades trying to forget.

Now they needed her to remember.

Tyler emerged from the bathroom, hair still damp but free of drywall dust. He'd hoped the days would be a little longer. It was Friday, and all week, Andy had been ready to call it quits by seven o'clock. Tonight it had been even earlier. Nine years Tyler's senior, maybe Andy was slowing down. Or maybe he'd been thinking about Joan's cooking and couldn't hold out any longer.

Tyler drew in a slow, fragrant breath. The scent of baking roast beef that had plagued him since he stepped onto the front porch wrapped around him again, and his stomach growled. When he entered the kitchen, Andy was already there, helping Joan cut up salad ingredients.

She smiled over one shoulder. "Dinner will be ready in twenty minutes. You guys messed me up coming home early."

The doorbell rang, cutting off his response. Leaving them to their meal preparation, he made his way to the front door. When he swung it open, Nicki stood on the porch, Callie next to her. A smile spread across her face and lit her eyes, sending an odd warmth straight to his core.

"I was walking Callie and saw you guys were home." She shifted her weight and cocked her head to the side. "You said you like to stay busy. How would you like to do a few projects for me?"

"Sure. What do you have in mind?"

"Several things. When you get a chance, stop by and I'll show you what I'm looking for."

He stepped onto the porch and closed the door behind him. "I've got almost twenty minutes till dinner. And if I'm a few minutes late, I'm sure Joan and Andy will save me some."

Nicki walked several feet down the driveway, then cut across the yard and into the woods. She glanced back at him, grinning. "Shortcut."

"Yeah, I found this one myself." It was the same route he'd taken Monday morning after seeing her to her door.

When they reached her yard, she pulled a set of keys from her pocket. "I used to not worry about locking up if I was just stepping outside for a few minutes. Now if the house is out of sight at all, you can be sure it's locked."

"That's a good idea."

He followed her into the house. Before Monday night, he'd made an assumption based on the simple block exterior. But on the inside, the place looked like something out of one of Joan's home decor magazines. A leather sectional sofa wrapped around an oak-and-glass table set on a wrought iron base. A marble-type floor tile in varying shades of brown and beige met three walls the color of Dijon mustard, the fourth a deep burnt orange. Two curio cabinets held a variety of figurines, and a floor lamp with amber globes bathed everything in a warm glow.

"This looks great." Whatever projects she had in mind, they probably didn't include this room.

"Thanks. The prior owners made some updates but never finished. I like the floor tile, but they'd painted all the walls a boring off-white." She grinned over at him. "I had to jazz it up a bit."

"That picture is perfect." He tilted his head toward the seascape hanging over the sofa. It was a sunset scene, depicted in colors that complemented her decor.

"Thanks. I had Meagan Kingston, a local artist, do it for me. It was my birthday present to myself."

"Happy belated birthday. And what about the stained glass wall hangings?"

"Those are mine."

"I thought so. I saw your supplies when I was checking the window locks."

"That's my hobby. Or maybe it's more than that, since I sell them. I've got them downtown at the Cedar Keyhole Artist Co-op and Darci's Collectibles and Gifts."

She led him into the kitchen. "The prior owners stripped and refinished the cabinets and replaced the appliances. I had the granite countertops put in. But I've got to get rid of that light fixture."

"Yeah, it looks sort of industrial. Do you have something picked out?"

"Not yet." She walked from the room and headed down the hall. "I plan to make one trip and do it all at once." She stopped at the open door to the bathroom. "Pedestal sinks look great, but they're not very practical. I'd like to replace it with a vanity and a cultured marble top. Are you up to it?"

"Sure." He was more than up to it. The broken arm had mended, and the burns were as good as they were going to get. All that was left of the smoke inhalation was some shortness of breath if he overexerted. Most of the damage to his body had healed. The effects on his mind, not so much. Splints and bandages couldn't blot out the images.

Or justify his returning home when his men hadn't.

He shook off the thoughts and followed her into the bedroom across the hall.

"This is technically the guest room, but it's where I sleep. So I'd like to get some more space in the closet."

"Closet organizers?"

"Yep." She opened the louvered doors. "On this side, I'd like the top shelf raised to make room for double rods. I'll keep a single rod on this side. In the center, I'd like a small set of drawers with a shoe cubby above. Twenty or thirty slots, if possible."

He eyed her with raised brows. "You got enough shoes?"

"You don't know the half of it." She grinned up at him.

Warmth filled his chest, and he grew serious. "It's good to see you again, Nicki."

"Yeah, same here. I've missed you."

He held her gaze for several moments. The years melted away, and they were once again connected by that invisible bond that tied his heart to hers. Distance hadn't severed it and neither had time. Did she feel it?

She turned, and he followed her into the hall. When she reached the large room at the end, she made a wide sweep of her arm. "As you can see, this is my work area."

He walked to a table where a partially completed stained glass scene lay. Peaks and valleys rose and fell, outlined in what looked like copper. Some kind of flowering trees occupied the foreground.

"The room has a *his* and a *hers* closet." Her words drew his attention, and she swung open one of the doors. "I'll leave the smaller one as it is, with the rods and all, because if I ever have company, this is where they'll sleep." She motioned toward the daybed against the far wall, then turned back to the closet.

"I want to have several shelves installed on all three sides here. Right now, I'm storing a lot of stuff in bins, and it'll make my life a lot easier to have everything more accessible."

"Let me know what you want, and I'll build it."

"Awesome." She pulled a pushpin from the corner of the bulletin board and handed him a sheet of paper. "Here's my wish list. Do you think you're up to it?"

"And then some." The work she'd laid out would keep him occupied for quite a few evenings. And it would give him somewhere pleasant to focus his mind, far away from the horrors of war.

"Are you out for good now?" She walked from the room and headed down the hall.

He followed her into the living room, shaking his head at her uncanny way of reading his thoughts. "I'm out for good."

"They can't call you back?"

"Nope." They'd retired him. And he was still trying to find his purpose.

She leaned back against the entertainment center. "I thought your first months or years out, they can always recall you."

"Not always."

His clipped answers weren't what she was looking for, and he knew it. But he didn't want to talk about it.

The progression from enlisted to retired didn't happen overnight. Those things never did. They reassigned him to a warrior transition unit for a year. The cast eventually came off his arm, but the skin graft procedures seemed to go on and on. Finally the doctors decided he was as good as he was going to get, and the medical board made their determination. He could no longer do the job. And that was that.

He shifted his gaze to the window overlooking her front yard. Drapes in earth tone patterns hung on each side, connected by a matching valance. Lacy sheers occupied the space between, partially obscuring whatever lay in the lengthening afternoon shadows. Another task he would add to his to-do list—installing some blinds behind the sheers. The bedrooms had them, but the living, dining and kitchen areas didn't.

"How should I go about getting the materials you need?"

Her words pulled his attention from the window, but movement in his peripheral vision snapped it back. For a brief moment, a vague shape hovered at the left portion of the sheers, then disappeared. He tensed and raised a hand. What had he seen?

"Stay here."

He made a dash for the door, jerked it open and pulled it shut behind him. As he rounded the corner of the house, a figure melted into the woods lining the back of Nicki's property. Tyler pounded through the grass and ran into the tree line a few moments later. Seeing no one, he stopped to listen.

A rain-scented gust whipped the trees around, the steady *shhh* drowning out the rustle of the intruder's movements. He turned slowly, all senses on alert. Some distance to his right, the snap of twigs underlay the steadier sounds of nature. He moved in that direction, his own footsteps little more than a whisper. His pulse picked up as he closed in on his prey.

Soon a voice drifted to him, soft and distinctly femi-
nine. Then another, this one male. Both young. And a
flash of clothing. Moments later, two figures came into
view, and he shook his head. He'd followed a couple of
teenagers on an early evening hike. And the intruder
had gotten away.

As he approached, the guy took her hand, pulled her
to a stop and drew her into his arms. Fifteen years ago,
that had been him and Nicki. The hanging-out, walking-
through-the-woods part, anyway. The other had been
only in his dreams.

He cleared his throat, and they both started.

"Did you see anyone pass by in the last few min-
utes?"

They shook their heads. There was no sense con-
tinuing his search. Nicki's Peeping Tom was long gone.
And she was probably inside wondering if he'd lost his
mind. He hadn't taken the time to explain.

When he got back, though, Nicki wasn't in her house.
She was standing at the edge of the sidewalk, face an-
gled downward. She looked up as he approached.

"You were supposed to stay inside." His tone was
stern.

"I did, for a minute, anyway. What's going on?"

Judging from the furrows in her brow and the con-
cern in her eyes, he could have asked her the same
thing. He cast a glance down. A wicked-looking knife
lay in the flower bed, partially obscured by the day-
lilies planted there.

"Where did that come from?"

"It's my chef's knife. It's been missing since my
house was broken into. I thought I'd misplaced it."

He frowned. "Someone was at your window. By the

time I got around the side of the house, he was disappearing into the woods. I took off after him, but I didn't get a good look at him."

"Find anything?"

"'Fraid not. I ended up following a rabbit trail." At the question in her eyes, he continued. "I heard something, which led me to a couple of teenagers." He glanced back down at the knife. "We need to call the police and have that fingerprinted."

Another gust swept through, the rain even closer, and Nicki moved toward the front door. "The intruder must have taken the knife, then dropped it the night he broke in. I've been in and out this way with Callie, but I wasn't paying any attention to the flower bed at the time. So I didn't notice it."

He nodded. That was one explanation. Except he didn't buy it. His own interpretation was much more sinister. He stepped onto the porch and opened the door for her, then followed her inside. "Maybe you're right and he dropped it the night he broke in, or…"

"Or what?"

He turned her to face him and took her hands. He would do everything he could to protect her. But she needed to be armed with the facts.

"Maybe he took it with him the night he broke in, then brought it back tonight, fully intending to use it."

THREE

Blood.

So much blood.

It covered the woman's body, seeping outward in an ever-expanding circle. She lay facedown on the floor, hand curled into a fist, as if she was spending the final moments of life in an angry protest against the void creeping over her.

She drew in a final shallow breath. The fist tightened, then released.

Nicki bolted upright with a gasp and pressed a hand over her racing heart. It was only a dream. One nightmare of many. This one was probably triggered by the visit from the two detectives and all the talk of her mother's murder. The knife lying in the mulch might have played a part, too.

She slid from the bed and bent to stroke Callie's head, trying to shake off the final remnants of the dream. She was no stranger to nightmares. Scary movies triggered some of them, the evening news others. Growing up, she'd seen things no child should ever see, watched movies that would terrify the most hardened adult.

But often her dreams held elements of the past—leering grins, sinister glances and whispered threats. Louie had landed a starring role in more than one.

As she removed a T-shirt and shorts from the chest of drawers in the corner, her gaze slid toward the closet. She'd left the doors open last night. Shoes lined the bottom, and her clothes hung in organized sections, although packed in way too tightly. Lavender once again occupied his spot on the shelf.

She hadn't been able to bring herself to throw him away. So she'd bought a needle and some matching thread and set to work. Now, with the exception of dozens of tiny stitches crisscrossing his belly, he was back in the same condition he'd been in before the attack—one eye missing, pale purple fur matted and stuffing so compacted his head listed pitifully to one side.

All these years, she'd held on to him. He was the only thing from her early childhood she'd managed to keep. She'd started out with a bin of personal belongings, but through the series of foster homes, one by one, the items disappeared. Some she accidentally left behind, but more often, other kids took them. Once someone tried to take Lavender. The foster mom had to pull her off the other child. The next day, she was on her way to another home with her beloved stuffed rabbit.

Callie nudged her hand, letting her know she'd dallied long enough. It was time for a walk. And after that, breakfast. Like most dogs, she approached both with equal enthusiasm.

Once showered and dressed, Nicki hooked up the leash. As soon as she stepped outside, uneasiness sifted through her. She scanned the yard, then shifted her gaze to the flower bed. Nothing was there, no threatening objects. She tried to shake off the apprehension. It was broad daylight. And Callie was with her.

But finding her chef's knife lying in the mulch Friday night had shaken her more than she wanted to admit. And although neither she nor Tyler had seen hide nor hair of the intruder in the day and a half since, tension continued to wrap itself around her body.

She glanced toward Andy's, then headed down her drive. Tyler was probably back inside, having long since finished Sasha's walk. Maybe she should try to coordinate Callie's walks with Sasha's. She would feel safer, and the company was nice. Reconnecting with Tyler had been a pleasant surprise.

But he was different from the boy she'd known long ago.

Friday night, when she'd asked him about his military service, she could feel him shutting down. Her questions had been innocent. But he'd clammed up so tight she couldn't have pried the information from him with a crowbar.

He never used to be that way. During those balmy days, sitting in the tree in her backyard, sharing stories as daylight became dusk and finally darkness, there'd been no secrets between them. But those experiences had happened a lifetime ago. That Tyler was gone. Maybe that Nicki was, too.

When she reached the road, she looked in both directions. She hadn't gotten up as early as she did during the week. Maybe if she had, she could have avoided the nightmare. If that was the case, the extra hour of sleep hadn't been worth it.

She took in a deep breath and increased her pace to a jog, giving Callie the opportunity to work out some of that inexhaustible supply of energy. Yesterday after Tyler had finished his work at the inn, they'd made a run to Crystal River for materials. Today he had the day free and planned to tackle her bathroom vanity installation in the afternoon, as soon as she got home from church. Andy refused to work on Sundays. Tyler didn't have any such compunctions.

Callie skidded to a stop so suddenly, the leash jerked Nicki's arm backward before she could halt her forward movement. She frowned down at the dog, who'd stepped off the pavement and was busy sniffing the ground. "A little bit of warning would be nice."

Nicki let her gaze drift down the street. A short distance away, a car sat parked against a patch of woods. When Nicki started moving again, the engine cranked up. The driver made a U-turn and sped away, heading toward downtown.

Her chest tightened, and she tried to push aside the uneasiness. The driver was probably a lost tourist consulting a map, then discovering he was on the wrong part of the island. That was a logical explanation.

Except for the break-in and the note and the knife left near her living room window.

Unfortunately, she hadn't gotten close enough to make out the tag. Other than the fact that it was small to medium size and white, she couldn't even say what kind of car it was. She wasn't good with car models. She'd always been a truck girl herself.

A few minutes later, she turned around and headed in the direction of home. Callie would keep going if Nicki let her, all the way to town. But long walks alone had lost their appeal. There were too many deserted stretches along Hodges.

Back at the house, she opened the front door and removed Callie's leash. The dog made a beeline for the kitchen, then stood watching her enter, eyes filled with eagerness. After opening a can and dishing up a generous serving of a smelly concoction named Savory Beef Stew, she poured herself some cereal and sat at the kitchen table.

Yesterday's mail was still piled at the edge. She'd been busy cleaning when she saw the mailman stop and hadn't taken the time to go through it. Then she'd set to work on one of her stained glass projects until Tyler arrived to take her to Home Depot.

She picked up the top piece and tore open the envelope. Central Florida Electric Cooperative. The charges were every bit as high as she'd expected. Summers in Florida were hot and it showed on the power bill. Of course, that was all she'd ever known. At least she had air conditioning, which was more than she could say for her early years.

The next envelope contained a credit card offer, which she intended to run through the shredder. Beneath that was something from Chase. One of her credit cards was through them. But the page showing through the windowed envelope looked more like a letter than a statement.

As she scanned the type, dread slid down her throat, lining her stomach with lead. Someone had applied for a credit card in her name, likely before she'd placed the fraud alert. She hadn't gotten home till Sunday night. And she'd called them Monday morning. If her intruder had come in on Friday, he'd had two whole days to wreak havoc with her credit.

She laid the sheet of paper on the table and sat back

in her chair. She'd have to call Chase and cancel the request. This was what she'd feared the moment she saw her information spread across the table. One week had passed, and it was already starting.

The doorbell sounded, and her tension ratcheted up several notches. Who would be ringing her bell at eight-thirty on a Sunday morning? She looked through the peephole, and the tension dissipated. When she swung open the door, Tyler stood on her front porch.

He wasn't smiling. In fact, his jaw was tight, and vertical creases of concern marked the space between his eyebrows. When he spoke, the concern in his features came out in his tone. "Are you all right?"

"Yeah, other than the fact that someone just applied for credit in my name."

Of course, Tyler wouldn't have known about her identity theft concerns. Something else must have put those creases of worry on his face. "What's going on?"

He held out a folded sheet of paper, which she hadn't noticed until that moment, and a chill passed through her. "What is it?"

"Whoever has been harassing you has apparently decided to carry it next door. I don't think this is aimed at my brother, even though he's the one who retrieved it from the front door a few minutes ago. It wasn't there when I walked Sasha this morning."

She took what he held and unfolded it. Like the other note, it was written in all caps with bold, angry strokes that could belong to almost anyone.

WATCH THE COMPANY YOU KEEP. IT CAN GET YOU KILLED.

Her blood turned to ice and her heart almost stopped.

She looked up at Tyler, her jaw slack. Her heart had resumed a frantic pace, and moisture coated her palms. "He was watching us. He saw us leave for Home Depot together." She took a step back, shaking her head. "You have to stay away from me."

He moved closer until he was standing at the threshold. "Do you really think I'm intimidated by this creep who's too much of a coward to show his face?"

"Maybe *you're* not intimidated, but *I* am. I'm not willing to risk you getting hurt. This is my battle, not yours." Although she had no idea what she'd done to get drawn into it.

He took a step closer and put both hands on her shoulders. Now he was inside her entry area. "It's *our* battle. Friends stick together. Or have you forgotten that?"

She dropped her gaze. No, she hadn't forgotten. When some of the snooty rich girls at school had given her a hard time about being adopted, he'd gone to bat for her. And she'd returned the favor when those same girls and their boyfriends had egged the principal's house and tried to pin it on Tyler.

He laid a finger against the underside of her chin, encouraging her to look at him. His eyes held a warmth that had never been there before. Or maybe it had and she'd been too young and naive to recognize it.

When he finally spoke, his tone was low, the words heavy with meaning. "I never run from danger. Especially when it involves someone I care about."

She swallowed hard, unable to look away. His words suggested more than simple friendship. So did his tone.

The thought scared her more than anything had as yet.

* * *

Tyler moved through the darkness at a brisk walk, the beam of his flashlight illuminating the road ahead of him. It was 1:00 a.m. on a Monday morning, and Hodges was deserted, all the houses dark except for the soft glow of porch lights shining from a few of them. Gulf Boulevard didn't show any more signs of life than Hodges had. According to Andy, a lot of his neighbors escaped the heat and humidity and spent summers up north. In the wee hours of the morning, that sense of isolation was even more acute. Most sensible people were in bed.

He'd tried. For almost two hours, he'd chased sleep. Finally he'd grown tired of tossing and turning and had slipped out into the quiet night.

He should have been tired. Actually, he was. Physically, anyway. He'd worked hard all afternoon and evening, pushing to get Nicki's new sink and vanity installed and the plumbing hooked back up. He'd even started on the shelves in the master bedroom closet. But when he'd dropped into bed at eleven, his brain had gone into overdrive.

The note Andy had pulled off the front door that morning was in the hands of the police. But they probably wouldn't be any more successful lifting the intruder's prints from it than they had been from the first one. Or from Nicki's house, for that matter. All the viable prints belonged to her. Her intruder had apparently worn gloves.

Tyler slowed his pace to catch his breath and cross to the other side of the road. He'd walked about a mile and a half. Maybe by the time he got back, he would be ready to sleep.

But the tension that had coiled through him as he lay staring into the darkness was still very much there. The second note had disturbed him as much as the first. Not because of what it meant for him. He wasn't afraid for his own life. The note was likely an empty threat. But he understood the purpose behind the words. Whoever wrote them was trying to isolate Nicki from her friends. To weaken her and make her a better target.

It wasn't going to work. It would take more than a written threat to tear him from Nicki's side. It would take mortars, RPGs and a couple of Abrams tanks. And even that wouldn't stop him if he could help it.

As he neared her house, he cast a glance in that direction. Light trickled through the trees that bordered her yard. She would be sound asleep inside, Callie nearby. The dog's presence brought him a measure of relief. Otherwise, he would insist on loaning her Sasha to stand guard. Or move in himself.

He dismissed the thought as soon as it entered his mind. The nightmares were too frequent. Too real. He'd gotten pretty good at waking himself up before the scream building in his throat escaped. But sometimes the terror refused to release its grip until it was too late. Though it hadn't happened yet, it was only a matter of time until he jarred Andy and Joan from a sound sleep. That was going to be embarrassing enough. He wasn't about to show Nicki how messed up he was.

He rolled his shoulders, then ran his hands through his hair. When he reached her property line, he again shifted his gaze toward the house. To the right of the front door, a rattan rocker sat bathed in soft yellow light. A short distance away, an American flag hung from a short pole attached to the corner post. Further to the right, her Ram sat in the carport.

In total darkness.

He drew his brows together. When he'd headed out thirty minutes ago, both the porch light and the carport light were on. Had she gotten up and turned the second one off? Or had someone else extinguished it, not wanting to be seen?

He clicked off the flashlight and squinted into the night, worry coiling in his gut. But beyond the glow of the porch light, everything was black. Clouds obscured most of the stars, and the sliver of moon he'd seen early yesterday morning wouldn't be visible until just before daylight.

He retraced his steps, then slipped into the trees bordering her yard. A twig snapped beneath his foot, the sound amplified in the silence. He hesitated. He had a gun. It just wasn't with him. With his flashbacks and nightmares, he'd figured it was best to leave his weapon with a friend for safekeeping. Only a week and a half had passed, and he was already rethinking that decision.

Staying within the tree line, he continued to move away from the road, eyes on the carport. Once he was even with her truck, he stopped, listening. The skin on his arms prickled. Someone was there, or had just been there.

Dropping to his hands and knees, he clicked on the light and shone it under the truck, then swept the beam side to side in an expanding arc. Seeing no one, he sprinted to the back of the truck, then crept around it.

When he shone the light on the door of her house, he heaved a sigh of relief. It was undisturbed. He shook the tension from his shoulders. Of course it was undisturbed. No one was getting past the lock he'd installed. At least not without an ax or sledgehammer.

So maybe no one had been there. Maybe the light had burned out. He reached into the fixture. The bulb was still hot. It was also loose. He rotated it a quarter turn and light flooded the carport.

His stomach tightened as he stepped back from the door. His first instinct had been right. Someone had been prowling around her house in the dark. He scanned the side of the house. The laundry room window was the only jalousie left. According to Nicki, the prior owner had changed all the others to single-hungs.

Icy fingers traced a path down the back of his neck. Two of the four-inch by three-foot panes of glass stood against the house. The metal tracks that had held them were warped and bent outward. And the intruder had started on a third. Another thirty minutes and some-one would have been inside, in spite of the locks he'd installed.

A sense of protectiveness surged through him, and he clenched his fists. Whoever wanted a piece of his longtime friend was going to have to go through him first. He stalked toward the front door, pulling out his phone as he walked.

After calling 911, he lifted his hand to ring the bell, then hesitated. That probably wasn't the best option. He'd startle her out of a sound sleep, and she'd be ter-rified, not knowing what threat stood at her front door.

He dialed her number, and she answered on the sec-ond ring.

"Tyler? What's going on?" Her tone held hesitancy.

"Come to the front door. I'm right outside."

A light went on some distance to his left, filtering

through the slats in her miniblinds. A minute later, the front door swung inward.

And his breath caught in his throat.

Nicki stood just inside, auburn hair framing her face in wild disarray. Her eyes were wide, fear swimming in their green depths, and it shot straight to his gut. She stepped back to allow him entrance, then stood motionless, her silk robe fluttering with every jagged breath. She looked so vulnerable.

And so beautiful.

As he stepped inside, he lifted a hand to reach for her, then mentally shook himself. She was his friend, nothing more. It was all she'd been back then, and there was even more reason to keep it that way now. In less than two months, he'd be finished with his business in Cedar Key and once again hit the road. In the meantime, he wouldn't lead her on with promises he couldn't keep.

"What are you doing here?"

He shut and locked the door. "I caught someone trying to get in your laundry room window. He already had two panes of glass out and was working on the third."

Blood leached from her face, leaving it with as little color as the pale ivory robe. She took a faltering step backward, shaking her head. "I didn't hear anything. Callie apparently didn't, either."

He closed the gap between them and took her hand. "The police are on their way. Let's sit." He led her to the couch, then eased down next to her. When he draped an arm across her shoulders, she leaned into him. A faint floral scent teased his senses. He closed his eyes and forced himself to focus.

"You need to think about moving in with Andy and Joan."

"I don't want to impose." She leaned away to look over at him. "Will you stay for a while, though? Just tonight?"

He pulled her against him again. "I'm not going anywhere. If you want to try to get some sleep after the police leave, I'll be right here on your couch. Come daylight, I'm picking you up a more secure window."

In some areas, changing windows required a permit. If that was the case in Cedar Key, he'd beg forgiveness later.

Because nothing was going to stop him from doing what he needed to do. Come nightfall, the house would be secure. Nicki would be safe.

And that was all that mattered.

Nicki shut off her computer monitor and pulled her purse from the bottom desk drawer. It had been a hectic day. But she wasn't complaining. Busy days went faster. And she was thankful for the job. The week she'd moved to Cedar Key, the receptionist at city hall had moved away, leaving the position open. With Nicki's five years in management, she was overqualified. But the pleasant people and the laid-back environment were just what she needed.

Now that the day was finished, fatigue was creeping over her. She'd barely been asleep two hours when Tyler called. Though she'd been back in bed less than two hours later, sleep had been a long time coming.

She hated to even speculate about what would have happened if Tyler hadn't walked by when he had. She never did ask him what he was doing outside at that time. That should have raised her suspicions, but it didn't. Something told her she wasn't the only one with nightmares—memories kept at bay in the daylight, waiting to invade the subconscious in the wee hours of the morning.

She slipped her purse strap over her shoulder and moved toward the double glass door, but before she could get there, a female voice stopped her.

"Nicki, can you come into my office for a moment?"

She stopped midstride to face her boss, Miranda Jacobs. Nicki's chest tightened, and she tried to shake off the uneasiness. There was no reason to be nervous. She hadn't done anything wrong. Not that she knew of, anyway. But there was something in her boss's tone, a cool professionalism, hinting that there might be a reprimand coming.

"Have a seat." Miranda motioned toward one of two chairs, then settled herself behind her desk. "I've been very happy with your work performance. You're catching on to everything quickly."

Nicki nodded, waiting for Miranda to continue. Why did she sense an imminent *but*?

"I received a complaint this afternoon, though."

Nicki frowned. "What kind of complaint?"

"A woman called, a Jane Wilson. Do you remember helping her this morning?"

"No, I don't. But I'd have to look back through my notes to be sure. Did I do something wrong?"

"She said you were rude to her."

Her jaw dropped. "Rude? I haven't been rude to anybody."

Miranda gave her a sympathetic smile. "Dealing with people all day long can be stressful. But no matter how annoying someone is, we have to bite our tongues and be pleasant, even if it's the last thing we feel like doing."

Nicki shook her head. "I promise you, I wasn't rude to anybody. What did I supposedly say?"

"She claimed that she asked you some questions and you were short with her, that you cut her off and said you didn't have time for her."

Nicki snapped her mouth shut. It had sagged even further during Miranda's explanation. "That's not true. She's making things up."

"Why would someone do that?" Miranda's brows were raised in question. Or maybe it was suspicion.

"I don't know why." She drew in a shaky breath. Someone was out to get her.

"Have you made any enemies?"

"No." Well, maybe one. Peter hadn't taken it very well when she dumped him. He somehow thought it reasonable to expect her to wait for him to do his time, then pick up where they left off.

But it wasn't Peter who'd made the complaint. It was a woman. Of course, he could have put someone up to it.

She drew in a deep breath. "I apparently have an enemy I don't know about, because I promise you, I haven't been rude to anyone. You've heard me talk to people who come in, and you've listened to my side of phone conversations. Have I ever been at all short with anyone?"

Miranda hesitated before responding. "No, you haven't."

"Please believe me when I tell you I wasn't this time, either."

"All right." She gave her a small smile. "I have to admit, when the woman called, what she was describing didn't sound like you at all, even though she mentioned you by name, first and last."

"When I'm helping people, I always identify myself by my first name only. This Jane Wilson, if that's even her real name, apparently knows me outside of work."

Miranda nodded. Nicki wished her farewell and walked from the office. After climbing into the Ram, she backed from the parking space, mind still spinning. Who would want to get her in trouble and possibly fired from her job? The same person who was leaving threatening notes and had tried to tamper with her credit. Someone had set out to destroy her. But she had no idea who.

She pressed the brake and eased into her turn onto D Street. Over the years, she'd stuck her neck out a few times, provided help to friends who needed a little extra gumption to walk away from good-for-nothing men. Maybe it was coming back to bite her.

Or maybe it was her own good-for-nothing man. Peter had gotten pretty angry the last time she talked to him. He was out on bond, still awaiting trial, and before she left for Miami, he'd called to make one last-ditch effort to talk her into staying with him. His pleas hadn't worked. But was he that vindictive? Something about the scenario didn't ring true.

Maybe it wasn't anger driving him. Maybe the threats and attacks were all part of an elaborate plot to send her running back to him. The notes, the break-in and subsequent attempts, the knife left behind—it was all unsettling. In fact, she was scared. She'd be lying if she said otherwise.

And the attack on her credit and her job were almost as disconcerting. If she ended up unemployed, with her credit destroyed, she'd soon find herself in serious financial trouble, in spite of the little nest egg she'd inherited from her parents.

She squared her shoulders and tightened her grip on the wheel. Peter was underestimating her. She'd been through a lot worse and survived. No matter what happened, she didn't need a man to take care of her.

She made the final turn on her four-minute commute. Hodges wasn't in a subdivision. Most of the houses were spaced far apart, some almost hidden in the trees. The secluded setting was what she'd wanted. A month ago, anyway. Now one of those postage-stamp-size lots in the city had a lot of appeal.

But she had good neighbors. Andy and Joan had extended their friendship the day she moved in, with freshly baked cookies, and had made regular visits since. Now Tyler was there, at least for the time being. He and Andy wouldn't be home yet. But she'd see him tonight. He was determined to have the laundry room window changed out before she went to bed.

And he was equally determined to ignore the threat against him. She pursed her lips. The note had said, "Watch the company you keep. It can get you killed."

Was Peter capable of murder? She hadn't thought so. But she hadn't thought he was capable of embezzling a hundred grand from his employer, either. Which proved one thing—she really didn't know him at all.

She pressed the brakes and made a right turn into her driveway. She'd unwittingly given Peter a reason to go after Tyler in earnest. Late Saturday afternoon, she'd left with Tyler and not come back for three hours. They'd even had dinner out. It had been totally professional. Their *date* had consisted of roaming the aisles of Home Depot.

But Peter wouldn't know that. He'd think she'd found someone new, which would make his chances of winning her back zilch. Of course, they'd been nonexistent anyway. But Peter wasn't one to give up easily.

She drew in a stabilizing breath. As soon as she got inside, she'd call Amber, or maybe Amber's brother Hunter. He'd been a Cedar Key cop a lot longer. She wasn't ready to file an official report, because she didn't have enough evidence to make an accusation. But Hunter would be able to advise her.

As she moved up the drive, she scanned the house's concrete block face. Everything looked the same as it had when she'd come home at lunchtime to take Callie out. Except...

Dread wrapped around her like a cloak. Something was attached to her front door.

Heart pounding in her chest, she jammed on the brakes, jumped from the truck and hurried to the porch. A sheet of paper was folded in half, its creased edge affixed to the door with a small piece of tape. She extended her arm. She wouldn't risk destroying prints. Touching only the top edge, she folded it back and scanned the words.

YOUR WORLD UNRAVELING? YOU HAVEN'T SEEN ANYTHING YET.
YOUR HOME, YOUR JOB, YOUR FRIENDS, YOUR LIFE.
I WILL TAKE IT ALL.

Bile rose in her throat, and she stepped back, clutching her stomach. Why would Peter go after her like this? The first note had said, "The party's over." But he, better than anyone, knew her life had been anything but a party. She'd told him a little about her childhood and her years in foster care. Not all of it. There were some things she hadn't told anyone except Tyler.

But Peter knew enough. And he'd been there the night she got the news of her parents' deaths. She'd had plenty of hardships over her twenty-nine years and fought far too many battles to get where she was.

None of that mattered. She knew that now. Peter was a lover spurned. He was selfish and angry, maybe even a little off.

It was a combination that could turn out to be deadly.

FOUR

Nicki turned back the cover on her notebook and passed it across the table to Meagan Kingston. "It's just a rough sketch, but what do you think?"

Meagan studied what she held, then showed it to Hunter next to her. He was dressed in his police uniform, on break during his shift. Besides enjoying dinner with his wife, he'd be dispensing some advice. Nicki had already forewarned him.

Meagan tapped the page with her other hand. "I like it. But I think I want a little more detail on the trees."

Nicki nodded. She'd treated herself on her birthday with a Meagan Kingston painting, and now Meagan was ordering some Nicki Jackson stained glass to hang in her dining room. The three of them sat on the back deck of the Blue Desert Café, two half-eaten medium pizzas in the center of the table. Usually in July, the deck would have been unbearably hot, even at dusk. But a thunderstorm brewed somewhere off the coast, sending refreshing gusts of cooler air over the water.

After wiping her fingers on a paper napkin, Meagan removed a pencil from her purse, then held it poised over the paper. "Do you mind?"

"Not at all. You're the artist."

"Looking at what you have displayed at Darci's and the co-op, I'd say you are, too." She put the pencil to the paper and sketched some lines, then did some shading.

While Meagan worked, Nicki took a bite of pizza, then lifted her gaze to the dock extending out over the shallow water. Near the shore, palmettos partially obstructed the view. Further out, other greenery broke the horizon. Cedar Key was a series of islands, some connected by bridges, others accessible only by boat.

Meagan handed her back the pad. "Is that doable?"

"Definitely. Now for colors." She pulled several pages of swatches from the back of the notebook and, after handing them to Meagan, turned her attention to Hunter.

"You've probably heard about what's been happening around my place."

"The break-in and the notes, yeah. We've been having units drive through and patrol the area."

"I appreciate it." She cut off a piece of pizza but didn't put it in her mouth. "Yesterday I had another note."

"I heard." Hunter frowned. "Those were some pretty serious threats. Any ideas on who could be making them?"

She opened her mouth, but the words stuck in her throat. When she'd made the decision to talk to Hunter, she'd been sure of her course of action. What if she was wrong? Peter was in enough trouble without her adding to it with false accusations.

But what if she was right? What if he refused to accept that it was over and would stop at nothing to get her back? Or worse, what if he had accepted it and decided if he couldn't have her, no one else could, either?

She drew in a deep breath. "Let's just say there's a guy who isn't very happy with me right now."

"An ex-boyfriend who can't seem to walk away?"

"Fiancé. I was supposed to have gotten married last month."

Meagan looked up from the color blocks, concern in her eyes. From what Nicki had heard, her new friend had her own horror story involving an ex-fiancé. "I take it you're the one who broke it off."

"Yes." At least she was trying. She wasn't sure she'd accomplished it yet. "He thinks I should give him a second chance."

Hunter didn't respond, just waited for her to continue, which was turning out to be a lot harder than she'd thought it would be. It was as if Peter's bad choices were somehow a reflection on her.

In a way, they were. They showed what a bad judge of character she was.

She pursed her lips, then continued. "He got caught embezzling from his company and was arrested. He was shocked I wasn't going to stand by him through it. First he tried playing the sympathy card, blaming it on being poor and deprived growing up and needing to feel secure. Then he tried to guilt me into staying with him, telling me that he did it all for me."

She stifled a snort. Material possessions had never ranked high on her list of priorities. The first nine years of her life, she hardly had any. When she finally landed in the Jackson home, there were too many other new things to experience—love, security and life without fear. Baubles didn't mean much. Peter knew that as well as anybody.

She pushed a bite of pizza across her plate with her fork, then again met Hunter's eyes. "When that didn't work, he got angry. That was the last conversation I had with him, about two weeks ago." She'd witnessed a side of him she'd never seen before. Once she'd made it clear it was over, he called her several choice names and disconnected the call. Was he angry enough to attack her in the way someone had in recent days? Angry enough to want to kill her? It was hard to imagine.

"Did he make any threats?"

"No, just said some pretty hateful things. I figured he was hurt and was lashing out." But maybe it was more serious than that. Maybe over the next few days he'd let the anger simmer and had plotted ways to get even.

She sank back in her chair. "I'm not sure what to do. I don't want to accuse him in case he's innocent."

Hunter nodded. "Where does he live?"

"Crystal River." An hour away. Too close for comfort.

"I'll check out his mug shot and be on the lookout for him. I could also go talk to him, see what he's been up to. If he *is* the one behind everything that's been going on, maybe having a cop show up on his doorstep will be enough to convince him to stop."

"That sounds good." She released a small sigh. A little bit of the weight lifted.

Hunter popped the last of his pizza into his mouth and stood. "I'd better get back out there."

She smiled up at him. "Thanks for letting me talk shop during your dinner break."

"Anytime." He pulled a pad from his pocket. "Give me your ex's name."

"Peter Gaines."

"I'll check him out." He bent to give Meagan a kiss, then stepped off the deck and headed up the narrow gravel drive toward the road.

Meagan slid her chair closer and laid the samples on the table between them. "I think I have my colors picked out."

By the time they finished their pizza, several color names surrounded the sketch, with arrows drawn and notes in the margins. "I should have this finished in about a month." Nicki tucked the notebook into her bag and flagged the waitress to bring their checks.

Meagan rested her chin in her hands. "I'm nervous about you staying at your place alone."

"I'm not alone. I've got Callie."

"Callie doesn't carry a .45."

Meagan had a point. "I do have someone keeping an eye on me." And he likely did carry a .45. Or something comparable. "Andy's kid brother." Since they all went to the same church, Meagan knew Andy and Joan.

Her brows shot up. "Oh, yeah?"

"No, not like that." She'd made a vow. No more serious relationships. She was through with men. "We're just friends."

Meagan grinned. "I've heard that before."

Nicki sighed. Meagan was enjoying giving her a hard time. "I'm serious. We were friends as kids, in Crystal River. Then he and his mom moved away, and we lost contact."

"And now he's back. Well, I'm glad he's there."

Yeah, so was she. Their childhood friendship made

him a little more than a concerned neighbor. Over the past few days, he'd spent a lot of his spare time at her house. Of course, he'd had a good excuse. He'd gotten through most of the work she'd assigned him.

In fact, he was there tonight, installing a closet organizer in her bedroom. She'd left him with his tools, a pencil tucked over his ear and the room in total chaos. She'd probably be sleeping on the daybed tonight, unless he worked really fast.

She looked out over the water. The trees were now dark silhouettes against a sky stained shades of orange and pink. Soon dusk would fade to darkness. By then, she'd be headed home. Tyler would likely still be there.

He'd changed a lot since those early days. That ever-present chip on his shoulder seemed to have lessened. Maybe with maturity, his anger with the world had evolved into acceptance.

It wasn't an easy acceptance. Tension emanated from him, a brooding silence that hadn't been there before. Beneath the adult confidence was a tortured soul, something he'd never be able to hide from her, because she knew him too well. And she knew herself. Their shared traumas formed the invisible cord that would always tie them together.

When she looked at Meagan again, she was wearing a knowing half smile. Nicki shrugged it off. Let her think what she would. She valued Tyler's friendship too much to throw it away on yet another failed attempt at something more.

After they'd paid their checks, Nicki rose and followed Meagan off the deck.

"I'll keep you posted on my progress. I've got two other projects to finish first, but they're small."

Meagan leaned against the passenger side of her car. All the parking for the Blue Desert Café was along the street. "No rush. We're still dealing with remodeling dust. My goal is another two weeks, but a month is more realistic."

Nicki's gaze drifted past Meagan to the house across the street. "Then it should be perfect ti—" She stopped midsentence, tension spiking through her. A figure stood in the shadow of a tree a few yards from the side of the house.

Meagan turned. "What's wrong?"

"Someone's watching us." Either that, or he'd stepped outside for a smoke and she was letting her imagination run away with her. Between the distance and the shadows, she couldn't say what he was doing or see any kind of identifying characteristics.

Moments later, the person scurried away, moving deeper into the woods. Meagan pulled her cell phone from her purse with one hand and grasped Nicki's arm with the other. "Stay here. I'm calling Hunter."

"Trust me, I'm not going anywhere." She wasn't the type to follow a stranger into the woods unarmed. She'd leave the heroics to the cops.

The cops showed up in the form of Hunter ten minutes later. He'd searched the area and found no one suspicious. She wasn't surprised. Whoever had been watching her from the shadows was the same person who was making all the threats. She had no doubt. If he was smart enough to not leave behind any prints, he wouldn't stand around and wait for the police to arrive.

She climbed into the driver's seat of the Ram and started the engine, thankful she wasn't going home to an empty house. But Tyler wouldn't be around indefi-

nitely. Eventually he and Andy would finish their work
on the inn. And Tyler would be gone.

She pulled from the parking lot, an odd sense of loss
stabbing through her. It wasn't just the thought of the
protection she'd no longer have. And it wasn't the loss
of the companionship she was growing accustomed to.

No matter how she tried to fight it, Tyler was becom-
ing much more than a friend.

Andy turned his truck onto Hodges, and Tyler took
off his baseball cap and laid it in his lap. It was covered
in drywall dust. His clothes had been, too, but he'd man-
aged to brush off the majority of it before getting into
Andy's truck. A cool shower had a lot of appeal. Then
he'd see what Nicki was doing.

He'd finished the closet organizer project late Tues-
day night, after she'd come in from dinner with her
friends. Last night she'd gone to church. Nicki had in-
vited him twice, Andy and Joan more than that. But
each time he'd come up with an excuse.

It wasn't like he'd never been. After his father left,
his mother hadn't known how to deal with his anger,
so she found a small white church two blocks away and
started taking him. It didn't help. He hated not getting
to sleep in Sunday mornings and resented giving up
time hanging with his friends.

When his mom got sick, though, everything changed,
and he tried to make a bargain with God. If God would
keep his mother alive, he'd be in church every time the
doors opened. Hey, he'd even have been willing to be-
come a preacher if that was what it took.

Apparently God didn't listen to angry teenage boys.
Because in spite of his mother's good fight and his own

pleas and promises, the cancer took her anyway. And he hadn't darkened the door of a church since.

"So what are your long-term plans?" Andy's words cut across his thoughts.

"I don't have any."

"Are you thinking about maybe settling in Cedar Key?"

He shrugged. "Hadn't considered it. Why?"

"I don't know. You've been spending a lot of time with Nicki. I figured you might think about staying here permanently."

Tyler slanted his brother a glance, but Andy's attention was focused forward.

"I've been spending a lot of time with Nicki because I've been working for her."

Now Andy did look at him. "You know, you're going to have to stop running at some point."

Tyler nailed him with a glare. "Twenty years ago, you were bigger than me, so you got away with bossing me around. It's not going to fly now."

Andy lifted his shoulders and let them fall. "Have it your way. But as long as you're here, I'm going to work on you. I want you to be happy, bro."

"I *am* happy." He crossed his arms in front of him, then dropped his hands to his lap. The first pose had looked anything but happy.

When they approached Nicki's house, she was walking down the driveway with Callie. Tyler lowered the passenger window, and Andy eased to a stop. When Tyler called a greeting, Callie picked up the pace, tail wagging, pulling Nicki with her. She stopped at the side of the truck, then stood up, resting her front paws on the door. The dog had taken a liking to him. Or maybe she just associated him with her buddy Sasha.

He reached through the open window to pat her head while he talked to Nicki. "Will you be home tonight? I was going to see if I could stop over."

"Make it after eight. I'm feeding Callie, warming up some leftovers for myself, then heading up to The Market for groceries."

"Let me get cleaned up, and I'll go with you."

She waved away his offer. "I'm sure you have better things to do than follow me around the grocery store."

"It's no trouble. I need to go myself. I'm sure Andy and Joan are out of something. If not, I'll pick up another jar of peanut butter." He grinned. "You can never have too much peanut butter."

She returned his smile. "All right. In that case, I'll let you tag along. Come over in about forty-five minutes."

After Nicki pulled Callie away from the truck, Andy took his foot off the brake and gave him a crooked smile.

Tyler shrugged. "She's in danger, and I'm right next door." A touch of defensiveness had crept into his tone. His brother knew about the break-in and notes and didn't need to be giving him a hard time.

Andy pulled into his driveway and turned off the truck. "She's a nice girl. I'm glad you're taking an interest."

Tyler responded with a grunt.

A short time later, he was on Nicki's front porch, clean and pleasantly full from Joan's cooking. Before ringing the bell, he'd scanned the area, making sure they were alone. It appeared they were. Of course, with woods all around, he couldn't say for sure.

Nicki grabbed her purse and, after giving Callie her usual command to behave herself, closed and locked the door. She pressed a button on her key fob and the locks on the Ram popped up. "How is the work at the inn coming along?"

"Right on schedule." He slid into the passenger seat next to her. "Actually a little ahead of schedule. We've been at it almost two full weeks. If everything goes as planned, another five should do it."

She nodded, her lower lip pulled between her teeth.

He reached across the cab of the truck to rest a hand on her shoulder. "Nicki, I'm not leaving until I know you're safe."

"Thanks." She gave him a half smile. "Under normal circumstances I'd tell you not to change your plans on account of me. But I feel a lot better having you around."

She cranked up the truck but didn't back from the drive. "I might know who's been doing this."

He studied her in the growing afternoon shadows. "Who?"

"Peter, my ex-fiancé. I broke things off with him about three months ago. The first few weeks, he was pretty persistent, trying to get me to go back to him."

His gut tightened. He'd heard too many stories about vindictive exes. And he wouldn't mind getting his hands on this one. "Have you given his name to the police?"

"I told Hunter about him Tuesday night. He's Amber's brother, also works for Cedar Key. Anyhow, he called me this afternoon and said he'd talked to Peter. Apparently he hasn't been outside Citrus County. Even has the witnesses to prove it."

"So our only lead has been eliminated."

She shifted the truck into Reverse and backed into the street. "Not necessarily. These people aren't with him twenty-four seven. He could drive over here, stay a couple of hours and be back before anybody misses him. Or maybe he's getting someone else to do his dirty work."

Tyler shook his head. Neither scenario sounded good. No, leaving Cedar Key before this was resolved was out of the question.

A few minutes later, Nicki pulled into a parking space. The Market at Cedar Key was the only grocery store on the island. It wasn't big, but it had all the basics and then some. Which was good, since Joan had come up with a fairly lengthy list.

Nicki tilted her head toward the Prius next to them. "Meagan's here. I'll introduce you."

As soon as they were inside, Nicki waved him forward and made a beeline for the cash register. A woman with long blond hair gathered three bags, looping two of them over one arm before picking up the third. Her face lit up when she saw Nicki. She shifted the single bag to her left hand to give her a hug, then extended her hand his direction.

"Meagan Kingston. You must be Tyler. Nicki told me about you." She smiled. "It was all good. I promise."

After the women chatted for a minute or two, Meagan glanced down at her bags. "I'd better get this stuff home."

Nicki nodded. "I'm glad we ran into you. When I saw that shiny silver Prius out there, I knew you were inside here."

Meagan frowned. "The poor thing had to be towed yesterday."

Nicki's brows went up. "You broke down? You haven't had it that long."

"No, the engine was fine. It was the tires, all four of them. I got up yesterday morning, and someone had taken a knife to them."

Nicki's jaw dropped and the blood leached from her face. "Someone slashed your tires?" She pressed her hands to her cheeks and took several steps back. "This is my fault. You were with me Tuesday for dinner. And he was watching. We saw him. He's watching everything I do." She looked frantically around her. "He retaliates against anyone who dares to be seen with me. You have to stay away."

Meagan rushed toward her, then stopped Nicki's flow of words with a hand on her arm. "You don't know that."

Nicki jerked her arm away and backed up further. "Tyler and I left for the evening to go to Home Depot, and the next morning, there was a note on his door telling him to watch the company he keeps, that it could get him killed. Anyone who dares to be seen with me will pay for it. I should leave."

Tyler draped an arm across her shoulders and pulled her close. "Whoever is doing this will follow you. He's trying to isolate you. If you leave Cedar Key, you'll be playing right into his hands. You need to stay here where you have friends, people looking out for you."

"Tyler's right. I won't abandon you, and I'm sure if we talked to our other friends, they'd say the same thing. And I know for a fact that the Cedar Key police are working on all this." Meagan looped the last bag over her arm so she could take both of Nicki's hands. "Promise me you'll stay." When Nicki didn't respond, Meagan spoke with more force. "Promise me you'll stay. Give Hunter and Amber and the others a chance to solve this. Okay?"

Nicki nodded. Her face was still pale, her eyes wide and filled with fear. "I don't want anyone getting hurt. If anything happened to any of you guys, I'd never forgive myself." She hesitated, eyeing him with raised brows. "You carry a gun, right?"

"No, I don't."

"Do you have one?"

"Not here."

She studied him, brows raised in question at his clipped answer. But he didn't talk about his experiences in Afghanistan with anyone. And he certainly didn't discuss the mental and emotional issues that had followed him home.

He dropped his arm from her shoulder to take her hand. "Come on. Let's get our shopping done."

Whoever was tormenting her meant business. By spending so much time with her, Tyler was putting himself in the line of fire, especially if her tormentor was a jealous ex.

That was a chance he was willing to take.

All through their friendship, he'd been there for her. And she'd been there for him. He wasn't about to let her face this alone.

FIVE

A man knelt in the semidarkness, straddling the figure beneath him. He raised his arm, and a shaft of light caught the blade of a knife. For one tense moment, he held it suspended. Then he plunged it downward. The figure on the floor jerked, and a high-pitched scream pierced the night.

The arm rose and swung down a second time. The head lifted from the floor, and stringy hair fell over the side of the woman's face as another scream was wrenched from her throat. Again and again, the knife plunged into her back. The screams became gurgles, then faded to silence.

Nicki came awake with a start, her own scream dying on her lips. The remnants of the dream held on, chilling her all the way to her core.

This was the second time she'd dreamed of a woman being killed. Twice in less than a week. The other time, she didn't witness it, just saw the aftermath. The woman's final breath. And the blood. Lots of blood.

Callie nudged her hand and released a small whimper. The dog had gotten into bed with her sometime during the night. Nicki pushed herself to a seated position and patted Callie's head. "It's okay, girl. It was only a nightmare."

Where were the dreams coming from? And why now?

She was under a lot of stress. The constant uneasiness, the sense of being watched. The threats against friends. Maybe she hadn't been able to turn it all off when she crawled into bed at night. And the detectives reopening her mother's murder case gave her mind the fodder it needed to congeal all the fear and anxiety into one terrifying scenario.

She glanced at the clock on the nightstand, its red numerals glowing in the darkness: 4:45. She didn't have to get up for another hour. But trying to go back to sleep would be pointless. Her heart pounded in her chest, and tension still threaded through her muscles.

She swung her feet over the edge of the bed, trying to shake off the final tendrils of the dream. Callie jumped to the floor with a thud, then trotted to the open door, tail wagging. For Callie, morning meant two things, both equally exciting—a walk and food. It wasn't time yet for breakfast. And since Nicki didn't know who was lurking in the darkness, taking her for an early run alone was out of the question. Callie would have to wait.

Nicki stood and padded from the room. She'd work on one of her stained glass projects before starting her day. She always found the work therapeutic. Anything creative calmed her. Over the years, she'd spent many hours hunched over her sketch pad.

Sometime later, she sat back in her chair and stretched her arms skyward. She'd gotten a lot accomplished. While she worked, the nightmare had gradually released its grip. It wasn't daylight yet, but it was time to quit.

She rolled the chair back from her work table, and Callie perked up. For the past hour, she'd lain with her head resting on her front paws, eyes closed. Now that she knew a walk was imminent, she pranced from the room and down the hall, casting backward glances as she went.

The doorbell rang, and Nicki smiled. All week long, Tyler had been there at 6:00 a.m., like clockwork. After finding someone at her window, he'd insisted they time their walks together. She hadn't argued. The dogs hadn't objected, either.

She swung open the door and greeted Tyler with a smile and Sasha with a firm scratch behind the ears.

He lifted a brow. "You look perky this morning."

"I probably look perkier than I feel. I've been awake since shortly after four-thirty."

"Trouble sleeping?"

"Nightmare."

He grimaced. "I can relate."

Yeah, he probably could. Though he'd never mentioned it, he'd probably had more than his share of bad dreams.

At the end of her drive, she scanned Hodges in both directions. Tyler was doing the same thing. But the street was deserted. They turned left and headed down the road.

"Any new news?"

"Since ten o'clock last night?" She grinned.

He returned her smile. "Patience has never been one of my virtues."

"I think I remember that." She kicked a piece of gravel along the asphalt. "Since the Peter lead was a dead end, I'm guessing there won't be any opportunity for breaks until whoever is harassing me tries something again."

His smile faded. "You might be right."

When they'd once again reached her drive, he hesitated. "How about letting me take you to work?"

"Thanks, but I think I'll be safe driving in broad daylight. Besides, I don't want to be without my truck. I'd be stranded until you came to get me."

"Let me at least see you from your house to your truck."

She gave a sharp nod. "That I can do. I'll call you when I'm ready to leave."

She stepped onto her porch and bade him farewell, but he still seemed hesitant. She rested a hand on his forearm. "I'll be fine."

When she slipped out the side door forty-five minutes later, he was waiting next to her truck, this time without Sasha.

"I wish I could be here when you get home every night."

"I'll be all right. I'll keep my eyes open and won't get out of the truck until I'm sure I'm alone. Then it's only a few feet to the kitchen door." She pressed the fob and strolled toward the Ram. "And if all goes as planned, when I get home tonight, I'll be armed."

He raised his brows. "You bought a gun?"

"No. I don't know how to use a gun." She didn't like them, either. One of the men her mother brought home had one. Used to get it out regularly, too, wave it around and make threats with it. Several times he aimed it at her mother, explaining that with a twitch of his index finger, her brains would be all over the wall behind her. He'd even pointed it at Jenny once.

"When I got home from the Blue Desert Café Tuesday night, I went online and ordered some mace. I had it shipped to the office and paid for two-day delivery. According to the email confirmation, it went out Wednesday and will arrive today."

Relief flashed across his features. "That makes me feel a little better. Not as good as being here myself, but better than the thought of you walking in unprotected."

She climbed into the truck and fastened her seat belt. "I don't know how to use a gun, but I can handle a tube of mace. And if I ever feel threatened, I won't hesitate." She grinned at him. "So make sure you never sneak up on me."

"Thanks for the warning."

She held up a hand in farewell. "Later."

He closed the door, patted the roof twice, then watched her back from the carport. By the time she reached the end of the drive, he was halfway through his trek back to Andy's. The two men would be leaving shortly and wouldn't return until after seven. At least, that had been their usual schedule.

She backed onto Hodges, then headed toward town. She wasn't in a hurry. She had fifteen minutes to make the four-minute drive. Her to-do list waited on her desk, completed the afternoon before. No matter how crazy things got, she never left work without outlining her tasks for the next day. She wouldn't hold to it—her plans would change a hundred times. But starting with everything laid out in black and white gave her a sense of control.

And control was important. Maybe because the first nine years of her life, she'd had none.

She turned onto D Street and stepped on the gas.

Some distance ahead, a group of six or eight people stood beside the road, waiting to cross. Tourists, more than likely.

As she approached, the man standing at the head of the group stepped into the road, and the others followed. None of them looked to be in a hurry, another indication she'd been right in labeling them tourists.

Nicki depressed the brake pedal, then, with a gasp, released it to jam it down again. Both times, it went all the way to the floor. Panic stabbed through her as the distance between her and those ambling across the road decreased. Hand on the horn, she grabbed the lever beside her and jerked it upward, but the emergency brake was as useless as the other.

A half-dozen faces turned in her direction, then registered the same panic spiraling through her. She jerked the wheel to the right and bounced up over the curb and onto the sidewalk. Not twenty feet away, a telephone pole stood framed in her front windshield. Before she could react, a deafening crash mingled with her own scream, and the truck jerked to an abrupt halt.

For several moments, she sat motionless, drawing in calming breaths and trying to still her racing heart. She'd almost hit those people. When she shifted her gaze to the side mirror, one of the men in the group stalked toward her, face red and arms flailing.

She groaned. She'd just had one of the biggest scares of her life and now had to face some stranger's wrath. As soon as she opened the door, the words assaulted her.

"What were you doing, lady? You could have killed us."

She stepped from the truck, and for a brief moment, her legs threatened to collapse under her. Steadying herself against the door, she lifted a hand. "I'm so sorry. It was my brakes." She drew in another shaky breath. "I pressed the pedal and didn't have any."

Her words apparently didn't soothe his anger. "Brakes don't just go out like that." He snapped his fingers on the word *that*.

She squared her shoulders, her own patience growing thin. She didn't need this. "Well, mine did. I had new pads put on six months ago, and the brakes were working fine until just now."

He dropped to his hands and knees in front of her door. After inspecting the underside of the truck for a half minute, he rose, then went to the back. His head and shoulders again disappeared under the truck. When he stood a minute later, he was rubbing his right thumb and fingers together.

"Lady, you got a problem."

His tone was somber, all traces of anger gone. A cold block of fear moved through her, leaving a frozen trail. She preferred the anger. "What do you mean?"

"I've been working on cars since I was sixteen, and it looks to me like somebody punctured your brake lines."

Her chest clenched. "They're cut?"

"Not cut. Judging from the way brake fluid is sprayed all over the undercarriage, someone poked holes in them, front and back. If we went around to the passenger side, we'd probably find the same thing. This way, instead of the fluid all leaking out in your driveway, your brakes wouldn't fail until after you'd depressed them a time or two." He pulled a tissue from his pocket and wiped the oily substance from his fingers. "The mess under there was intentional, because whoever did this also cut the cable to the emergency brake." He shook his head.

"Somebody wants you dead."

Tyler's tennis shoes pounded the pavement, and his breath came in heavy pants. The moon rested low on the horizon, a swollen crescent, waiting to be pushed aside by the morning. But even at that early hour, a solid sheet of moisture hung in the air, promising another hot and humid day.

Andy and Joan were still asleep. At 4:30 a.m., so was Sasha. He had been, too, until about twenty minutes ago, when the whoosh of incoming RPGs had invaded his dreams. After a series of brilliant flashes and earth-rocking explosions, he'd sprung from the bed and slammed into the wall, a scream clawing its way up his throat.

So he'd thrown on some clothes and shoes and headed outside. Exercise helped. Movement of any kind helped. It almost gave him the illusion that he could outrun the memories tormenting him.

He slowed to a stop, then stood bent at the waist, hands on his knees, trying to catch his breath. Two years ago, a run like he'd just done wouldn't even have left him winded. Now, with the slightest exertion, his damaged lungs worked overtime, never quite able to keep up with what his body demanded.

He moved again, this time at a more reasonable pace. No sense sapping all his strength before getting the day started.

Today would be a shorter workday. Saturdays always were. But first, he'd check on Nicki. She'd been pretty shaken yesterday after her accident. Actually, *he'd* been pretty shaken. She'd again resisted his pleas to move into Andy's place, but she was at least going along with his demand that she not go anywhere alone. In another hour, he'd be on her doorstep with Sasha. This afternoon, they'd take another walk, then make a trip to Enterprise in Chiefland to get her a rental car. The Ram was repairable, but it was going to be out of commission for some time.

The hum of an engine sounded in the distance, and he cast a glance over his shoulder. There was no sign of headlights. In fact, the closest street lamp was some distance away. And the dim glow of the porch light on the nearest house wasn't much more help than the sliver of moon barely visible over the treetops.

He shrugged it off and continued walking. Sometime between those morning and afternoon walks, he needed to talk to Bridgett. His sister hadn't called in almost two weeks, which was unheard of. Of course, she probably had some level of comfort knowing he was staying with Andy. At least she knew he wasn't dying under a bridge somewhere.

The hum grew louder and closer, and he cast another glance over his shoulder. Still nothing. What was he hearing? It was too close to be someone's air conditioner kicking on. And if a car were approaching, there would be headlights, especially on such a dark night.

Moments later, the hum raised in pitch and volume, building to a roar in the span of a second. Now he had no doubt. It was a car. And it was close.

His heart beat out a jagged rhythm, sending blood roaring through his ears. He shot sideways toward the woods a few feet away. Blinding light engulfed him, and he swiveled his head. The car was right on him.

In a split-second reaction, he threw himself onto the hood and rolled up the windshield, then landed in the grass with a thud. The car careened back onto the road, and the taillights brightened. The driver was hitting the brakes.

When he tried to sit up, his battered body protested. His right leg and hip were bruised, maybe even broken. Already his back muscles were drawing up, and pain shot through his left shoulder and wrist with the slightest movement.

He pulled his cell phone from his pocket, and his heart fell. A strange pattern of psychedelic colors shone from behind the shattered screen. Twenty yards away, the car made a U-turn. The headlights again went black and the engine roared.

It was coming back.

With a groan, he rolled onto his hands and knees and scrambled into the woods. The car raced past. He plopped onto his side and lay motionless in the underbrush. If the driver got out to finish what he'd started, Tyler would be doomed. He was in no shape to fight.

He pushed himself to a seated position and clenched his fists. He didn't survive three tours in Afghanistan to be taken out by some driver with an ax to grind. Or a jealous ex-fiancé.

The car made one more pass to head toward town and probably off Cedar Key. And for several minutes, Tyler sat there, testing joints and taking inventory. By the time he crawled from the woods, the promise of dawn touched the eastern sky, now a pale charcoal.

With the help of the nearest tree, he pulled himself to his feet, then took a small step. Everything still worked. Apparently nothing was broken.

He put a shaking hand to his chest, trying to calm his pounding pulse. That was no accident. The extinguished lights, the racing engine, the erratic path off the road—it left no doubt. Someone had tried to kill him.

But this wasn't about him. He didn't have any enemies. Not on this side of the Atlantic, anyway. This was about Nicki. And the note. He'd been warned to stay away from her or else. Tough. No way was he letting her face this creep alone.

He stepped away from the tree that had been supporting him for the past couple of minutes and limped toward the road. He was a good mile from Andy's. Stumbling back with every joint and muscle screaming at him was going to be pure agony.

By the time Nicki's driveway came into view, the eastern sky had faded from black to gray, the first hint of approaching dawn. He'd call the police from Nicki's house. Already he was probably ten or fifteen minutes late for their morning walk, and he didn't want her heading out alone.

He'd made it three quarters of the way up the drive when the door swung open and Nicki called his name. She eyed him with concern. "What happened? Where's Sasha?"

He stepped onto her porch and winced. "I left early to go for a walk and almost didn't make it back. Someone tried to turn me into a hood ornament."

Her mouth fell open and her brows drew together. "Are you all right?"

"I don't think anything's broken, but I can pretty much guarantee you, come tomorrow, I'll wish I'd stayed in bed."

She took his arm and draped it across her shoulders,

then looped hers around his waist. Once she had him inside, she locked the door and led him to the couch. "Have you called the cops?"

"The impact killed my phone."

She pulled hers from her pocket and, without further comment, punched in the three numbers. There would be nothing the police could do. The car was long gone. And he couldn't even describe it. Year, make, model, even the color—it was all a mystery. The only lead he could give them was to look for a car with a body-sized dent in the hood and roof.

While she waited for the dispatcher, her gaze swept him. "You need to go to the hospital."

"I'll be fine. I just need some ice." Several bags. Maybe an ice bath. Because his body was now beyond protesting. It was shouting obscenities.

After reporting everything, Nicki pocketed the phone and headed toward the kitchen. When she returned a minute later, she held two dish towels and zippered bags filled with ice. He wrapped both packs, trying to analyze which body parts hurt the worst. Probably his hip and shoulder.

"What about Callie?"

"I'll take her out in the front yard when the police get here."

"You don't have to work?"

"Not on Saturday."

Oh, yeah. She was off. And unless he did some incredible mending over the next hour or two, he'd be off, too.

She sank onto the couch next to him and put her face in her hands. "This is my fault."

He dropped the ice pack from his shoulder into his

lap so he could give her leg an encouraging pat. He'd known this was coming, that once she was no longer occupied with taking care of him, she'd heap the guilt on herself. "That didn't look like you behind the wheel."

"You know what I mean. You were told to stay away from me. You should heed those warnings." She stood and started to pace. "I'm putting everyone in danger. I need to leave."

He once again pressed the ice pack to his shoulder. "We've already had this discussion. I'm sticking with you through this. And so is everyone else. We're going to catch this guy."

She stopped pacing to stare at him, her eyes wide and filled with worry. "And who else will be hurt in the meantime?"

"We'll all be careful. I'm sure the police will be stepping up surveillance, too." And he was going to see to it that they checked out this Peter character. He'd better have a pretty watertight alibi for where he was between the hours of four and six this morning.

He forced a smile. "How about getting us some breakfast?" She needed to occupy herself with activity again and stop all this ridiculous talk of leaving.

For several moments, she stood motionless, eyes swimming with indecision. Finally she gave a sharp nod and disappeared into the kitchen. Moments later, the clanging of pots and pans announced the beginning of breakfast preparation. Soon the police would arrive and make a report. Meanwhile, he'd rest. Now that his pulse rate had returned to normal and his system had absorbed all the extra adrenaline, exhaustion was creeping over him. He hadn't gotten enough sleep. Or maybe it was having almost been killed.

He let his head fall against the padded back of the couch and closed his eyes. As the pleasant aromas of frying bacon and eggs wafted through the house, an odd sense of contentment slid through him, that cozy warmth synonymous with home. It wrapped around him, holding him in its soothing embrace.

Home. What every soldier dreams of during each seemingly endless stint. The reason to survive against all odds.

He moved the ice pack from his shoulder to his knee and pushed the thought from his mind. He wasn't even going there. Because home didn't last. That was life.

Good things ended way too soon.

And the fewer attachments he formed, the better.

SIX

Nicki slashed through the final envelope, the rip of paper eclipsing the other office sounds. She'd just come back with the morning mail and was determined to get it dispersed before lunchtime. It had been a busy morning. One more day and the week would be over.

She laid the letter opener on her desk and removed the contents of each envelope. There were the usual items—invoices, customer payments, letters and other business, along with a healthy stack of junk mail. She began separating everything into stacks based on recipient. One letter, however, was simply addressed to "Manager." That was typical for form solicitation letters. But this one looked more personal.

She leaned forward and began to read. Below the City's address were the words "Re: Complaint about employee."

Uneasiness chewed at the edges of her mind. Last week, someone else had made a complaint. About *her*. That one had come from a Jane Wilson. This letter was from a man, a Thomas Abbott, according to the bottom of the letter. The return address portion of the envelope was left blank.

As she read, the uneasiness morphed to dread in one swift stroke. The first sentence pointed out the offending employee—Nicki Jackson. The author of the letter claimed to have applied for a permit for which he had to pay one hundred fifty dollars, but that when he arrived home, he found the receipt had been made out for seventy-five dollars.

Nicki's jaw dropped, and a cold lump settled in her stomach. She wasn't being accused of simple rudeness this time. The author of the letter accused her of dishonesty.

The next paragraph began, "Clearly she pocketed the other seventy-five." And he had his own opinions about how to handle it, suggesting that she be terminated and investigated for embezzling.

Nicki dropped the sheet of paper on her desk and flopped back in her chair, her thoughts tumbling over one another. Although she wanted nothing more than to make the letter disappear, she couldn't do it. She had to give it to her boss. Maybe Miranda would see it for what it was—nothing more than a vendetta. Peter had embezzled, and she'd refused to stand by him. So he was accusing her of the same crime.

She rose and headed toward her boss's open door. She'd been able to convince her the first time. But she was a new employee. And this was the second complaint in a week and a half. How many more would she be able to ward off before Miranda gave in and let her go?

As soon as she stopped in the doorway, her boss motioned her in. Maybe she should have given the letter to the police. But what was the point? The envelope had been handled by too many people. She stepped forward and handed Miranda both the letter and the envelope. "This came in the mail today."

Without speaking, Miranda took what she held. When she finished studying them, she looked up, brows raised, a question in her eyes.

Nicki steeled herself, ready to make her defense. "Lies. Every bit of it."

"I'd tend to agree."

The tension drained from her body. "You would?"

"No return address on the letter or the envelope. No contact phone number. He claims he was bringing in the paperwork for his sister, who is the one having the work done, but didn't give us her name, so there's no way to verify any of this. I smell a skunk."

Nicki slumped against the doorjamb and released a sigh. Her job was safe. For the time being.

After thanking Miranda, she headed back to her desk to retrieve her purse. No more trips home at lunchtime to walk Cassie. The dog was now spending her days with Joan and Sasha. And Tyler was watching Nicki come and go from the house each morning and afternoon.

But a short walk downtown in the middle of the day would be safe. Today, especially, she needed the break from the office. She'd do lunch out, maybe text Tyler to see if he had time to talk.

She stepped outside and looked both ways down Second Street. The car she'd rented on Saturday sat parked at the curb. Several people strolled down the sidewalks.

She crossed the street then headed toward Tony's Seafood Restaurant a block away. In an hour, she'd return, refreshed, settled and ready to work. She opened the wooden door and drew in a fragrant breath. Yes, this was what she needed—a bowl of Tony's world-famous clam chowder. And a long talk with her oldest and dearest friend.

Friend. That was all Tyler was. That was what she had to keep reminding herself. Especially with the way he looked at her. The gentle concern he showed. That fierce protectiveness.

She sighed, then moved to one of the small tables. After the server had taken her order, she pulled her phone from her purse. Tyler hadn't been without his for long. The day he was hit, she'd driven him to Chiefland for a replacement. He'd wanted to be easily reachable if she needed him.

When she swiped the screen, ready to place the call, her phone showed one text received. The number belonged to her private investigator, and the message was short and sweet—Call when you get a chance. Her pulse picked up. Tyler would wait.

When Daniel answered, she dispensed with the pleasantries. "You have news?"

"Sort of." He paused. "I caught up to her in Gainesville yesterday, met her face-to-face. She was waitressing in a small mom-and-pop place. I told her who I was and why I was looking for her. This was about four o'clock. She said she'd get off at seven and I should come back then."

"You came back, and she was gone."

"I never left. I took a seat in a corner booth, got the Wednesday special, and settled in to wait her out. Shortly after five, I didn't see her anymore. Checked, and she'd slipped out the back. At first no one would tell me where she went. They all seemed to be covering for her."

"Then?"

"Then one of the women broke down and gave me what I needed. She and her brother had been separated when they were young and recently reunited, so she has a soft spot for siblings trying to find each other. She didn't have the address, but she'd picked Jenny up for work a few times when Jenny's car broke down, so she was able to give me the name of the apartment complex and the location of the apartment."

"I take it by the time you got there, she'd run again."

The waitress returned with a glass of tea, and Nicki swirled the ice with the straw. The investigator had gotten close this time, had actually gotten to meet Jenny. But the rest of the story was going like all the previous times. Jenny still didn't want to be found.

"Yes. Jenny's roommate was there. She said she didn't know Jenny, that she lived alone. Of course, the neighbors said otherwise. I staked out the place all night, until about eleven o'clock this morning, and she never returned. When I went to the diner, I learned she was scheduled for the breakfast and lunch shifts and never showed up."

As Nicki listened, an idea began to form. Jenny's roommate was protecting her. With all the trouble Jenny had been in, who knew what she was running from? She'd view any stranger looking for her as a threat. Even Daniel. After all, he could be a cop, his story about looking for a long-lost sister nothing but a cover to get information.

But if a woman showed up on the roommate's doorstep, someone who bore a strong family resemblance to Jenny, maybe she'd talk. Even with the five-year age difference, Nicki had looked like her. They'd had the same green eyes, the same small bone structure, the same angled features.

"Give me the roommate's name and address. I'm going to pay her a visit and see if she'll talk to me. I'm sure Jenny's gone, but maybe the roommate has a clue where she went."

Nicki pulled a piece of paper from her purse and jotted down the information, then disconnected the call. Gainesville was a little more than an hour away. She'd leave right after work. She didn't have her truck back yet, but the rental car would get her there just fine. Now to call Tyler.

He answered on the first ring.

"Am I pulling you away from work?" she asked.

"No, we just broke for lunch. What's up?"

"I'm going to Gainesville."

"What's in Gainesville?"

She smiled. "Jenny's roommate. I got a call from the PI. Jenny has disappeared again, but I now have her roommate's name and address. I'm going to pay her a visit."

"When?"

"I'm leaving right after work."

"I'll get off early." His tone was emphatic. "I'm going with you."

"Won't that put Andy in a bind?"

"Andy will survive. I'm not letting you drive over there alone."

The determination and protectiveness behind his words sent an odd warmth coursing through her. She tamped it down. He'd always been protective of her. It didn't mean any more now than it had then.

"It *will* be nice to have some company."

The waitress returned with a steaming bowl of clam chowder and placed it in front of her.

"My lunch just arrived."

"What are you having?"

"Tony's clam chowder."

"I haven't tried it."

"You need to." She spooned some into her mouth and savored it. "Spicy. The best."

"Better than my cold bologna sandwich?"

"Living with Joan, you're not eating bologna."

"You're right. Today is beef stroganoff. I was trying to drum up some sympathy."

She grinned. His quirky sense of humor was usually buried under a pensive soberness, but occasionally it slipped through, giving her a glimpse of the old Tyler. "It didn't work."

When she'd finished her soup and paid for her meal, she took a final swig of iced tea. "I've got to get back to work."

"Me, too. I'll meet you at city hall at five."

"Sounds good." She crumpled her napkin and stood. "Later."

"You always say that. I've never heard you say *bye*."

"*Goodbye* is too final." That was what she'd told her parents the night before they were killed—*bye*. She hadn't meant it. What she'd meant was *see you later* or *talk to you tomorrow* or any number of other ways to sign off. Instead, she'd told them *bye*, and that was what it had ended up being, their final goodbye.

What she'd said hadn't made a difference. She knew that, at least logically. But she hadn't been able to bring herself to mouth the word since.

She walked out the door and headed toward the

office, pushing the thought from her mind. She had more important things to think about. After over six months of searching for her sister, with countless ups and downs, a reunion might be in the near future. The thought brought eagerness mixed with trepidation.

Nicki wasn't kidding herself. Jenny was messed up. Even with love and a stable environment, she wouldn't be right for a long time. Maybe ever. Reaching out to Jenny might saddle her with Jenny's problems for years to come. But she wasn't about to quit now.

Finding Jenny had become even more important with the visit from the detectives. Given that Jenny was five years older, she probably remembered more. She was possibly home at the time of the murder. Maybe even witnessed it.

Whatever faults their mother had possessed, she hadn't deserved to die in the way she had. For twenty-two long years, someone had gotten away with murder. But now, justice might soon be served.

When it finally happened, Nicki would be able to close the door on the past.

Then maybe the nightmares would stop.

Andy pulled into a parking space in front of City Hall, and Tyler stepped from the truck. His F-150 was still sitting in the driveway at his brother's place. He wouldn't need it. This trip was Nicki's deal, so she'd insisted on driving.

He moved up the front walk, stiff after his short ride there from the inn. Although six days had passed since the car had struck him, he still had some sore joints and ugly bruises. He reached up to rub his shoulder, then glanced in through the glass door. The room was the obvious site for town meetings. A table stood at the front, several microphones positioned along its length. Wooden pews arranged in neat rows provided seating for attendees.

To the left, a window opened into Nicki's work area. She stood there talking with someone, papers spread out on the counter between them. Nicki looked in his direction and gave him a quick smile before returning her attention to the customer.

He turned to his right, where three glass-encased bulletin boards lined that side of the walk. He was a couple of minutes early. And if the paperwork on the counter was any indication, Nicki was going to be more than a few minutes late.

The first case held meeting agendas—city commissioners, historic preservation board and local planning agency. The second held a variety of announcements, from Scrabble at the library to vacation Bible school next month. The sleepy town of Cedar Key was more active than he'd realized.

He'd just moved to the third board when the door opened and the man Nicki had been helping walked out. A few minutes later, Nicki was ready to leave, too. He smiled at her as she came out the door. "You got through your work quicker than I thought you were going to."

"I planned it that way." She grinned. "I figure if we get there before dark, this Gina Truman will be more likely to open the door."

"You're probably right." He followed her to the rental car. "So, what do you know about her?"

"Her name and address."

"That's it?" He raised his brows. "I'm glad I'm going with you."

"I don't think I have a whole lot to worry about. She's more likely to avoid me than mug me."

She started the car, then dropped it into Reverse. "I had another attack today."

His stomach clenched. "You didn't tell me."

"I was going to. Then I talked to the PI, and that has consumed my thoughts ever since."

"What happened?" He scanned the length of her body. She didn't look injured in any way, so it must not have been a physical attack.

"Another complaint at work. This time it was a letter, someone claiming I'd charged him a hundred fifty dollars for a seventy-five-dollar permit. The letter said I should be fired and investigated for embezzling. Fortunately, my boss didn't take it seriously. There was no return address on the letter or the envelope."

His tension uncoiled. The threat was serious. Someone had made some grave allegations. But this time it was her job instead of her life. He suppressed a relieved sigh. With Nicki facing the possibility of losing her means of supporting herself, she probably wouldn't appreciate the gesture.

An hour later found them in a less-than-desirable part of downtown Gainesville. The businesses had bars on the windows, and trash littered the edges of the road.

Tyler frowned over at her. "Are you sure you're in the right place?"

"Positive. I pulled up the directions on MapQuest and also plugged it into my GPS. They agree, so that's a good sign."

He nodded, his uneasiness over her quest increasing with every passing minute.

Nicki succeeded in driving them directly to Jenny's

apartment complex. It was two stories, made of concrete block covered in peeling paint. A metal stairway zigzagged up the side of the building, its railing continuing all the way across the front.

Nicki pulled into a parking space and turned off the car. "Stay here, at least for the time being. She'll be more likely to open the door if it's just me standing there."

He crossed his arms. "I don't like you going in there alone."

"You don't have a choice. Now that I've gotten this close, I'm not going to risk you scaring her off."

He frowned. With that determination in her eyes, arguing with her would be pointless. But if she went inside and didn't come out within ten minutes, he was going to break the door down.

She looped her purse strap over her shoulder, and as she stepped out of the car, he opened his own door. They were parked a couple of spaces over but from his vantage point in the car, he could see Gina Truman's apartment door and hear any conversation that took place. Until Nicki disappeared inside. His stomach clenched. It was going to be a long ten minutes.

But before Nicki had even reached the front bumper, the door to apartment 112 swung open and a young woman stepped out. If there was any family resemblance at all between Nicki and her sister, the woman he was looking at wasn't Jenny. The woman on the front stoop was short, not much over five feet, but solid, a little on the chunky side. Chances were good they were looking at Gina Truman. If so, Nicki wouldn't even have to go inside.

Nicki moved in her direction, and their words drifted back to him.

"Gina?"

"Yeah?" The single word held a lot of hesitation. Her gaze flitted over the parking area.

"I'm looking for Jenny. I'm her sister."

Gina's eyes snapped back to Nicki's face, and she visibly relaxed. They stood facing one another, both in profile to him.

Gina nodded. "Y'all look enough alike. I can see you're sisters. So the guy yesterday was telling the truth." She shook her head. "I couldn't take any chances. A while back, Jenny crossed some bad people down in Miami. If they found her, it wouldn't be good."

Tyler's gut tightened. So Jenny wasn't just running from the police. Her problems were more serious. Worry circled through him, settling in his chest. With a crazy ex after her, Nicki had enough to handle without exposing herself to her sister's mess of a life.

Nicki shifted her weight to the other foot. She was still dressed for work. Her black dress pants and modest heels were a sharp contrast to Gina's short shorts and flip-flops. "I don't know how much Jenny told you about her childhood."

"Not much. She's a pretty private person. Tough, but private."

"When she was twelve, our mom was murdered. We got put into different foster homes and haven't seen each other since. About six months ago, I started looking for her." Nicki paused, studying the other woman. "I'd like to help her if I can."

Gina sighed. "I wish I could tell you where she went, but I don't know."

"What did she say when she was leaving?"

"Nothing much. She came tearing through the front door and ran straight to our room. Then she started throwing her stuff in bags. She said they were closing in, so it was time to run again."

"Did she give you any hint about where she was headed?"

"Not at all. She just said she had to disappear. But first she was going to see a wrong made right."

"Any idea what she was talking about?"

Gina shook her head. "I asked her, but she was being real mysterious-like. I got the idea it was something before all the Miami stuff. Something from a long time in her past."

"If you hear from her, will you let me know?"

"Sure. Give me your number."

While Nicki fished in her purse for a pen and paper, a door opened upstairs. A woman stepped out and moved down the walkway, five-inch heels clicking against the cement floor. Her leather miniskirt stretched taut across her hips, and the thin tank she wore left little to the imagination. She made her way down the stairs, weaving between three young men who sat at varying heights, sharing a smoke. Based on the sweet smell that wafted to him, it wasn't tobacco. When she reached the bottom of the stairs, she moved toward the parking lot.

Tyler shifted his gaze back to Nicki, but not before taking in the sunken cheeks beneath the woman's heavy makeup and the creases around her eyes and mouth. She probably wasn't more than thirty, but she'd lived a hard life.

Nicki climbed into the driver's seat and cranked the

engine. "She doesn't know where Jenny went, but she's going to call me if she gets word from her."

"Yeah, I heard." He studied her for several moments. She wasn't going to like what he was about to say, but he couldn't keep quiet. "Gina said Jenny has some bad guys after her. Doesn't that worry you?"

"A little." She backed from the space, then headed out the same way they'd come in.

"Whoever is after her, you don't want her to lead them to you. Maybe you should stop your search. Sometimes it's better to leave well enough alone."

Her hands tightened on the wheel, and her eyes filled with that determination he knew so well. "I won't turn my back on her."

"You've got enough of your own problems. Do you really want to take on Jenny's?"

"I want to find her, whatever it involves. You have a brother and a sister. I have no one."

You have me. The thought shot through his mind, but he immediately dismissed it. She *didn't* have him. She had his friendship, at least for the time being. Then, once this was over, once Nicki was safe and the work on the inn was complete, he'd be gone.

A block away, she braked to ease around an old man pushing a heaped-up shopping cart down the edge of the road. "These people have it rough."

"A lot of them choose the lifestyle they have."

"No, they don't. It chooses them." She stopped at a traffic light, then turned to look at him. "Do you think they want to live that way? Like the woman who walked past you a few minutes ago. She'll spend the night turning tricks. Maybe she'll still be alive in the morning."

The light changed, and she stepped on the gas. "Even

Gina. On the surface she seems okay. But you didn't look in her eyes and see the hopelessness there."

He smiled over at her, but her expression didn't soften. "You've always stuck up for the underdog."

"That's because I've been the underdog, more times than I can count."

Yes, she had. So she would always have a heart for those less fortunate. It was innate, an intrinsic part of her.

And that was one of the things he loved about her.

SEVEN

It was dark, except for a narrow shaft of light spilling into the room from somewhere down the hall. But it wasn't silent. There was a tussle, panting, then curses.

A woman ran into the room, a man right behind her. He pushed her to the floor and pinned her there.

Light glinted off the blade of a knife. He raised it and plunged it into her back, again and again. Screams echoed through the room, then fell silent.

The woman lifted her head and turned it to the side to mouth a single word—"Run."

Nicki jumped from the bed and stumbled backward until the dresser stopped her. Bile pushed its way up her throat, and she clamped a hand over her mouth. The scene was the same as the other two times she'd had the nightmare. Just as real, just as bloody.

But what had chilled her the most was the woman's face—the pain and fear and desperation.

And her own recognition.

The face had belonged to her mother.

Cassie nudged her hand, then pressed her body against Nicki's legs. Nicki dropped to her knees to wrap both arms around the dog's neck and bury her face in the soft fur. For several moments, she clung to her, the lifeline linking her to sanity. Gradually her racing pulse slowed and her spinning thoughts stilled.

What had just happened?

She'd dreamed of her mother's murder, as real as if she'd been there. And her mother had warned her—or somebody—to run.

Was it more than a dream? Was it a memory?

No, that was impossible. She hadn't been there. She'd been next door, with Lizzie and her family. While Lizzie had waited in the doorway to her room, Nicki had gotten her things together—pajamas, clothes to put on in the morning, her toothbrush and toothpaste, a brush and ribbons and barrettes for Lizzie and her to play beauty parlor. She'd never forget that night, because it had been the end of an era. After that, everything had changed. Her whole life had been turned upside down.

The next morning was just as clear in her mind. She'd woken up to Mrs. McDonald shaking her gently, the woman's face streaked with tears, telling her that something awful had happened, that her mother was gone and people would be coming to get her, people who'd love her and take care of her.

So why was she dreaming about her mother's murder as if she'd been there and witnessed it?

She pulled a T-shirt and pair of shorts from the dresser. It was four thirty on a Saturday morning. She should go back to sleep. But that was the last thing she felt like doing. What she wanted to do was walk.

She moved to the nightstand and picked up her phone. At this time of night, most normal people were asleep. But there was a good chance Tyler wouldn't be. She keyed two words into the phone.

You up?

The return text came moments later, a frowny face.
Her thumbs slid over the screen again.

Walk?

Be right there.

By the time she finished dressing, brushed her hair
into a high ponytail and clipped on Callie's leash, Tyler
was at the door with Sasha. She stepped onto the porch,
and he looked at her with raised brows.

"Another nightmare?"

"Yeah. You?"

"Yeah."

"What about?"

He shrugged. "Just stuff."

She released a sigh. He was as tight-lipped as ever.
But she didn't expect otherwise. She stepped off the
porch and headed down the drive. "I've had nightmares
most of my life. But the ones I'm having lately are dif-
ferent." She was going to sound crazy, but she needed
to talk to someone. And if there was anybody she could
be herself with, it was Tyler.

If only he could be himself with her.

"I keep dreaming I'm seeing my mother's murder."

"Since when?"

"The last couple of weeks."

He nodded, his expression thoughtful in the light
of the half moon. "After all these years, the event was
probably pushed to the back of your mind. The visit
from the detectives a couple of weeks ago put it front

and center. And all the stress you've been under hasn't helped."

What he said made sense. But it was more than that. "I don't know. Aside from the fact that I'm just an observer, it doesn't feel like my other nightmares. It seems so real. It's almost like I'm...remembering."

He looked over at her, brow creased. "You said you weren't there."

"I know."

"Is it possible you were?"

"No. I distinctly recall going to Lizzie's house. My memory isn't the slightest bit foggy on that. She came home with me to get my stuff together. Then we went to her house. We took turns fixing each other's hair, and her mom made chocolate chip cookies, brought them to us hot out of the oven."

She smiled at the memory. The time spent with Lizzie and her mother had been the one bright spot in an otherwise dreary and terrifying childhood.

"A little while later, we went to bed. The next thing I remember is waking up and Mrs. McDonald breaking the news to me."

In the distance, headlights angled toward them, someone coming from the direction of town. Tyler grabbed her arm and pulled her into a neighbor's yard. The dogs followed without hesitation. All while she had spoken, he'd listened with tense alertness, his eyes taking in their surroundings. They ducked behind a tree, and the vehicle moved past at a normal rate of speed. It was an SUV. As it neared her house, it didn't slow or make any other suspicious moves.

Tyler let out a breath. "False alarm." He led her back

toward the road. "Cars in the dark make me a little more nervous now than they used to."

She cast him a sympathetic smile. "With good reason."

By the time they returned to the house, the first hint of dawn had touched the eastern sky. He stepped onto her porch and watched her unlock the door.

"What are your plans for today?"

She shrugged. "Some cleaning, laundry. Work on a stained glass project or two." The problem was, none of what she mentioned appealed to her in her current state of mind. "Maybe I'll go into town, bum around some of the shops. Or hang out at the park." Anywhere that would take her thoughts away from threats and nightmares for a while.

"If you go this morning, I'll go with you."

"You have to work."

"Andy's doing a half day today, not going in until this afternoon. Joan's got him tied up this morning."

"In that case, how about a trip to the park?" Sitting on a bench overlooking the water, with the happy voices of children drifting to her from the playground, would go a long way toward soothing her frayed nerves. Especially with Tyler sitting next to her. As long as he was there, he wouldn't let any threats near her. "Nine o'clock?"

"Nine o'clock." He lifted a hand in farewell.

"Later."

After breakfast, she dove into her housework. In spite of her lack of enthusiasm, she managed to get quite a bit accomplished over the next three hours. When the doorbell rang, she'd just finished putting away the laundry and had all the cleaning except the vacuuming done.

She was apparently looking forward to this outing with Tyler more than she'd realized.

After checking the peephole, she swung open the door. He stood on her porch, this time without Sasha. His black F-150 sat in her driveway.

He motioned in that direction. "I brought my truck over. You seemed a little cramped in the Fiat." He grinned. "Not to mention me with my long legs."

"I'm supposed to get my Ram back Monday or Tuesday." She walked with him to his truck. "I've always had trucks, never owned a car. My first vehicle was a blue Silverado pickup with chipped paint and several dents. But I was so proud of that thing."

He walked her to the passenger's side, and when she had climbed in, he closed the door. As he backed from the drive, she continued.

"At sixteen, I got a part-time job at the ice cream parlor in town. For over a year, I saved every penny I made, until I had enough to buy myself a vehicle."

The Silverado hadn't looked great, but she'd paid for it herself, and that had made all the difference. Some of her friends had gotten new cars for their sixteenth birthdays. Six months later, half of them had wrecked those same new cars. But the Silverado got her all the way through college and was still chugging when she'd traded it in four months after graduation.

Tyler shifted into Drive and headed down Hodges toward town. "I didn't have to buy a vehicle until I got out of the Army. When I was a teenager, we didn't have the money, with Mom being sick and everything. By the time I hit seventeen, she wasn't driving anymore, and I was helping my aunt get her to and from her chemo and doctor's appointments. So her Camry sort of became mine."

Nicki watched him as he spoke. His tone was casual, but she wasn't fooled. His mother's illness and death had devastated him. She could see it in his eyes, in the hard lines of his jaw.

Tyler eased around the curve from Dock Street onto A, then pulled into a parking space. On the grassy area in front of them, a father worked with his boy to get a kite airborne. Beyond them, children scurried over a variety of playground equipment painted cheery shades of yellow and blue. Beyond that was the beach. The water was like glass, the line between sea and sky blurred, except for the green mass that was Atsena Otie Key.

Nicki stepped from the truck, then walked with Tyler toward the beach. Mornings and evenings were popular times at the park, when the July heat and humidity were much more bearable.

After a leisurely walk on the beach, she sank onto a wooden bench overlooking the water, and Tyler sat next to her. A barely there breeze whispered past them, and Nicki closed her eyes. But instead of drawing peace from the sights and sounds of nature, she had the opposite reaction. Tension wove through her body, drawing her nerves taut. Out in the open, she was too exposed, too vulnerable.

She glanced nervously around her. A short distance down the beach, a man and woman held fishing poles, two buckets between them. In the other direction, a young couple stood, hand in hand. At the playground, parents conversed with one another while keeping one eye on their charges. A man stood alone near the pavilion, leaning against a tree. Was he watching them?

When Tyler's arm came across her shoulders, she jumped.

"Are you okay?"

"Yeah, just a little tense." She rolled her shoulders, then gave him a shaky smile. "I guess I need to chill, huh?"

She settled in against his side, reveling in the safety she felt there. She shouldn't. If Peter was watching...

But he wasn't. She'd looked. Aside from the one guy standing near the pavilion, all the park's visitors seemed to be involved in their own activities, oblivious to Tyler's and her presence.

His arm tightened around her. "That's better."

She tilted her head to the side to smile up at him. "I guess I can always relax when you're around, huh? You stay alert enough for both of us."

"I try." He paused. "How about hanging out with Joan this afternoon?"

"I've got work to do at home. I promise I'll stay locked inside all weekend. Except for church." She cocked a brow at him. "You could go with me."

"Or you could ride with Andy and Joan."

"You act like I'm trying to drag you back into battle or something. Something must have turned you off."

He shrugged. "I don't see any purpose in it."

If that were the case, he'd be apathetic. She straightened on the bench so she could turn to face him. The set of his jaw and the stubbornness in his eyes said the opposite.

"I think you're angry with God. What happened?" When he didn't respond, she continued. "You feel He let you down."

He crossed his arms over his chest. "Will you stop trying to psychoanalyze me?"

The angry response told her she was uncomfortably close to the truth. "He's not Santa Claus, you know."

"What is that supposed to mean?"

"You can't give Him a list and expect Him to give you everything you ask for."

"So what you're saying is God *doesn't* answer prayer."

"That's not what I'm saying. God always answers prayer. But sometimes the answer is *no* or *maybe*."

The sound he emitted was halfway between a sigh and a snort. "You're letting God totally off the hook."

"Look, I don't have all the answers. I'm new at this stuff myself. But there are a few things I've figured out. One is that bad things sometimes happen to good people. It doesn't mean God has turned a deaf ear to their prayers. We don't always understand why things happen the way they do. We don't see the big picture."

She studied him for a moment. If she was getting through to him, he wasn't letting it show.

"The second thing is that whatever happens, God walks with us through it. We don't have to face anything alone. He gives us strength and comfort, and when we come out on the other side, we're better people. But that part's up to each of us. We can let the bad stuff make us better or we can let it make us bitter."

For a long minute, a heavy silence hung in the air between them. Finally he stood and held out his hand. "I need to get home or Andy's going to be upset with me."

She put her hand in his and forced a smile. "Thanks for coming here with me. I needed this."

"Anytime."

When they arrived home, he walked with her onto her porch. She unlocked the front door and swung it open. Callie was waiting just inside, tail wagging furiously.

"I'm going to take her out."

"Then I'll hang around a few minutes longer."

Nicki stepped inside and hooked up the leash. When she walked back out, her gaze shifted to the side. At the edge of the woods was a flash of movement, with a simultaneous *phsst*. Callie let out a squeal, and Nicki dropped to her knees. Blood seeped from a wound behind the dog's left shoulder.

"Callie's been shot!" She jerked in a jagged breath, heart beating double-time.

Tyler grasped her arms and pulled her to her feet. "Inside, quick." He half dragged her over the threshold, tugging on the dog's leash. Callie yelped again when she put weight on the injured leg, then lay on the tile floor. Nicki ran to get a towel and dropped down next to her dog. Tyler was already on the phone, reporting the incident.

When he finished the call, Nicki looked up at him. "We need to find a vet." She should have established herself with one long before now. But Callie's shots weren't due for another eight months, and there'd been no reason to take her.

Now Callie was in trouble, and she had no idea who to call. She pressed the towel to the wound. The dog whined but didn't resist.

Tyler still held his phone, touching the screen several times. "I'm not pulling up any vets on Cedar Key, but there are some mobile vets who service the area."

"She might need surgery to remove the bullet."

"Our best option is to get her to a vet in Chiefland who's open on Saturday." He fiddled with his phone for another couple of minutes. "Family Pet Vet. They're open till noon. I'll let them know we're on our way."

While he waited for the call to connect, he knelt and inspected the wound. "Pellet gun."

"Are you sure?"

"If it was a regular bullet, Callie would be dead. They'll remove the pellet and she'll be fine."

Relief swept through her, mixed with anger. She'd been attacked in almost every way possible—her job, her finances, her friends. What kind of person would take out anger on a defenseless dog?

Peter wasn't an animal person, something he'd admitted right from the start. But he'd never been cruel. At least, she didn't think he had.

But maybe the shot wasn't intended for Callie. Maybe she or Tyler was the target. If that was the case, the shooter meant to harm, not kill. Otherwise he'd have chosen a different weapon. The realization didn't bring the comfort she longed for.

Tyler pocketed his phone and handed her his keys. "They're expecting us." He bent to scoop up Callie. "You drive and I'll hold her."

As she opened the front door, a Cedar Key police cruiser pulled into the driveway. Relief rushed through her. If their attacker had had any thoughts of hanging around for another shot, he was likely gone now.

Nicki locked the front door, and when she turned back around, Amber was stepping out of the car.

"We've got to get Callie to the vet. She's been shot." Of course, Amber probably already knew that.

"Where did the shot come from?"

Nicki pointed, then climbed into Tyler's truck. She'd get Callie the help she needed and leave Amber to do her investigation.

At the park this morning, she'd been tense, worried about what threats lurked in the shadows.

She'd been wrong. No one had been watching them at the park. While she and Tyler were there, someone was right here, waiting for them to return. Looking for the right moment to exact vengeance.

Poised and ready to strike when the moment came.

And Callie was the victim.

It was bound to happen eventually.

Tyler stalked down the street, his tread heavy. He didn't have Sasha with him, but the dog was awake. Andy and Joan were, too, thanks to him. He'd known it was just a matter of time. But that didn't make his shame any less.

Once again, his mind had taken him back to the place of darkness and smoke and the stench of burning flesh. His own screams had mingled with the screams of his men. And Andy's had, too. Apparently Andy had stood there for some time, hollering his name, smart enough to stay out of harm's way, but determined to release his mind from the prison holding it.

Several blocks down, he turned around and headed back toward his brother's house. He was going to have to face them. Might as well get it over with.

When he stepped inside, Joan was in the kitchen making a pot of coffee. Andy sat in his recliner, a magazine open in his lap. He looked up from what he was reading.

"Feeling better?"

Tyler shrugged and sank into a chair. "Better than I was thirty minutes ago. Sorry I woke you guys up."

"No need to apologize. From everything I've read and seen, it's to be expected."

Yeah, it was, but that didn't make it any easier.

"How about going to church with us this morning?"

He stifled a snort. "You think that's going to fix me?"

"It sure can't hurt."

Andy had invited him every week since he got there. Joan had chimed in a couple of times, too. Even Nicki had asked him to come.

But religious platitudes weren't going to fix what was wrong with him. Neither had counseling or anything else he'd tried. In fact, his therapists had been pretty up-front about the battles he was going to face. They'd warned him the flashbacks and nightmares could go on for years, maybe even a lifetime.

He pushed himself to his feet. "No thanks. I'll hang out here."

"Why are you so dead set against going with us?"

"Let's just say I'm keeping a promise."

He ignored Andy's raised brows and strode to the kitchen. After pouring himself a cup of coffee, he moved down the hall. He'd been in such a hurry to get away from the house, he'd stayed in the gym shorts he'd slept in and thrown on the first shirt he could find. But he wanted to make himself more presentable before meeting up with Nicki.

When he returned to the living room, Sasha lay next to the recliner, waiting for the scratches Andy regularly delivered over the side of the chair. Tyler removed the leash from the coat rack by the front door, then clapped his hands. "Come on, girl, it's time to meet Callie. You'll just have to be easy with her."

He walked out the door and looked toward Nicki's. The sun sat low on the horizon, blocked by the trees separating the two properties. They'd agreed to a later meet-up time since it was Sunday. After yesterday's scare, starting the walk in daylight had a lot of appeal.

When he rang Nicki's bell, a half minute passed before the door opened.

"How's Callie?"

"Sore. She's limping, and she hates the cone."

He smiled. "They always do. But without it, she'd have those stitches pulled out in no time."

He'd been right about it being a pellet gun. The object had lodged in the soft tissue right behind the shoulder joint. The vet had removed it, put in three small stitches and sent them home with an antibiotic, some pain medication and the plastic cone around her neck.

"Last night we didn't go much past the front door. This time we'll see if she can make it all the way to the end of the driveway."

Letting Callie set the pace, they moved toward the road. The limp wasn't as pronounced as he'd expected. Another week or so and she'd probably be back to normal.

He frowned over at Nicki. "I'd feel a whole lot better if you'd move in with Andy and Joan and me." They'd had the conversation yesterday, and he hadn't gotten anywhere with her. Moving in with any of her Cedar Key friends was out of the question. She wouldn't put them in danger. And she wouldn't consider staying with someone off Cedar Key because she wasn't willing to give up her job. Moving in to one of the area hotels wasn't doable, either, because of cost.

"I'm not going to impose on them like that."

"It's not imposing. I already talked to them, and they agreed." Maybe he needed to have Andy and Joan walk over and appeal to Nicki themselves.

"There are only two bedrooms."

"You and Callie can have mine. I'll sleep on the couch."

She shook her head. "I'm not putting you out of your room." She sighed and continued. "I'll be all right. I'm being careful. And you're next door."

"Nicki, someone shot your dog." His exasperation came through in his tone. Sometimes she was too stubborn and independent for her own good.

"With a pellet gun. If he'd intended to kill Callie or me, he'd have used something a lot more lethal."

"Maybe next time he will."

When they reached the end of the drive, Callie stepped off into the grass and squatted. This was likely as far as she'd go. Once she finished her business, she'd be ready to head back to the house.

"What time are you leaving for church?" He might as well drop the other topic of conversation. Convincing Nicki to move in with Andy and Joan wasn't going to happen. Her mind was made up.

"Around ten." She raised her brows, hope in her eyes. "You thinking of coming with me?"

"No, I just want to make sure no one bothers you on the way to your car."

"What about from the car into the church and from the church back to the car?"

She had a point. "That's why I suggested riding with Andy and Joan."

"They go a lot earlier than I do."

He frowned. This conversation wasn't going much better than the other one had. But she was right. Andy played guitar for worship and practiced before the service, and Joan taught Sunday school.

"Okay, I'll go."

"Awesome!" A victorious smile spread across her face.

Yeah, her victory, his defeat. But not really. He wasn't reneging on his long-ago vow never to set foot inside a church. He was going to see to her safety. He had no intention of paying God any kind of homage.

As promised, he was back at her house at ten o'clock sharp. She swung open the door, and his breath caught in his throat. She was elegant, sophisticated, beautiful. And utterly feminine.

Growing up, he'd never seen her in anything but jeans and shorts. Except for the dress pants and blouses she wore to work, that was still her usual attire.

Not today. Apparently she wore dresses to church. This one was made of some soft, silky fabric with bold splashes of color. It was sleeveless, V-necked and cinched at the waist with a wide blue belt. The flared skirt fell just below her knees, swirling as she moved. High-heeled sandals the same shade of blue as the belt put her eye level with him.

"You look great."

She stepped out the door and pulled it closed behind her. "Thanks."

As he climbed into his truck, he glanced at his watch.

This wasn't how he wanted to spend his Sunday morning. But in another two hours, it would all be over.

They arrived fifteen minutes before the service would begin. As soon as they stepped from his truck, a short, perky woman, whom Nicki introduced as Darci Stevenson, ran over to greet her with a warm hug. Her husband Conner was with her, along with their two sons.

Inside, Nicki introduced him to several other friends. He'd met Meagan previously, along with her husband Hunter and his sister Amber. The rest of them, he didn't know. He eased himself into a seat between Nicki and Meagan and looked around. Several people conversed softly, faces animated, as if they wanted to be there.

After an opening prayer, the musicians led the worshippers in several songs. The music wasn't what he'd expected. He'd intended to shut it out. But it wove its way past his defenses, catchy tunes that made him want to sing along in spite of the worshipful lyrics.

And when the pastor finally took his place, there was nothing irrelevant about his message. The theme was "Cast your cares on Him, because He cares for you." There was something appealing about the whole idea. Tyler couldn't say he believed any of it, but he wasn't able to ignore it, either.

Church was different from what he remembered. Or maybe *he* was different. He was no longer an angry teen being forced to do something he thought was pointless. Instead, he was a floundering adult, here by his own free will. Sort of.

When the service was over, everyone filed out of the rows, and several people gathered in groups to chat.

Nicki led him out of the building behind Hunter and Meagan. Once outside, Meagan faced them.

"Game night's at Blake and Allison's this month." She winked at him. "You're welcome as Nicki's date."

Nicki smiled at him. "The last Friday night of the month, there's a group of us who get together for games. It'd be nice to not be the odd man out for a change."

He glanced at those around them. They all seemed to be couples. He nodded. "Sounds like fun."

After farewells, they all headed toward their vehicles. Darci and Conner were parked two spaces over. They stopped at their car, but instead of getting in, removed something from the windshield.

Tyler frowned, lead settling in his gut. All the notes he'd seen lately hadn't been good. He watched Darci as she skimmed the page, the color leaching from her face. Hunter apparently saw it, too, because within moments, he was next to her.

"Don't handle it." He took it from her, touching only the corner. "We'll try to get prints."

"What does it say?" Nicki's voice was paper-thin.

Darci's hands shook as she read. "'Stay away from Nicki Jackson, or harm will come to those little boys of yours.'"

Nicki stepped back, her face now as pale as Darci's. She held up her hands, her eyes darting from face to face. "You have to stay away from me. I can't be near any of you. I won't come here anymore. I won't put all of you in danger."

"No."

Tyler turned toward the female voice at his back. Sometime after Darci had pulled the note from her windshield, Allison and Blake had stepped up behind them. So had Sydney and Wade, two other friends.

Allison continued. "You can't stay away. It's times like this when you need your church family more than ever. I can't speak for everyone else, but Blake and I are standing with you."

Wade stepped forward, holding his wife's hand. According to Nicki, he was a Cedar Key firefighter. "Sydney and I are with you, too."

Hunter spoke next. "We need to leave Darci and Connor out of this. They have the boys to think of. But Meagan and I are with you, too."

Tyler put his arm around her and pulled her close. "And you already know where I stand."

The three couples formed a circle around Nicki and Tyler and joined hands. When Tyler looked at Darci, standing to the side with her small family, her eyes were moist.

A tear slipped down her cheek. "Nicki, when I was in trouble, you were there for me. I don't know what I'd have done without you. Now you're the one who needs help, and I'm turning my back on you."

"No," Nicki argued. "Don't worry about me. Take care of your boys. They come first."

Darci nodded and got into her car. Tyler pulled Nicki even closer. She'd refused to give up her search for her sister, because Jenny was the only family she had left.

She was wrong.

Maybe Nicki didn't share any blood with these eight people.

But they were family, in the truest sense of the word.

EIGHT

Nicki sat in Tyler's truck, staring out the front windshield, conflicting emotions tumbling through her. She was a danger to everyone. She should leave and start over somewhere else.

But it wasn't that simple. A good bit of her inheritance was tied up in her house. She had her job and two great outlets to sell her artwork. If she walked away with nothing but her reduced savings account, she'd starve before she got on her feet. And who was to say the person tormenting her wouldn't find her again as soon as she got settled somewhere else?

Tyler pulled out of the parking lot, then reached across the truck to squeeze her shoulder. "You okay?"

She swallowed hard. "I don't know what to do. I'm putting everyone in danger by staying here. But I don't know where to go."

"You need to stay right here in Cedar Key. Hunter and the others are going to catch whoever is doing this. It's been only three weeks. We need to give them time."

How much time, and who'd be hurt in the interim? It wasn't just her own life. There were too many others who could be caught in the crossfire. All of her wonderful new friends. Darci's autistic little boy. Conner's nephew Kyle who'd already experienced far too much heartache before Darci and Conner adopted him.

Tyler squeezed her shoulder again. "Okay?"

She nodded slowly. What else could she do? Leaving was out of the question. And she couldn't isolate herself. Her friends wouldn't let her.

She laid her head back against the seat and closed her eyes. Her friends. They were more than friends. Allison had referred to them as family, her church family.

All through foster care, *family* had seemed like some glittering concept that would remain forever out of reach. Then, against all odds, she'd landed in the home of Doris and Chuck Jackson. And the impossible dream had become a reality.

The moment she learned her adoptive parents had been killed, her whole world had collapsed into the giant black hole left by their absence. And soon, the desire to reconnect with the last living person who could fill the role of family had been overwhelming.

But Tyler was right. Bringing Jenny into her life would also bring all of Jenny's problems down on her. Was that what she wanted? Her own problems would be over once the police caught whoever was harassing her. But Jenny's problems would go on indefinitely.

Tyler's gasp cut across her thoughts, and the engine revved. She opened her eyes. Ahead and to the right, smoke billowed into the sky. Her back stiffened, and she leaned forward in the seat, straining to see where the billowy charcoal-colored column was coming from.

Someone's house was on fire.

Her heart pounded out an erratic rhythm, picking up speed the closer they got. It was either her house or the one on either side of hers. Within moments, she had no doubt. Her house was engulfed in flames.

Callie!

She hooked her purse strap over her shoulder, gripping it until her fingers cramped. Without waiting for Tyler to bring the truck to a complete stop, she swung open the door and stumbled out. Her sandal contacted the edge of the pavement, and her ankle twisted, throwing her sideways into the grass. Without pausing to survey the damage, she pushed herself to her feet and ran up the drive. Pain shot through her right ankle with every step, but she didn't slow down. Callie was inside. She had to get to her.

As she neared the house, high-pitched barking punctuated the ominous crackle of flames. She pulled her keys from her purse and, with shaking fingers, inserted one into the lock. The next moment, a deafening explosion rent the air as the living room window exploded outward in a burst of flames just ten feet away.

Strong arms wrapped around her, pulling her backward, and she fought for all she was worth. She couldn't let Callie die in the flames.

"Let me go!" Her voice was loud and shrill. She twisted and brought her right elbow backward. It connected with Tyler's ribcage with a solid thud. She followed it with several more blows.

They didn't even faze him. With his arms still wrapped around her waist, he picked her up and carried her away from the house. She continued to scream at him and kick her feet. Several times her heels connected with his shins, and he swore under his breath.

"Stop fighting me." He forced her to the ground and pinned her there. "You can't go in there or you'll die."

She stopped resisting and let the tears flow. "Callie's in there. You can't let her burn to death."

"I'll see what I can do. But you have to promise me you won't try to go in."

She drew in a sobbing breath and nodded her head.

"I'm going to release you, but you've got to promise me."

She nodded again. "I promise." Her eyes widened. "We need to call 911."

He glanced to the side, and she lifted her head to follow his gaze. Andy rushed toward them from the road, where he had left his truck, his phone pressed to his ear.

Tyler released her and stood. "I think my brother already has."

She pushed herself to her feet and followed Tyler to the house, staying back several feet. The barking had become even more frantic and seemed to be coming from the master bedroom.

When Tyler reached the house, he pressed his hands to the bathroom window. "She's in here, and the glass is cool."

He peeled off his shirt, and her eyes locked on his bare back. He'd never talked about that final mission and the injuries he'd sustained. But now she knew at least part of what had sent him home. Pale skin stretched across his upper back, down toward the curve of his waist and up over his right shoulder. Some places were mottled, others unnaturally smooth. All of the mended area was different from the surrounding olive-hued skin. He'd been badly burned and likely undergone months of painful skin grafts. And now he was going in to save her dog.

He wrapped the shirt around his fist and thrust it

through the window. One blow shattered the glass. After ripping the miniblinds from their brackets and tossing them aside, he knocked the remaining shards of glass free from the frame. Then he ducked his head and shoulders inside. Moments later, he backed out, and a blond head and front paws followed him.

Nicki rushed forward in an exclamation of laughter mixed with tears. Sliding her hands under Callie's stomach, she helped Tyler lift her through the opening. Then they moved away from the house, Tyler carrying Callie.

After putting her down on the lawn, he shook out any shards of glass clinging to his shirt and put it back on. "It's a good thing you had Callie closed up. That helped keep the majority of the smoke away from her."

She looked at him sharply. "I didn't. I always let her have the run of the house. At least, I do now that she's well past her destructive phase."

He drew his brows together. "That's odd. She was in the bathroom with the door closed."

She nodded. "She closed doors a couple of times at the other house. When I first got her, she'd start playing, chasing her tail and whatnot, and bump into all kinds of things. I'd say she went back there today, trying to get away from the fire. Then, as she got more and more frantic, she hit the door and slammed it shut."

Sirens sounded in the distance, and Nicki glanced up the road. Over the next couple of minutes, they grew closer, then stopped as a fire truck came to a halt in front of her house. The next moment, the crash of shattering glass split the silence. On the carport side of the house, the roof collapsed, and a swirl of sparks rose into the sky.

Two firemen ran toward the house, pulling the hose

as it unreeled behind them. One was Wade Tanner, his firefighting gear probably thrown quickly over the clothes he'd worn to church.

Moments later, a thick stream of water shot from the end of the hose, traveling in a gentle arc. A sharp sizzle rose above the other sounds, and smoke billowed into the air as the water extinguished the flames.

Nicki stood frozen, watching it all. Pain shot through her, so intense it brought her to her knees. She wrapped her arms around Callie's neck and buried her face in her fur. Everything was going to be a total loss—all her stained glass supplies, the incomplete projects, her clothes and dishes and furniture. The figurines and jewelry and everything else that had belonged to her parents. And the pictures—years of photo albums holding precious memories.

A sob welled up in her throat, and she tried to tamp it down. Callie was still alive, unhurt. Her possessions would be replaced by insurance. The memories of her parents, she'd forever hold in her heart. No one could take those from her.

She raised her head to look at Tyler, and her blood ran cold.

Although he was standing right next to her, he was somewhere else. His fists were clenched. His jaw was tight, and his eyes were squeezed shut. Sweat ran down his face, far more than what could be blamed on the heat and humidity.

She rose to her feet. "Tyler?"

"No." He shook his head, but he wasn't communicating with her. He was reacting to whatever was going on in his mind. "No, no, no." Each word was louder than the last. He lifted his arms to press his palms against his ears.

"Tyler." She gasped, her thoughts spinning. What was he seeing? She moved to stand in front of him, her back to her smoldering house. "Tyler, it's Nicki. Look at me."

She put her hand on his arm, her touch featherlight, and he started. He opened his eyes and looked at her. But not really *at* her. More like *through* her, to something only he could see.

She slid her fingers beneath his. "Tyler, you're here with me. And Callie." She pulled his hand away from his ear and lowered it to Callie's head. "See? Callie's here."

His gaze gradually cleared. "I'm all right."

She continued to study him. His posture was stiff, his focus straight ahead. He *wasn't* all right. Her jaw went lax. Her fire, his burns… "Watching my house burn, you were reliving that last mission, weren't you?"

He swallowed hard, his Adam's apple bobbing with the action, but he didn't respond.

"It might help to talk about it."

He answered without meeting her eyes. "No war stories, okay?"

She wrapped her arms around his neck and pulled him to her. Her heart broke for him, for the agony he'd lived through that refused to release him. And it broke for herself, for all that lay destroyed in the smoldering ruins behind her.

"Hold me," she whispered. The words slipped out of their own accord.

She pressed her cheek to his, feeling his breath in her hair, and his arms came up to circle her back. He tightened his hold, and she reveled in the security she felt in his embrace.

Maybe she'd one day escape the clutches of the past, and he would, too.

Maybe together they'd find healing.

Tyler sat on the couch, feet propped up on the coffee table, Nicki next to him. She was sitting close, tucked under his arm, which was draped across the back of the couch. Callie and Sasha lay at their feet. An older romantic comedy played on the TV, something light and fun and a little bit senseless. Just what he needed after the day they'd had. A period of zoning out would probably do Nicki a world of good, too.

It had been a crazy afternoon. Amber had shown up shortly after the fire was out and called Hunter, who'd had the day off. He then told Meagan, who got in touch with Allison and Blake. Soon half the people he'd met at church that morning were in Nicki's front yard, offering their support.

Allison was tall like Nicki and the closest to her size. So after Nicki had answered the investigator's questions and called her insurance company, Allison had loaded her in her car and taken her home. Forty minutes later, they returned with several bags of clothes. Allison even had shoes Nicki could wear. Then Tyler had taken her to the Chiefland Walmart to stock up on anything else she needed, mostly toiletries and underclothes.

Nicki still hadn't been inside the house. That wouldn't happen for some time yet. Since everyone suspected arson, Chief Robinson had called in the state fire marshal. The scene wouldn't be released until the investigation was complete. The first time into the house would be heart-wrenching for Nicki, but Tyler planned to be right by her side.

He glanced over at her. Her head was tilted back, resting against his arm, and her eyes were almost closed. She was exhausted. He could relate.

He'd had his own ordeal that afternoon. As he'd watched the flames consume her house, he'd suddenly been back in Afghanistan. Explosions rocked the landscape, brilliant flashes of fire lighting up his surroundings. Smoke enveloped him, pungent and suffocating. Then came the screams of the trapped and dying—gut wrenching howls of agony that went on and on.

Nicki had brought him back.

She'd stood in front of him, understanding shining from her eyes, the gentle breeze lifting her hair and swishing it about her shoulders. When she wrapped him in her arms and drew him to her, he'd wanted to melt into her and stay there forever.

The shame he'd expected to feel over his display of weakness hadn't been there. They were two of a kind—lost souls trying to find their way through the quagmire of life's circumstances.

When the credits began to roll, he looked again at Nicki. Her chest rose and fell in the steady rhythm of sleep. Her eyes were closed, her lashes fanned out against her cheeks. Some pale blue shadow covered her lids. The peach lipstick she'd applied that morning for church was long gone, but a hint of color still touched her cheeks.

Her eyes fluttered open and she turned her head to look at him. "I missed the last part of the movie."

He smiled. "I like watching you sleep."

"I hope I didn't do anything embarrassing."

"No, you didn't snore. There weren't any snorts or other strange noises."

She swiped her hand across her chin. "And I didn't drool, so I guess I'm okay." She pushed herself to a more upright position. "I guess I should let you go to bed."

"No rush." He liked having her sitting there with him. After almost two weeks of trying, he'd finally convinced her to move into Andy and Joan's house.

"I feel bad running you out of your room."

"You didn't run me out. I left willingly." He patted the cushion beside him. "The couch is quite comfortable."

"I still feel like I should be the one sleeping out here, not you."

"Absolutely not." He stood and held out his hand to help her up. "Ladies need their privacy. Us guys, we can crash anywhere."

She let him pull her to her feet. "I have to admit, a nice, soft bed sounds really good about now."

He watched her disappear down the hall, then fluffed the bed pillow lying on the end of the couch. He'd changed into a pair of shorts and a T-shirt as soon as he'd gotten home. He'd sleep in them just fine.

After turning off the lamp, he swung his legs up onto the couch and lay on his back. Moonlight washed in through the front door's oval glass inset, casting the room in its soft glow.

A welcome sense of contentment washed through him, the result of having Nicki so close.

Partly because he could now keep her safe.

And partly because that was where he'd always wanted her to be.

*** *** ***

He slipped silently into the kalat *and stopped, M4 at the ready. Tension spiked through him as he scanned the shadows. Five others filed in with him, each with a preassigned sector. He moved toward a doorway and stepped inside the adjoining room, weapon swinging around in a controlled arc.*

The telltale whistle of a mortar round rent the silence, the explosion following a fraction of a second later. Pure adrenaline spiked through him. He spun back through the open doorway and strained to see into the cloud of dust and smoke that enveloped the area. The rugs had ignited, and flames licked at the pillows and cushions lining the room. A gaping hole in the front wall gave a clear view of the outside.

Small arms fire erupted, and he snatched his radio from his vest, struggling to make out his men in the haze. Three were crouched, having moved to positions away from the front wall. Two were down. Marty lay faceup on the cushions at the back of the room, bloodstained hands clutching his stomach. Steve sat against the wall nearby, empty space where the lower part of his leg should have been.

Tyler raised the radio to his face. "This is Wildcat two-one. We're caught in an ambush and receiving fire. Over."

The cushion beneath Marty erupted in flames. Tyler stepped in that direction as another mortar round whizzed into the room. The explosion threw him backward, slamming him into the side wall. A bone snapped, and pain shot through his left arm. The staccato rhythm of AK-47 fire continued, and another man went down. Where was that other squad?

An agonized scream rose over the sounds of the small arms fire. Marty was engulfed in flames. Steve would be next. With his left arm hanging, Tyler moved toward them on his knees, firing off several shots through the damaged wall. Another mortar round slammed into the building. Mud bricks and debris crashed over him, knocking him flat.

The next moment, a series of creaks sounded above him. That section of the roof was giving way. He threw his good arm over his head just before the full weight of it crashed down on him. Steve's screams joined Marty's, forming a hideous chorus.

He tried to rise, but he was pinned. Flames spread to the newly fallen support beams, and his own screams mingled with those of his dying men. He had to get out. His men needed him.

Suddenly his arms were free. He threw his hands back, fighting his way through the debris holding him. His fist connected with...something.

The screams faded and disappeared, replaced by barking. Dim light crept into the room from somewhere else. He blinked several times. He was in Andy's living room. A figure lay on the floor on the other side of the coffee table, barely visible in the glow of the light seeping in through the front door. A dog flanked each side, still barking.

"Nicki?"

He flew to his feet and clicked on the lamp, a vise clamping down on his chest. If he'd hurt her...

"Are you all right? Tell me I didn't hurt you."

The dogs settled down but still eyed him warily. Nicki pushed herself onto her hands and knees and sat back. Her left cheekbone was turning an angry shade of red. Callie gave her several sloppy kisses on the side of her face. Nicki grimaced, then ran a shaking hand down the dog's back.

He dropped to his knees and gathered her into his arms. "Oh, sweetheart, I'm so sorry."

"It's not your fault."

"Yes, it is. I hit you."

His brother appeared at the end of the hall, followed by Joan. "Everything okay? We heard a scream."

Nicki spoke. "Tyler had a nightmare. Everything's fine."

"No, it's not. I hit her." And he hated himself. He was a danger to those around him. He'd thought if he just kept his weapon locked away, he couldn't hurt anyone. He'd been wrong.

"I shouldn't have approached you." Her eyes held concern mixed with understanding. "I was awake and heard you thrashing around. By the time I got out here, you were talking in your sleep. Something was apparently going horribly wrong." She cast a glance at his brother. "Andy and Joan would probably appreciate me not repeating your exact words."

He cringed. "Sorry about that."

"Your talking got louder and more agitated, and I tried to wake you up by calling your name. When that didn't work, I put my hand on your shoulder and shook you. Then you screamed and started swinging. I tried to twist away, but I didn't escape fast enough."

He shifted his gaze to the coffee table, and his stomach filled with lead. "I hit you hard enough to knock you over the table."

"Not totally. I was already off balance, my weight

shifting that direction. You just helped." She started to smile, then winced.

Apparently having decided the danger was over, Andy and Joan disappeared back down the hall. The dogs must have sensed it, too, as they lay back down. He tightened his hold on her and buried his face in her hair. "I'm so sorry."

"Don't apologize." Her words were the softest whisper.

She turned so she could wrap her arms around him, and for several minutes they sat, locked in a comforting embrace. He breathed in the faint floral scent of her shampoo, letting her soothing presence drain away the last of his tension.

He'd cherish it while it lasted. Because like every other good thing, his time with Nicki would be all too fleeting. Soon he and Andy would finish their work on the inn. Eventually whoever was tormenting Nicki would be caught. Then Tyler would leave.

He'd entertained thoughts of staying, of trying to make Nicki feel something more than friendship. That had been nothing but a pipe dream. Tonight had proved it.

Because if he stayed, if they became more than friends, he'd never know when he might hurt her. He'd always be a threat.

Maybe as much of a threat as whoever was after her.

NINE

Nicki couldn't help shaking her head as she hung up the phone. Tyler was still sitting at the kitchen table, and she plopped into the chair next to him. After he and Andy had worked a short day at the inn, the four of them had had a late lunch, and Andy and Joan had run into town. Tyler was probably thankful for the afternoon off, since they'd stayed out way too late last night. At least he'd enjoyed his first game night with her friends.

She turned to him now. Almost a week had passed since the fire, and she'd just gotten her first piece of news. "That was Chief Robinson. The preliminary report shows the right rear burner under the pan I'd fried eggs in was left on medium high."

Tyler raised his brows. "You forgot to turn off the stove?"

"No, I didn't." She was too much of a double-checker to walk away with her stove on.

"Maybe you were distracted."

"I'm positive I turned it off. Besides, I fry eggs on medium, not medium high."

She rose from the table and began to pace, a knot forming in her stomach. She'd hoped it was faulty wiring or some other accidental cause. This proved otherwise.

Tyler nodded, mouth set in a firm line. "If that's the case, someone turned it on, maybe trying to make it look like a grease fire to hide the fact that it was intentionally set." He drew his brows together. "Would Callie let a stranger into the house when you're gone?"

"I doubt it. But if someone broke the kitchen window, he could stretch across the counter and reach the knobs without even coming inside, since they're on the back of the stove."

It was a distinct possibility. The kitchen window had been broken. So were several others. The day before yesterday, she'd gone in with Tyler and taken a look around. The tour had been heartbreaking. Ashes littered everything, charred remains of most of her earthly possessions.

The room she used as her workshop had been the least damaged, leaving her stained glass tools and supplies salvageable. There was a lot of smoke damage, but fortunately, the insurance company had arranged for cleanup.

The rest of the house hadn't fared so well. The kitchen and living room were a total loss. The curios holding all her collectibles were reduced to a few warped and charred pieces of wood and blackened panes of glass. The figurines lay in pieces amid the destruction.

Her bedroom was almost as bad. The flames had swept through the room, turning everything fabric to ash. It was all gone—curtains, blankets, bedding, clothes. And Lavender.

Nicki sighed. After the first attack, she'd carefully

stitched the rabbit's belly back together and returned her to her place on the shelf. This time there would be no repairing her. Lavender was gone.

She sank back into the chair and laid her phone on the table. "The investigator said the glass is still being tested to determine whether it was shattered from the outside first or burst from the inside due to the heat. Since the doors were still locked, I'm guessing they'll find that at least one window was shattered from the outside." She was pretty sure it was the one in the kitchen.

Before Tyler could respond, her phone lit up and the ringtone sounded.

"You're popular today."

She frowned at the phone. She didn't recognize the number. She swiped the screen and said a tentative hello.

"Nicki?"

Her pulse began to race. There was something familiar about the voice, a certain lilt that, even after twenty-two years, she'd never forgotten.

"Jenny?"

"Yes, it's me."

She closed her eyes and clutched the phone more tightly. After seven long months of searching, and a couple thousand dollars, her dream was about to become a reality. She was going to be reunited with her sister. "Where are you?"

"On my way to Cedar Key. I just need your address."

The front door opened and closed, and several moments later, Andy and Joan stepped into the kitchen. Nicki sprang from her chair and pointed at the phone, mouthing her sister's name. Now that she'd gotten over the initial shock, she could hardly contain her excitement. She gave Jenny directions, then moved into the living room at a half skip.

"How soon will you be here?"

"About thirty minutes."

"I can't wait."

After disconnecting the call, she bounded back into the kitchen. "Jenny's on her way here."

Joan squealed and hugged her. Andy patted her shoulder. "That's wonderful news."

Only Tyler didn't share in her joy. He sat with his arms crossed and his jaw tight. Annoyance slid through her, and she tried to tamp it down. He was just concerned. Once he saw that everything was going to be okay, he'd be happy for her, too.

At least, she hoped everything was going to be okay. Because the doubt chewing at the edges of her mind was hard to ignore.

For the next thirty minutes, she alternated between pacing and parting the blinds to stare out the window. When she thought she could stand it no longer, a small white car pulled into the driveway. She opened the door and stepped onto the porch.

The driver's door swung outward, and a woman climbed out. Platinum-blond hair brushed her shoulders, and long legs emerged from cut-off denim shorts. A baggy T-shirt ended a couple of inches above the frayed hem. Sunglasses hid her eyes. She stopped just before reaching the porch.

Nicki closed the remaining distance between them and wrapped her in a tight hug. Tears sprang to her eyes, and she had to choke back an unexpected sob. Jenny returned the hug, but not as enthusiastically as Nicki had initiated it.

Nicki released her. Jenny was holding back. Nicki understood that. They had so much catching up to do. After twenty-two years, they were virtual strangers.

"Come on in. I want you to meet my friend Tyler and his brother and sister-in-law."

Once inside, Jenny moved her sunglasses to the top of her head. Her eyes were the same green Nicki remembered. But there was a hardness to them, and creases fanned out from the outer edges. Jenny had other wrinkles, too, vertical troughs between her eyebrows and frown lines around her mouth, signs of the hard life she'd led.

Nicki made introductions, and Joan extended a warm handshake. "Can I get you something to drink?"

"No, thanks. I had something on the way over." She gave everyone an apologetic smile. "I was hoping Nicki would show me around Cedar Key. I feel like the two of us have so much to talk about, I don't know where to begin."

Tyler stepped up. "How about if I chauffeur you? Then you guys can relax and enjoy the ride and not have to worry about a thing."

Jenny patted Tyler's arm. "I'd like some alone time with my sis. I appreciate the offer, though."

A hardness settled in his eyes, and Nicki flashed him a warning glare. He was entitled to his opinions about her sister, but he needed to keep them to himself. She'd been waiting months for this reunion and she wouldn't let him spoil it.

She put her phone back into her purse, then followed

her sister out the door. When she removed her keys, Jenny stopped her.

"I'll drive. Just tell me where to go."

"All right." Nicki slid into Jenny's passenger seat. "So, what would you like to see?"

"You pick. Show me whatever you think is note-worthy."

"How about if we start at the co-op?"

Jenny's brows went up. "Co-op?"

"The Cedar Keyhole Artist Co-op. It's where local artists sell their work—pottery, jewelry, leather, metal, paintings, you name it. I have some stained glass there. I'd love for you to see it."

Jenny shrugged. "Sure."

Nicki directed her through a few turns until they reached Second Street. Two blocks down, Jenny pulled into a parking space, and Nicki led her into the color-ful building.

Over the next several minutes, she introduced her to several people, pride swelling inside. *My sister.* She shook her head. It still seemed surreal, probably would for a long time.

After stopping to study some blown glass, she grinned over at Jenny. "I could live in here. Every time I come in, there's something different." She pointed ahead. "There's my stained glass."

Jenny followed her but seemed distracted, almost agitated. Or maybe she had no interest in art and was bored.

"Is there something else you'd rather do?"

"I was thinking it would be nice to go for a walk somewhere, just the two of us. We've got a lot of catching up to do. I want to hear all about what you've done over the past twenty years."

"Sure." She swung the door open and held it for Jenny to walk out ahead of her. "The Railroad Trestle Nature Trail would be perfect. It's quiet and peaceful and private. It's one of my favorite places to go."

When they arrived at the trailhead, the single parking spot was empty. Jenny stepped from the car and looked around her. "You're right. This is perfect."

Nicki slipped her phone into her pocket and headed into the woods, Jenny next to her. "You wanted to hear everything that's happened since we got separated." She grinned. "I'll give you the abridged version." She picked up a piece of a broken limb and tossed it away from the trail. "Foster care was the pits. By the time I got out of there, I was ready to fight anybody and everybody, no matter how big."

"Yeah, if you don't learn how to stick up for yourself, you can get eaten alive."

Nicki continued her story without slowing down to admire the scenery. Along the sides of the trail, a couple dozen signs identified many of the plant species there. She'd read them before. But not this time. If looking at the endless variety of art had bored Jenny, she wouldn't care to read botanical signs.

By the time they reached the end of the trail, Nicki had just finished telling her about losing her parents and inheriting the house. She looked out at the old trestle posts poking up through the shallow bay, remnants of the bridge that had carried the trains across the water. Now she would hear Jenny's story. And maybe through the process of telling it, Jenny would find healing.

Nicki headed back down the trail the way they'd

come. "So did my PI catch up with you, or did you talk to Gina?"

"Both. Gina gave me your number yesterday. But your investigator found me a few times before. Though we didn't personally talk, his messages got to me. At the time, I wasn't ready to see you." She hesitated, and an odd coldness entered her eyes. "Now I am."

Unease darkened Nicki's thoughts, a shadow passing through her mind. She shook it off. Jenny had no reason to want to hurt her. They hadn't even seen each other in over twenty years. Before that, they weren't close, but that was because of the five-year age difference. They'd gone to separate schools, had their own friends and varied interests.

Besides, even if Jenny did feel some kind of animosity toward her, she wouldn't be stupid enough to try anything. Too many people had seen them together.

Nicki cast her an uneasy glance. Jenny stared straight ahead, her whole body radiating tension. Finally she spoke.

"We both got shipped off to foster homes the day after Mom was killed. That's where I spent the next six years. Messed-up twelve-year-olds aren't nearly as adoptable as cute little seven-year-olds."

Nicki's uneasiness ratcheted up several notches at the bitterness in Jenny's tone. She put her hand over her back pocket, which held her cell phone. If things got too bad, maybe she could shoot off a quick text to Tyler.

Jenny continued, the bitterness increasing. "I never had the opportunity to go to college. And I never had a cushy job."

"I did go to college, but I've always had to work my

tail off at my jobs." She forced a laugh. "If you find out where the cushy ones are, let me know."

Jenny moved ahead as if she hadn't spoken. "I never owned my own home, either. Of course, I never had anyone to leave me everything when they bit the dust."

Nicki's jaw dropped, and anger surged through her. "I'd give it all back for another day with my parents."

Jenny ignored her again. "Always surrounded by friends and family. You have no idea what it's like to have no one." She shook her head and continued. "Two sisters. One given all the advantages. The other nothing. Do you think that's fair?"

Nicki gasped, realization slamming into her with the force of a freight train. No, it wasn't fair, so Jenny was here to level the playing field.

It wasn't fair she had the "cushy" job, so Jenny tried to make her boss doubt her, even fire her.

It wasn't fair she had good friends, so Jenny threatened them, hoping to isolate her from them.

And it wasn't fair she had her home and all of her possessions, so Jenny set fire to it and destroyed it.

Jenny had told Gina she was going to see a wrong made right. And that was why she'd come to Cedar Key.

To make sure the sister who had it all would end up with nothing.

Including her life.

Nicki glanced around, heart pounding in her throat. They were at about the halfway point on the trail, with mangroves and water on one side, marshes and more mangroves on the other. And not another human being in sight.

She drew in a stabilizing breath. If she could keep

Jenny talking, maybe they'd be back to civilization before things got ugly.

"The problems I've been having, it's been you all along, hasn't it?"

Jenny snorted. "Finally figured it out? You're not the brightest bulb in the pack, are you?"

It had taken her that long to unravel the mystery because she'd focused her attention in the wrong direction. Peter was angry. But he wasn't vindictive. And he wasn't crazy.

Jenny apparently was.

In one smooth motion, Jenny pulled a folding knife from her pocket and extended the blade with a sharp flick of her wrist. Then she took a predatory stance, knees slightly bent, as if ready to pounce. "Now it's my turn."

Nicki raised both hands and stumbled backward, a cold knot of fear in her stomach. She curled her toes against her sandals, every instinct shouting at her to run. But she didn't stand a chance with Jenny in tennis shoes. And if she screamed, Jenny would kill her instantly.

Jenny's eyes narrowed. "Try to run and I'll slice you up and leave you for the vultures."

Nicki swallowed hard. "Jenny, you don't need to do this. Come back with me. You can move in with me, and we can be real sisters again. It'll be like old times."

"Old times?" Jenny released a disdainful snort. "Old times was Mom protecting you because you were the baby, while her men slapped me around. Or worse."

Nicki's heart fell. No wonder Jenny resented her so much. The anger began long before their mother's murder. She'd blamed their lack of closeness on the age difference and normal sibling rivalry.

Now she knew. They weren't close because Jenny hated her.

Her phone buzzed in her back pocket, and she started. "Someone sent me a text. Everyone's watching me. If I don't answer, they'll know something's wrong, and half of Cedar Key will come looking for me."

Jenny tightened her grip on the knife. "Read it to me."

She pulled her phone from her back pocket and swiped the screen. "It's from Tyler. 'Everything OK? Worried about U.'"

Jenny nodded, lips pursed. "This is perfect. Tell him this: 'Fine. Jenny left, but I'm hanging out. Will catch a ride home. Thanks for checking.' Let me see it before you send it. Try anything, and I'll kill you right here."

Nicki entered the words exactly as Jenny had dictated them, with one small exception.

What she'd done was so minimal, so innocuous, Jenny would never catch it.

She held up the phone. Jenny read the message and gave a sharp nod. As Nicki hit Send, a sliver of the tension slipped away, pushed aside by a desperate hope. Jenny had approved the message, just as she'd keyed it in.

Jenny didn't see the clue.

Unfortunately, there was a distinct possibility Tyler wouldn't, either.

Tyler stared at the phone in his hand, doubt circling through him. She'd said she was fine. So why the nagging feeling that something was wrong?

He read the text again.

Fine. Jenny left, but I'm hanging out. Will catch ride home. Tx for ckg. Bye.

He tried to shake the tension from his shoulders. She was fine. Even thanked him for checking. He laid the phone on the coffee table and began to pace. She wasn't with Jenny anymore. But with everything that had gone on in recent weeks, he hated to let her out of his sight.

He moved to the front window and parted the blinds, willing a familiar car to pull into the drive—Allison's Camaro or Meagan's Prius. Or any other mode of transportation, as long as Nicki was in it. But the driveway was empty except for Nicki's newly repaired Ram and his, Andy's and Joan's vehicles.

"Are you all right? You're like a caged tiger."

He started at the female voice behind him, then spun to see Joan watching him with raised brows.

"Yeah." Except for the ever-present tension coiled in his belly. He was too used to watching for danger, always on the alert, ever cognizant of the fact that every second could be his last. It had been almost two years since he'd seen combat, but sometimes it seemed like yesterday.

The only way he was going to shake the uneasiness was to see Nicki for himself. He snatched up his keys. He'd probably find her downtown hanging out with her friends. Or strolling through the artist's co-op, feeding her creative side. Perfectly safe activities in broad daylight.

When he picked up his phone, he scanned her words once more. A solid block of ice hit his core.

She'd ended the text with *bye*.

"Nicki's in trouble. I'm going to find her."

"What do you mean?"

Ignoring Joan's question, he ran out the door, dialing 911 as he went. As he made the short trip into town, his heart pounded out an erratic rhythm, and he gripped the wheel so tightly his knuckles turned white. The dispatcher probably thought he was crazy. He heard her hesitation when he explained how he knew Nicki was in trouble.

But he had no doubt. That single word was a code, a way to let him know she was in danger without raising Jenny's suspicions. Unfortunately, he had nothing to go on. He had no idea where they'd gone. Over an hour had passed since they'd left. They could be a good distance from Cedar Key by now.

And he didn't have Jenny's tag number. He'd watched them leave and hadn't even thought to look at it. If they were still in Cedar Key, the car would be easy to spot. It was a white two-door Sunbird that had seen better days. The driver's side had long scrape marks running its entire length. A twelve-inch section of the front bumper was caved in, bearing a permanent imprint of a pole or tree trunk, and the hood was warped as if something had been dropped on it.

Something heavy…like a body. *His body.*

Jenny was the one who'd hit him. The one who'd broken into Nicki's house and tried to get her fired from her job. The one who'd been threatening her and had tried to isolate her from her friends.

And now Nicki was alone with her.

He turned onto Whidden, then pulled into a parking space. He sat for several moments, staring at the Cedar Key water tower, trying to get control of the panic circling through him. He had to rein in his scattered thoughts. Focus.

He pulled out his cell phone and went to his contacts. A half minute later, Hunter answered. Nicki had given Tyler both Hunter's and Amber's personal cell numbers.

"You on duty?"

"Not till this afternoon. What's up?"

"I've figured it out. Nicki's sister is the one who's been threatening her. Nicki's with her now."

"Where?"

"I don't know. The two of them went off alone together. I sent Nicki a text. She said she was fine, then ended with *bye*. Nicki never says *bye*. She always says *later*."

"You're right." Hunter's voice was thick with concern. "Something's wrong."

"I know." He filled Hunter in on everything he'd given the dispatcher. "I'm sure they've set up a road block on 24, so they'll catch her if she tries to leave Cedar Key."

If she hadn't already left. Enough time had passed, so it was a distinct possibility.

He continued. "I'm going to drive around the island looking for the car. Beyond that, I don't know what else to do."

"You can pray. And rest assured, I will be, too. God's in control, and he can lead us right to her."

"Thanks." He disconnected the call and pulled back onto the road. He'd talk to people in town and see if anyone had seen them, starting at the artist's co-op.

And he'd leave the praying to Hunter.

Maybe Hunter's prayers would do some good. From

everything Nicki had told him about the man, he had that kind of faith.

Tyler eased to a stop in front of the artist's co-op. Hunter had said God could lead them to Nicki. Actually, Tyler couldn't argue the point. He'd always believed God *could* answer prayers.

The problem was, when it had mattered more to him than anything in the world, God *didn't*.

TEN

Nicki looked frantically around her, willing someone to come down the trail. Jenny had become more agitated with every word out of her mouth. She waved the knife as she spoke, several slashes coming much too close.

Nicki took another step back. "Why are you doing this?"

"Don't go acting all innocent here. You brought this on yourself."

"How?"

"You had to go and find me. You couldn't leave me well enough alone. I was minding my own business, had completely written you off. I figured I'd never see you again. But you pushed your way back into my life and forced me to check you out. When I saw your perfect existence with your nice house and comfortable job and disgustingly sweet friends, I had to do something. You think you're someone, don't you?" She gave an irreverent snort. "It's easy when you've had all the breaks."

Nicki shook her head. "I haven't had all the breaks. I've had to work hard for everything. But I'll share it with you. You're the only family I've got."

"Share?" Jenny spat the word. "I don't need to share.

When you're gone, everything will go to me anyway as the only surviving relative." She grinned, but the gesture was grotesque instead of reassuring. "I think I'll even see if I can get your boyfriend."

Jenny took a step forward, eyes blazing hatred. Nicki moved back further. Perspiration coated her body, and a watery weakness had settled in her legs. Nothing she'd said was working. She swept her gaze to one side, then the other, not taking her attention off Jenny for more than a second.

Her heart pounded harder. A limb hung three feet to her right, barely connected to the tree. If she could break it loose and swing, maybe she could disable Jenny long enough to get away. It was a desperate move. But she was out of options. *Lord, please let this work.*

Jenny's eyes narrowed. "After all these years, it's time for you to die and me to live."

She raised the knife and swung downward in an arc, aiming at Nicki's chest. With a scream, Nicki stepped to the side and spun in a full circle, grasping the tree branch on her way around. It held on for a fraction of a second, then broke loose with a crack of splintering wood. A half second later, it connected with the side of Jenny's head and shattered into several pieces.

Nicki didn't wait to see the result. She sprinted down the trail, terror pounding at her heels. The blow wouldn't slow Jenny down for long. The branch had been too rotten.

A searing pain shot through her back, and she stumbled and fell to her knees. Jenny had thrown the knife. The next moment, Jenny was standing over her.

Understanding hit Nicki like a bolt of lightning.

The dreams. They weren't memories. They were

warnings. She was going to be murdered the same way her mother had been. *Please, no.* She'd made her peace with God, but she was too young to die.

Another pain shot through her as Jenny pulled the blade free. Before she had time to react, Jenny threw her onto her back, dropped to her knees and raised the knife again. As she plunged it downward, Nicki screamed and rolled away.

"Nicki!"

The voice belonged to Tyler. He'd come for her. And there were sirens, too, in the distance. Relief rushed through her. Help was coming. She was going to survive.

But only if she could hang on until they got there. *Lord, please help me.*

She rolled over and pushed herself to her knees. But before she could get to her feet, Jenny slammed into her, knocking her to the ground.

She released another scream as weight pressed down on her lower back and fingers entwined in her hair. She was pinned.

Jenny was straddling her. Just like the man in her dreams.

No. She wasn't going out like this. Especially with Tyler moments away. She screamed again, twisted to the side and swung. The back of her fist connected with Jenny's jaw. Several expletives rolled from her sister's mouth, and her eyes blazed with fire. The hold on Nicki's hair tightened, and the knife came up again. Footsteps pounded against the ground, and a moment later, a body slammed into Jenny.

Suddenly Nicki was free. She pushed herself to a seated position, her breaths coming in short pants. A few feet away, Tyler lay on top of Jenny, wrestling the knife from her hand. The sirens had stopped.

More footsteps sounded and two uniformed officers came around the bend on the trail, Hunter right behind them. The officers cuffed Jenny and one of them tried to read her her rights. But Jenny wasn't listening. A steady stream of hate-filled words flowed from her mouth. Nicki dipped her head. All of the anger was directed at her.

Tyler dropped to his knees beside her and grasped her shoulders, his gaze sweeping her from head to toe. Then he wrapped her in his arms and rocked her back and forth. His cheek was against hers, his mouth so close she could feel his breath against her ear. "When I got your text, I was frantic. I'm so glad I found you when I did. God answered Hunter's prayer."

Hunter's prayer? She'd have to ask Tyler about it later.

Tyler started to release her, then froze. "There's blood. You're hurt."

She shifted her position and winced. "She got me in the back."

Tyler pulled out his phone, but Hunter stopped him. "They're already here. The fire truck with the paramedics pulled up just as I headed down the trail. An ambulance will arrive shortly."

As if on cue, Wade Tanner and another man jogged up next to her, carrying a gurney and a medical kit. After checking her wound, they loaded her on the stretcher and stood.

She reached for Tyler's hand. "How did everyone know where to find me?"

"I know how you love the artist's co-op. So I figured

that's where I'd start and see if you'd been there. You had, and on your way out the door, someone overheard you mention coming here."

She closed her eyes, emotion sweeping through her. God had answered *someone's* prayer. Whether hers or Hunter's, she'd take it. If she and Jenny had waited until they were outside to have that conversation, there was a good chance she'd be dead. Thankfulness swelled inside her. Her back was on fire. But she was alive.

Commotion nearby drew her attention to her sister. The officers had her on her feet, trying to lead her up the trail, but she wasn't having it. She kicked at one of them. He sidestepped and managed to avoid the blow.

Jenny twisted to throw a malicious glance over one shoulder, her eyes locking with Nicki's. "Someday you'll get yours. He's coming after you, you know."

Nicki pushed herself partially upright, unease chewing at the edges of her mind. "Who?"

"Mom's killer. He knows where you are. I told him."

"Wait." She held out a hand, and the officers dragging Jenny up the trail stopped. "You know who killed her?"

Jenny tossed her head and lifted her chin. Her eyes held an odd sense of pride, mixed with disdain. "I was there, but he didn't see *me*."

"Who killed her?"

"What do you mean *who killed her*?" Jenny looked at her for several long moments. Then her jaw dropped. "You're serious. You don't remember."

"Of course I don't remember. I wasn't there." She'd said the words with as much conviction as she could muster, but doubt wove its way through her mind, shattering the reality she'd held on to for so long.

She hadn't been there, right? Otherwise she'd re-member. There would be some sliver of recall, some disjointed image.

Like in her dreams.

Coldness settled in her core, and she closed her eyes. No, the nightmares were just that—dreams. Nothing more. They weren't real.

When she opened her eyes again, Jenny was smiling.

"Oh, you were there." The smile broadened.

"What's even better is that he knows it. And he knows how to find you."

Nicki leaned over the railing of the observation deck and stared into water tinted a bright aquamarine. Shouts rose from the swimming area, visitors enjoying the re-lief the cool spring water provided from the steamy August day.

As she leaned over farther, pain stretched across her back. But she wasn't complaining. She had a lot to be thankful for. Jenny had intended to kill her. Instead, she'd barely nicked her lung. Over the past few days, the pain had retreated to a dull ache, and other than three days in the hospital, a hefty insurance deductible and some residual soreness, she was fine.

Except for the nightmares.

Tyler had shaken her awake from two, and last night he'd insisted on taking her someplace where she could relax and put the events of the past five weeks behind her. After an internet search, he'd settled on Fanning Springs State Park in northern Levy County. Right after church, they'd traded dress clothes for shorts, T-shirts and tennis shoes and headed out with a picnic lunch. Andy and Joan were dog-sitting.

It was over. She was safe. Jenny's final words were nothing but a lie, a last-ditch attempt to steal her peace. It wasn't going to work.

She straightened and smiled up at Tyler. They'd made a pact to avoid discussing anything related to Jenny. It was a welcome break.

"How is the work on the inn coming?"

"We're ready for appliances. Next week we'll start rebuilding some decks."

"Sounds like you're winding it down."

He leaned against the railing, resting on one elbow. "Yeah. Another two weeks and that should pretty well do it."

Heaviness filled her chest. Was he still planning to leave? She couldn't bring herself to ask. Just the thought left a big hole in her heart.

He turned away from the railing and extended his arm, palm up. After placing her hand in his, she let him lead her down the wooden stairs. At the bottom, concrete steps led up away from the pool area. When they reached the top, he turned right and headed toward the picnic area.

He squeezed her hand. "Tell me what else you did after I left."

She smiled. She'd already told him several stories from her later teenage years. "I can't think of anything else."

"Tell me about your first real boyfriend."

She looked at him askance. "I thought you didn't like war stories."

"I like hearing other people's war stories."

"I have quite a few." More than she wanted to admit. "I seem to attract the users and the losers." When Peter came along, she thought she'd broken the pattern. He was attentive, romantic, good-looking and successful. But two other adjectives had been lacking—*honest* and *law-abiding*.

"My first real boyfriend was Junior. His idea of a romantic date was taking me to his friend's house so I could watch them play video games. Fortunately, his friend also had a girlfriend who was as bored as I was. One night, we both got tired of competing with Halo and gave up. She called her brother to come and get us. That was the end of Junior and me."

"Sounds like he needed to grow up."

"Yeah. I'm afraid that describes too many of the guys I've dated."

Tyler took a seat at one of the picnic tables, and she sat next to him. A small playground lay a few yards in front of them. Both swings were occupied, and four other children slid down green plastic slides. Midway between the playground and a pavilion, two adolescent boys stood talking, kicking pine needles and stray pieces of mulch.

Nicki angled her face toward Tyler and rested her chin in her hand. "Okay, now it's your turn. Tell me about your first crush."

"That's easy. My first crush was a scrappy eighth grader who always had a chip on her shoulder and would never back down from a fight, especially if her best friend was the one being threatened." He grinned and gave her a gentle nudge in the ribs with his elbow.

She elbowed him back. "Hey, I'm being serious. Tell me about your first girlfriend."

He shrugged. "I didn't have much time for dating. As soon as I turned sixteen, I got a job after school working at a local fast-food place. When school let out, I went to work with a friend. His dad owned a small construction company."

Nicki studied him as he spoke. But he wasn't looking at her. Instead, he faced straight ahead, his eyes taking in the activity on the playground and scanning the woods beyond. An underlying tension flowed through his body, a ready alertness.

She was used to it. The only time he seemed truly relaxed was inside Andy and Joan's home, with the doors locked and the blinds drawn.

He continued, his gaze shifting to the right, where the two boys she'd observed earlier appeared to be trying out some pseudo karate moves on each other.

"My friend's dad didn't let me run the power tools. Maybe he wasn't allowed to, since I was underage. But he taught me a lot. I worked with him two summers."

"Then you joined the Army."

He nodded, his attention still focused on the boys. "But not till October. I was supposed to start college in the fall, but Mom's cancer had spread, so I stayed with her."

Some distance away, the shorter boy kicked at his taller friend, who grasped his foot and flipped him onto his back. Tyler stiffened and sat up straighter.

"I'm glad you got the time with her."

"We were able to keep her at home until…" His voice trailed off.

"Tyler?" She followed his gaze to where the boys were tussling. The larger one pressed his friend's shoulders to the ground, then straddled him.

Tyler shot to his feet, stepped over the bench and stalked that direction.

"Tyler!"

She stood and followed him, shouting his name again. But he marched straight ahead, picking up his pace. He took the final few yards at a jog.

Before she could stop him, he grasped the taller boy by the shoulders and threw him aside, then stood over him glaring, fists clenched. Both boys sat up and scooted backward, eyes filled with fear. He took another step, closing the gap between them.

"Tyler, stop! They're just playing." Her voice was loud and shrill. If she didn't stop him, he was going to hurt one of them.

He took another step. Both boys scrambled to their feet and took off in a spray of sand. Tyler stared after them as if unsure what to do. She ran in front of him, grasped his arms and shook him.

Finally the wildness left his eyes. He twisted free of her grasp, spun and walked back the way they'd come at such a brisk pace, she had to run to keep up with him. He jogged down the steps toward the spring, taking them two at a time, but instead of continuing to the water's edge, he made a sharp right and headed down the boardwalk. His pace slowed to a brisk walk, and she moved up beside him.

"What happened back there?"

He kept walking, eyes straight ahead, jaw tight.

She grasped his arm. "Tell me what's going on."

Again he shook himself loose from her grasp. For another minute, they walked in silence. Cypress trees rose all around them, shading them from the afternoon sun. Hundreds of cypress knees protruded from the ground beneath, ranging in size from a few inches to five or six feet. The setting was almost magical. But she knew Tyler wasn't seeing any of it.

She heaved a sigh. Keeping everything buried inside couldn't be good for him. But getting him to open up seemed almost impossible. He refused to discuss any of his experiences in Afghanistan.

She glanced over at him. "Tyler, stop. Tell me what's going on."

He didn't slow down, and he didn't look at her. His features were set in stubbornness, his fists clenched.

She bit her lower lip. Soon he'd have to stop. He wouldn't have a choice. Up ahead, the boardwalk ended in a square, covered area overlooking the river. Two couples stood there taking pictures with their phones. As she and Tyler grew closer, the women glanced their way, and the four of them began to move back down the boardwalk.

Tyler stepped under the structure and stopped at the end, hands clutching the wooden railing. Several more moments passed in silence.

She put a hand on his upper arm. "Tyler, please talk to me."

His muscle twitched under her palm, but he didn't jerk away from her. His eyes held a steely hardness. "I'm all right."

"No, you're not. If I hadn't stopped you, you might have hurt one of those boys."

"I was breaking it up. I thought the bigger boy was attacking the smaller one."

"They were playing."

His gaze dropped to the water below. "I know that now."

"And everyone else knew it then. There was never any doubt in anyone's mind except yours."

He allowed her to turn him away from the rail, and she took his hands in hers.

"Anywhere we go, you look as if you expect to be attacked at any moment. You're always assessing your surroundings, looking for threats. I thought it had to do with me and all the things that have been going on in my life. But that's not right, is it? It started long before you came to Cedar Key."

His hands tightened around hers, but he didn't respond.

"Talk to me, Tyler."

He shook his head. "You don't want to hear this."

"If I didn't want to hear it, I wouldn't be asking. Come on, Tyler. Talk to me. We used to tell each other everything. If anyone can understand what you're feeling, it's me."

She released his hands and raised her arms to rest both palms against the sides of his face. "What happened over there?" She was no longer talking about the playground. Instead, her thoughts were focused halfway across the world. Judging from the distant look in his eyes, his likely were, too. "Tell me what happened that sent you home."

For some time, a silent battle ensued. Then all the tension flowed out of him, and he released a heavy sigh.

"It was our last mission. We were all shipping home the following week. That day, there was a meeting planned with community leaders in a nearby village. I was tasked with route clearance. We go ahead of the command representatives and secure the route, looking for IEDs and ambush sites. These meetings are usually held in the home of one of the leaders, and we go in and make sure there are no booby traps, look for security vantage points and so on."

He released her hands and turned back to the rail, resting his palms on its surface. "There were six of us. We loaded into two MRAPs. I was with Marty and Steve. We were all talking about what we were going to do when we got stateside, who'd be running onto the field to greet us."

He smiled down at her, but there was sadness behind the expression. "The deployment homecoming ceremony is a big deal. The whole unit goes home together, so there are around eight hundred of us. The families are all in the bleachers, holding signs and banners welcoming us home. We'd been downrange for just shy of twelve months, so there was going to be a lot of excitement and emotion. Marty had a wife and a four-month-old baby. Steve was making plans to propose to his high school sweetheart."

He fell silent, and she didn't prod him to continue. He'd finish his story when he was ready. She laid her hand over his and curled her fingers into his palm. Finally he continued.

"Everything was fine. There were no problems en route. Nothing seemed out of the ordinary going in. Then Taliban forces fired the first mortar round into the building, and the rugs and furnishings caught fire. More rounds followed, and this whole time, the enemy kept a steady barrage of AK-47 fire coming at us. That pretty well kept us pinned. I radioed the perimeter squad, but it seemed to take them forever to subdue the enemy."

He closed his eyes. "Marty and Steve were down after the first mortar round. Pretty soon, both of them were engulfed in flames." His hand tightened around her fingers, his other one clenching into a fist. "I listened to their screams as they burned to death, but I couldn't get to them. I tried. The explosion of another mortar round knocked me backward. Then the roof caved in on me."

"What about your other men?"

"Gone, every one of them. One took a mortar round and was killed instantly. Two others were taken out by small arms fire." He pushed away from the rail to sink onto the nearby bench, then put his head in his hands. "Every one of them had so much to live for— girlfriends, wives, children. All they had to do was make it through one final mission. They didn't and I did." He lifted his head to look at her. "How is that fair? I had no one, just Andy and Joan and my sister, Bridgett. So why did I come home when none of the others did?"

She sat next to him. "It wasn't your time yet."

"And it was theirs? Marty with a four-month-old baby who is never going to know her father? Steve at twenty-one, who hardly even got to taste adulthood? You're telling me it was their time? How?"

"Some things we just have to accept, because trying to find an explanation will make us crazy."

He pulled his hand from hers and rose to his feet. "I can't accept it. And I never will. I keep imagining Marty lying there with a hole in his belly, Steve with his leg blown off. Flames swallowing both of them." He shook his head. "When I was watching your house burn, I was back there in that *kalat*, listening to their screams."

She closed her eyes, her heart twisting in her chest. He'd experienced unimaginable horrors, and now, when it should be over, he was reliving them again and again. As a teenager, he'd been tormented. And she'd known what to do. Often just her presence and a listening ear would soothe his troubled heart.

That was nothing compared to this. He'd seen things no one should have to witness. And they'd scarred him. Maybe permanently.

She wrapped her arms around him, offering comfort in the only way she knew. "I want to help you. I just need you to tell me how."

His arms circled her waist, then tightened around her, and he buried his face in her hair.

"You were always there for me." His words were muffled against the side of her neck, his breath warm.

"We were there for each other." And more than once over the years, she'd missed it desperately.

He stepped back to meet her gaze. "We were crazy to let that go."

She nodded, ready to agree with his statement. But the words stuck in her throat. His eyes were warm, raw emotion swimming in their depths. Her stomach rolled over, and all the oxygen seemed to exit her lungs, leaving her breathless.

She'd hugged him numerous times in the past. And other times, he'd watched her without saying a word.

This was different.

The way he was looking at her wasn't how a friend looks at a friend. The intensity in his eyes said a whole lot more.

Before she had a chance to ponder it further, he leaned closer. A bolt of panic shot through her, followed by calm. Because whatever he was feeling, she felt it, too.

The next moment, his mouth slanted across hers. Sensation burst across her consciousness, bright and hot, searing a path to her heart. This wasn't the boy she'd known fifteen years earlier. This was Tyler now—one hundred percent man. Capable of setting her pulse racing with a single kiss.

But in many ways, he was the same. The same caring person who felt deeply and bore scars as a result. The one who could read her moods and instinctively know what she needed most.

Her best friend in all the world.

She stiffened and backed away. If they allowed their friendship to become anything more, there would be no turning back. Eventually their relationship would end. Her track record had proved that. His wasn't much better. He was as damaged as she was. When everything fell apart, there would no longer be any friendship to fall back on.

"What's wrong?" Concern filled his eyes.

She stepped out of his arms, letting her hands fall from his neck. "You're my best friend. I'm not willing to throw that away for a brief fling."

Hurt pushed aside the concern. "Why would it have to be just a brief fling?"

"Because good things don't last. You know it as well as I do. This is one season of your life. It'll pass and you'll be off on your next adventure."

For several moments, he stood silent and still. Then he gave her a sharp nod and started back down the boardwalk.

She fell in behind him, disappointment swirling inside her. She'd halfway hoped he'd argue with her, tell her that they could make it work, that they'd overcome all the obstacles together.

But he hadn't, because he knew she was right.

ELEVEN

Tyler held the two-by-eight joist in place and swung the hammer, the sharp thuds piercing the tranquility of the summer day. A bead of sweat ran down the side of his face. The bandanna did a pretty good job of keeping it out of his eyes, but within an hour of starting work in the summer heat and humidity, his shirt was usually soaked and plastered to his chest.

Especially when he was working like this.

He removed another twelve-penny nail from his pouch. After three good whacks, it was flush.

"You know, we have air tools for that."

Tyler cast a glance at Andy over his shoulder. He was sitting on a camp chair in the shade of a tree, a glass of iced tea in one hand and two of Joan's oatmeal cookies in the other. The open thermos still sat on the ground in front of him. Thirty minutes ago, it had held home-made vegetable beef stew. Now it was empty, every last savory drop scraped from the wide mouth. Tyler's own thermos was in the same condition. When it finally came time to leave Cedar Key, he was going to miss Joan's cooking.

That wasn't all he was going to miss. Reconnecting

with Nicki had been a bonus he hadn't anticipated. Or yet another means of torture.

Especially now that he'd kissed her.

During most of their two-year friendship, he'd longed for more, had wondered what it would be like to hold her with more than the comforting hug of a friend, had dreamed of kisses in the moonlight.

The actual experience was so much sweeter than all those childhood fantasies. And he was having a hard time getting it out of his mind.

He pounded in several more nails, then stood back to survey his work.

"You think the deck is going to last longer if you build it by the sweat of your brow?"

Tyler ignored his brother's taunt. The deck wouldn't last longer, but swinging a hammer was a great way to work out some of his pent-up frustration.

Andy screwed the lid on the thermos and, after dropping everything into the lunch tote, ambled toward the unfinished deck.

"Now that you've spent the last ten minutes beating the deck half to death, you want to talk about what's ailing you?"

"Nothing's bothering me. I'm fine." He wasn't about to discuss his woman woes with his brother. Or anyone else, for that matter.

Andy planted both hands on his hips. "I think my pretty neighbor has been getting under your skin the past few weeks."

Yeah, he had that right. He was just wrong about when. Nicki had gotten under his skin fifteen years ago. Now she was there again.

Or maybe that was where she'd been all along.

He'd always had all kinds of excuses for avoiding serious relationships—too little time to date because he was working and caring for his mom, the transient military lifestyle with its lengthy deployments, the nightmares and flashbacks that regularly plagued him.

Maybe the real reason was Nicki, the knowledge that having a relationship with anyone else would be settling, that he'd never be truly happy.

The fact remained, he was too messed up for an intimate relationship. He'd proved it a few nights ago, when he'd accidentally punched Nicki and knocked her over the coffee table.

And yesterday at the park. He'd watched the activity on the playground—the children swinging, climbing on the equipment, going down the slides. And the boys making up karate moves.

He'd seen a threat that wasn't even there. And eliminating the threat had consumed all his thoughts, trumping common sense. If Nicki hadn't stopped him, he might have ended up in jail for battery. Or worse.

No, he wasn't fit for anything more than causal friendship, no matter what he felt for Nicki.

Andy put a hand on his shoulder, drawing him back to the present.

"I don't know her whole story, but I think she's good for you." He gave Tyler a couple of rough pats and continued, his tone serious.

"Think about it. Maybe it's time to stop running."

Tyler pulled into a space at The Market and put the truck in Park. The gentle lecture his brother had given him that afternoon still circled through his mind. He tried to shut out the words. Andy didn't know what he was talking about. If running was what it took to avoid hurting Nicki, that was exactly what he would do.

"I owe you an apology."

Nicki's words cut into his thoughts, and he turned to look at her. "You do?"

"I didn't appreciate you being so distrustful of Jenny. I got a little annoyed at you."

He grinned. "I thought I was imagining it."

"I'm listening to you now."

Yeah, she was. And that was why she was with him. It was a quick trip to The Market for orange juice, something she'd forgotten to pick up the last time she went. But he still wasn't willing to let her out of his sight except when she was at work. He didn't want to let her out of his sight there, either, but he couldn't very well make himself a permanent fixture in the meeting area at city hall.

He stepped out and headed toward the passenger side. Nicki met him at the front of the truck. Fortunately she'd agreed when he insisted on taking her to the store, which was good, because he wouldn't have backed down.

Jenny had said their mother's killer was coming after Nicki. Was it the one the cops were investigating, this Louie character? Or was it someone else?

Or was it anybody? Nicki didn't think so. She was sure Jenny was just blowing smoke, trying to torment her by keeping her looking over her shoulder. Chances were she was right. But he wasn't confident enough to gamble with her life. Until the investigation was over and Louie was either exonerated or taken off the street, he wouldn't relax.

He swung the door open and motioned Nicki inside. Halfway down the aisle, a young woman stopped her.

"A friend of yours is looking for you. He came into Kona Joe's for brunch today. I waited his table."

Nicki's brows shot up. "Oh?" Tension underlay the word, a strong dose of caution.

"He asked if I knew a Nicki Jackson. I told him I did. He wanted to know where he could find you. He said he'd been by your house, but there'd obviously been a fire, and it was vacant." She gave Nicki a sympathetic smile. "I heard about the fire. I hope you didn't have too much damage."

Nicki tried to return the smile but wasn't quite successful. "Thanks. I'm afraid it was pretty bad." She paused, then continued. "So, did you tell him where he could find me?"

The young woman shook her head. "I didn't know. I figured you weren't in your house anymore, but I didn't know where you'd gone."

Nicki released a soft sigh, but her body was still rigid with tension. "Did he give you a name?"

"No. When I told him I didn't know where you were staying, I asked for his name and said I'd have you get in touch with him when I saw you again. But he told me not to worry about it, that he'd catch up with you eventually."

Nicki's face lost a shade of color, and he draped a protective arm across her shoulders. He didn't like the sound of that, either. If the whole situation was legit, the guy wouldn't have a problem with leaving his name.

He pulled Nicki closer. "Can you describe him?"

"Probably late forties, early fifties, dark hair with some gray."

"A big guy?" Nicki's voice held a slight quiver.

"Not heavy, just really muscular. He was sitting at the table, so I don't know how tall he was. But he'd definitely spent some time at the gym."

Nicki thanked her and headed toward the orange juice.

Tyler followed Nicki to the refrigerated case and stopped next to her. "Did that description sound like Louie?"

"I don't know. Louie was big. Muscular *and* heavy."

He frowned. Based on what she'd learned from the detectives, he'd spent two thirds of the past twenty-two years in jail. Maybe he'd lost a lot of his girth on the prison diet. Or maybe whoever was looking for her wasn't Louie at all.

She paid for her orange juice and followed him out the door. "It can't be Louie."

"Why do you say that?"

"Even if he *did* kill Mom, he has no reason to come after me. I didn't see anything. I wasn't there."

He walked her around to the passenger side of his truck and opened the door. "What if you were? What if you saw the whole thing but suppressed the memory?" It was possible. The mind was a complicated and unpredictable thing.

She climbed into the seat. "I wasn't. If I had been there, I'd have some sliver of memory, something."

"What about the dreams?"

She swallowed hard. Based on the set of her jaw, the thought hadn't been far from her mind. He circled around to the driver's side and got in next to her. "Try to remember everything you can about that night."

"I have. Again and again."

"Try one more time." He started the truck and backed from the space. He needed to get her home if Louie was the one looking for her. Sitting in the truck at dusk, they were too vulnerable.

She took a deep breath and expelled it, letting her head fall back against the seat. "It was a Friday. I'd gone over to Lizzie's right after school. We were playing with her dolls. Her mom invited me to stay for dinner, and Lizzie asked if I could spend the night."

She stopped speaking, and he glanced over at her. Her eyes were closed, her hands folded in her lap. When she started speaking again, her tone was wistful.

"The McDonalds were dirt-poor, as poor as we were, but I loved it over there. Those were the only times I truly felt safe."

She drew in another breath and opened her eyes. "As soon as we'd eaten, Lizzie and I ran over to my house to get my stuff together. No one was there but Mom and Jenny. I was glad. I hurried through what I needed to do, because I never knew when Louie or one of my mom's other men was going to show up."

He shook his head, his sympathy for the terrified little girl warring with his anger at the irresponsible parent.

"We packed up my stuff—pajamas, a change of clothes for the next day, my toothbrush and hair brush. And we got out of there as fast as we could. When we left, there was still no one there but Mom and Jenny. Lizzie and I took turns fixing each other's hair. Then we watched a Disney movie and went to bed. That's the last thing I remember before waking up the next morning to Mrs. McDonald telling me my mom had been killed."

She turned to look at him. "If Louie did it and thinks

I know something, why didn't he come after me sooner? Why wait till now?"

"You said he was in jail the first fifteen years after your mother's murder. By the time he got out, he probably figured he'd gotten away with it. It would have been riskier for him to hunt you down and kill you than to let it go." He pulled into the driveway and turned off the truck. "Besides, he wouldn't have had any idea how to find you. You didn't even have the same last name."

Nicki put her hand on the door handle, then sat motionless, staring straight ahead. "The risk wasn't there before, but it is now, with my mom's murder case being reopened and the detectives talking to me. After twenty-two years, that loose end would need to be tied up. And if Jenny was telling the truth, finding me won't be a problem."

Her eyes filled with fear. "I'm sure she's given him everything he needs to know."

Nicki watched Joan lay out cake ingredients, her attention split between the woman's cheerful chatter and Tyler's one-sided phone conversation. As soon as they'd stepped into the house, he'd called Hunter, insisting that neither of them make any decisions until getting advice from their law enforcement buddy. Until then, the one thing he'd been adamant about was that she wasn't leaving Cedar Key without him.

Now that she'd gotten inside and calmed her thoughts, her circumstances didn't seem nearly as dire. In fact, maybe there was no danger at all. The person looking for her could have been anyone. Someone she'd known in college, a former coworker, a past neighbor.

Maybe he didn't give Libby his name because he wanted his visit to be a surprise.

Tyler's voice drifted to her from the living room, louder now that he was once again facing the kitchen. Since beginning his phone call, he'd paced back and forth, his voice fading in and out. He'd finished telling Hunter about Louie and was currently relaying the conversation they'd had with Libby in The Market.

Nicki leaned against the counter as Joan pulled two mixing bowls from the cupboard, then proceeded to measure dry ingredients into the larger one. When finished, this creation was going to be a red velvet cake decorated with cream cheese frosting and pecan halves. Knowing Joan's skill in the kitchen, it would be as pretty as the one pictured in the cookbook.

Tyler's voice once again faded, and Nicki sighed. Jenny had done everything to destroy her happiness. And when all her attempts failed, she'd made one last desperate parting jab. Leaving her looking over her shoulder, terrified to step out of the house, was exactly what Jenny had wanted.

Joan cracked two eggs into the smaller bowl, then added the oil, milk and vanilla. The final ingredient was a one-ounce bottle of red food coloring. It split the oil, some penetrating to the bottom of the bowl, the rest spreading along the surface of the other ingredients.

Like blood.

Nicki closed her eyes against the image intruding into her thoughts. The woman being stabbed. Her mother. Blood everywhere. Pouring from her body, seeping into the carpet.

No. There was no reason for her to be haunted by

those images. She hadn't been there. She'd gone to spend the night with Lizzie next door.

And she'd forgotten Lavender.

The realization was a physical blow, knocking the air from her lungs. She'd forgotten Lavender and couldn't sleep without him. So while Lizzie and Mrs. McDonald slept, she'd slipped out, across the yard and to her own house.

All she'd done was grab Lavender and run back to Lizzie's, right? Surely she didn't see her mother's murder. She'd have remembered it if she had.

Without any effort on her part, the events of the night unfolded, playing through her mind like an old film reel. She followed the path of her younger self into the house, through the living room, down the hall and to her room, where she snatched Lavender from her bed. Jenny was asleep in the other one. In the bedroom at the end of the hall, loud voices erupted. Her mother and a man. An angry man.

She squeezed her eyes shut more tightly, and suddenly, it was all there, every gory detail dredged from the dark recesses of her mind. She leaned over the counter, hands splayed on the cool surface.

"Nicki?"

She straightened and spun in the direction of Tyler's voice. He'd apparently finished his conversation with Hunter and stood in the doorway to the kitchen. Her legs buckled, and she slid down the front of the cabinet to the floor.

Joan stood staring at her, mouth agape, a wire whisk in her hand. Nicki struggled in a constricted breath. With three large strides, Tyler crossed the kitchen, then dropped to his knees in front of her. "What is it, sweetheart? Tell me what happened."

"I was there." Her tone was flat. The shock and fear had drained away, leaving her cold and numb.

Joan knelt on the other side of her and rested a hand on her shoulder. "What do you mean?"

"My mother's murder. I was there."

Tyler's brows drew together. "How? You'd gone to your friend's house."

"I ran back home to get Lavender." And she'd seen everything. Jenny was right.

Tyler sat next to her and pulled her into his arms. Joan straightened and stood, one hand clutching the other fist, the whisk still trapped inside. For several seconds, her lips moved, but no sound came out. Knowing Joan, she was probably praying.

Nicki pressed the side of her face to Tyler's chest. His warmth surrounded her, helping to thaw the frozen places inside her.

"Before I could leave, there was a fight, my mom and a man. My mom screamed, and I ran from my room at the same time she ran from hers. A man was right behind her." Her voice dropped to a whisper. "I recognized him."

And she'd been terrified. All these years later, she could still taste the fear, knowing that if he saw her, he'd kill her.

"I couldn't make it to the door, so I slipped behind the recliner in the living room, planning to hide until he was gone. It was dark, except for some dim light coming from the end of the hall. I stood there and waited."

She drew in a shaky breath. "My mom ran past, but before she could get out of the room, he caught her, spun her around and threw her to the floor. He had a knife, and he stabbed her eight or ten... I don't know how many times. It went on and on."

A shudder shook her body, and Tyler's arms tightened around her. For several moments, she sat in silence, drawing from his strength.

"I saw the whole thing. I stood there frozen, staring over the back of the recliner, holding on to Lavender. Then Jenny was there, almost beside me. She looked at Mom and Louie, then at me. Then she disappeared down the hall. Eventually Louie stopped. My mom raised her head one final time, looked at me and mouthed the word *run*. That's when he saw me."

"Who?"

"Louie. He looked right at me. The light shining down the hall illuminated his face, and what I saw there was pure evil."

She shuddered again. Now that she'd remembered, she'd never forget. That menacing glare would haunt her for the rest of her life.

"I panicked. I had no doubt he was going to kill me just like he did my mother. So I ran back to my room, slammed the door and locked it. Jenny had been there when I'd gotten Lavender, but she was gone then. Or maybe she was hiding under the bed. A few seconds later, the doorknob rattled. Louie was trying to coax me to open the door, telling me he wouldn't hurt me. I didn't believe him." By the tender age of seven, life had taught her a lot of lessons, one of which was never to trust the men who wandered in and out of her home.

"I opened the window, pulled my desk chair over and climbed out. Then I heard a crash. Louie had kicked in the door. But I didn't look back. I ran as fast as I could to Lizzie's, jumped into bed and pulled the covers up over my head. For the longest time, I lay there waiting for Louie to step into the room with that bloody knife. Even though I'd locked the back door, I was sure he was going to come after me. But he never did, and I finally fell asleep."

And somehow over the course of the next few hours, the memory of what she'd seen had retreated to a remote corner of her mind, where it remained buried, undisturbed for twenty-two years.

Louie knew she was a witness. And he was coming after her. He was already in Cedar Key. It would just be a matter of time till he learned where she was staying.

And showed up on Andy and Joan's doorstep.

Her mouth went dry. Whatever happened, she wasn't going to bring Andy and Joan into it. Or Tyler, either, for that matter. Her mind raced. If she called the police, they'd likely put together twenty-four-hour surveillance.

But she was a sitting duck. All it would take was one well-aimed shot fired from inside the woods.

Or one shot that wasn't so well-aimed and took out the wrong person.

No, there was only one way to ensure her friends' safety.

Leave Cedar Key.

TWELVE

Nicki stiffened and pushed herself from Tyler's arms. When she twisted to look at him, her eyes were wide and lit with fear.

"He's coming after me. I have to go." She rose to her feet. "I can't stay. If I do, I'll lead him here."

Tyler stood, too, and grasped her hand. "You can't leave. If you're alone, you won't stand a chance."

"I won't put you guys in danger." She pulled her hand from his and spun away from him, then stalked toward her room.

He followed, leaving Joan standing in the kitchen. Andy had gone to the church for a men's meeting and wouldn't be home for some time yet, which was unfortunate. Tyler could have used the reinforcement.

He stopped in the doorway of the bedroom. "What do you think you're doing?"

"Packing." She snatched the duffel bag she'd gotten from Allison the afternoon of the fire and stuffed clothes into it.

His chest tightened. When Nicki had her mind made up, it took an act of Congress to change it. "Nicki, stop. Let's calm down and think this through."

"There's nothing to think through." She picked up the bag and pushed past him. "He'd kill you to get to me."

He waited in the hall while she pulled her toiletries from the bathroom medicine cabinet. "I'll take that chance before I let you walk out of here alone."

"I'm not giving you that option." She stuffed each of the items into the side pouch and jerked the zipper closed. "I'm not giving Andy and Joan that option, either. I need you guys to take care of Callie for me."

He followed her into the living room and put a hand on her arm. "Hang loose until I call Hunter. You need to tell the police what you know. Once Louie is behind bars, you'll be safe. In the meantime, the authorities will protect you."

She picked up her purse but didn't head for the door. Maybe he was starting to get through to her.

Joan stepped up beside him. "Tyler's right."

Several more seconds passed. Finally Nicki released a long sigh. "All right. Call Hunter."

A ringtone sounded, but it wasn't his. Joan waved a hand. "That would be my weekly call from my sister. I'll call her back later."

Nicki gave her a weak smile. "Go ahead. I'm all right now. I promise I won't run."

Joan paused, then dashed to the kitchen for her phone. When she headed down the hall toward the master bedroom, Sasha trotted along behind her, with Callie in the rear. Nicki sank onto the couch, and Tyler redialed Hunter.

He answered on the first ring. "I was getting ready to call you back. I have some disturbing news. I did some checking, and Louie has disappeared from Jacksonville. So there's a distinct possibility he's the one who was asking about Nicki."

The knot of worry in Tyler's gut grew to boulder size. "That's what I was afraid of. But there's more than what I told you before. Nicki was there the night her mother was murdered, and Louie is the killer. She remembered everything."

Hunter let out a low whistle. "We'll get a couple of units out right away. We need to get a report and make contact with the detectives who are investigating the other murder. Until Louie is picked up, Nicki is going to need around-the-clock protection. We'll call Levy County in."

Tyler breathed a sigh of relief. Between the two agencies, someone would be watching her every moment of the day or night. He didn't intend to let her out of his sight, either.

When he finished the call, he laid the phone back on the coffee table and filled Nicki in on what Hunter had said. Finally she nodded and rose from the couch.

"All right. I'll stay here." She gave him a small smile. "I guess I need to unpack."

Instead of heading down the hall, she veered into the kitchen and poured herself a glass of water, then sat down at the table. "I'll stay for now, but if I even think you guys might be in any danger, I'm out of here."

"Just trust the professionals. They know what they're doing."

He circled around to the other side of her. As he pulled the chair away from the table, he looked past her to the living room. A shadow passed in front of the oval inset of the front door.

He tensed, all senses going on high alert. It was too

soon for the police to have arrived, and Andy's meet-
ing would still be going strong.

The doorknob moved a fraction of a turn and back
again. Then the other direction. Someone was trying
the door.

"Nicki."

Though he'd whispered her name, she'd apparently
picked up on the urgency in his voice. She sprang to
her feet, eyes wide. He grabbed her hand and pulled her
further into the kitchen, putting a wall between them
and the front door. A boom split the silence—the thud
of a foot hitting the door, accompanied by the sound of
splintering wood. A fraction of a second later, the door
crashed into the hall tree next to it.

Nicki gasped but didn't scream. As quietly as pos-
sible, Tyler turned the lock and swung open the back
door. If they could make it out before Louie discovered
where they were, they might have a chance at escape. He
hoped Joan would have the presence of mind to stay
hidden in the back.

With Nicki's hand still in his, he darted across the
backyard toward the woods. As they reached the tree
line, a series of shots sounded, and bark splintered,
spraying him in the face.

Explosions sounded around him, a volley of mortar
rounds. Then small arms fire. He spun and dropped to
one knee, reaching for his weapon. It wasn't there. Why
didn't he have his weapon?

Hands clamped down on his shoulders, then shook
him hard. Someone said his name in a harsh whisper.

Nicki.

He pressed his palms to the sides of his head. He
wasn't in Afghanistan. He was in Cedar Key. And if he

and Nicki had any hope of making it through the night alive, he had to hold it together.

Heavy footsteps pounded in the distance, moving closer. He sprang to his feet.

"Run," he hissed. "I'm right behind you."

Louie was much too close. It was only a few seconds, but Tyler had lost them precious time. Thankfully, Nicki had brought him back. Again.

No matter what happened, Nicki would always bring him back.

Renewed determination surged through him. He'd sworn to protect his men. And he'd failed every last one of them. Now he had another vow to keep. The night he'd seen Nicki standing in her drive, shaken over her break-in, he'd sworn to protect her. She meant too much to him to do otherwise.

She was the best friend he'd ever had. But what he felt for her went much deeper than that. He'd loved her then, and he loved her now. Through all their years apart, he'd never stopped.

Whatever it took, tonight he would save Nicki's life.

Even if he had to sacrifice his own.

Nicki ran like she'd never run before, one hand stretched forward in the darkness, the other shielding her eyes against the branches slapping her in the face. Her breath came in heavy gasps, as much from fear as exertion. She didn't dare slow down. Heavy footsteps pounded behind her. She hoped they belonged to Tyler rather than Louie.

She cast a quick glance over her shoulder but couldn't see who was there. Beneath the trees, the darkness was complete. Her sense of direction wasn't the greatest, but if she wasn't too far off, she was probably paralleling 166th Court. Eventually she'd reach the water and have nowhere else to go.

Hopelessness washed through her. Tyler's phone had been lying on the coffee table when they'd run from the house, and hers was in her purse. And Tyler didn't carry a gun. *Lord, please protect us.*

The woods disappeared, and a distant streetlight cast a soft glow over the area. Tyler bounded up beside her. He was stumbling forward, slightly bent at the waist, struggling to take in quick gasps of air. She slowed her pace and cast a frantic glance around, trying to get her bearings. She knew this place. It was the Cedar Key Museum State Park. And it was much too open.

Pulling Tyler with her, she dove under one of the trees separating the parking lot from the museum grounds. If they could make it across to the area north of the buildings, they'd once again have cover.

Tyler put a hand on her shoulder. "Listen."

Other than the gentle rustle of the branches overhead, the dark night was quiet. She shook her head. "I don't hear anything. Maybe we lost him." Now they might have the opportunity to call for help. If they could find someone home. A lot of people headed north for the summer. And for the year-round residents, August was a popular vacation month.

After gesturing for Tyler to follow, she darted through the parking lot toward 121st Lane. The street came off at a sharp backward angle and, though well-shaded, was more densely populated than 166th. But the first several houses were dark.

Staying under cover as much as possible, she jogged through the front yards, Tyler next to her.

In the distance, a motor roared to life. She cast him a sharp glance. Based on the alertness in his eyes, his thoughts were following the same path as hers. If they could reach the boat before its captain headed out, maybe they could get some help.

He held out a hand. "Come on."

She let him lead her between two houses at a full run. Away from the streetlights, the darkness was thicker but not complete. Though the crescent moon she'd seen early that morning wouldn't appear for another several hours, the night sky was awash with stars, their minimal light trickling over the landscape. In front of them, the ground sloped downward to where the yard grasses gave way to marsh. A dock stretched out over the water, a boat tied to it. This one was empty and quiet.

Tyler made a left and ran toward the roar of the motor, pulling her with him. A few houses down, they located it. As they approached, the driver of the boat looked up. Her breath escaped in a rush. It was Wade Tanner.

He froze midway through untying the rear dock line and scanned the landscape behind them. "You guys look like you're running from something."

"We need to call for help." She'd explain later. "Do you have your phone?"

He stood and pulled it from his pocket. Tyler stepped onto the dock to reach for it at the same time a shot rang out. Ten feet away, the ground erupted in a brief fan-shaped spray.

Her heart leaped into her throat. Louie had found them. He was too far away to aim accurately, but he'd have that remedied in moments.

Wade tossed his fishing pole and tackle box onto the dock. "Get in, quick."

Tyler jumped in as Wade shifted into forward. The boat was already starting to move when she stepped in. Tyler grabbed her around the waist to keep her from toppling over the side, and she landed in his lap.

He pushed her to the floor. "Stay down."

She twisted in time to see Wade give the throttle a sharp turn. Instead of rising in volume and pitch, the motor sputtered and fell silent.

Another shot rang out, this one hitting the dock. Wood splinters sprayed into the boat, wrenching a startled scream from her throat. Wade gave the rope two sharp yanks. His efforts were met with the turning of gears, then silence. Louie fired a third shot.

"In the water, quick." Tyler stood, pulling her to her feet and throwing her overboard in one smooth motion. Her knees and feet met the sandy bottom at the same time her head plunged beneath the surface. The water was warm, only about three feet deep even though it was high tide.

The surface wasn't more than six inches below the deck boards of the dock. The frame came down even further. She slipped beneath, and moments later, Tyler, then Wade surfaced beside her.

For what seemed like forever, she crouched in the water, hardly daring to breathe. A tense silence permeated the air, broken only by the gentle sloshing of the waves against the dock posts.

Then there was a heavy footstep, boot against board. Louie had stepped onto the dock. A second footstep followed, and a third. Her blood turned to ice in her veins.

Sirens sounded in the distance, moving closer. Joan

had probably called them. Relief washed through Nicki, but hopelessness doused it immediately. The authorities would never reach them in time.

A shot rang out, accompanied by a splash near the shore. Three more sounded, each splash growing closer. Louie was shooting through the deck boards.

She looked frantically around her, heart pounding out an erratic rhythm. Tyler pressed the side of his face to hers and spoke in the softest whisper. "Duck under and swim. Don't come up until you absolutely have to."

She sucked in a huge gulp of air, dropped as close to the sandy bottom as she could and propelled herself through the water with short kicks and wide sweeps of her arms. Would Louie be able to see her movement in the dim starlight? Or would the relative darkness conceal her?

She continued to swim, each stroke taking her farther from danger. The urge to breathe became almost overwhelming. She needed air. Fear pumped through her with every beat of her heart, using up the oxygen even faster. Her lungs burned, and she willed herself to not breathe. Just a little farther.

Finally she turned and surfaced as quietly as she could, resisting the urge to burst from the water. She drew in huge gulps of air, her gasps sounding amplified in the quiet night air.

Louie stood in the center of the dock some distance away, little more than a menacing shadow in the semi-darkness. With pistol raised, he spun in her direction. As she dipped back beneath the surface, he fired off three more rounds, their muffled sounds reaching her through the water.

She changed the angle of her path. Louie couldn't see her. Otherwise he'd have hit her by now.

But what about Tyler and Wade? Worry tightened her gut. In the brief moments after she'd surfaced, she hadn't seen them. If anything happened to either of them, she'd never forgive herself.

No, they had to be swimming, the same as she was. If Louie had shot them, they'd be lying on the beach or floating on the surface of the water. *God, please keep them safe. And please let the police get here in time.*

She knew they were nearby. She'd heard the sirens. But they'd have gone to Andy and Joan's. Unless someone else had called to report gunshots.

She surfaced again, and almost immediately, a shot sounded. The resulting splash a foot away sent a surge of adrenaline through her. She ducked back beneath and lunged sideways. Louie fired two more shots, and she swam, praying the panicked half breath she'd taken would somehow last.

When she surfaced the third time, her heart almost stopped. Tyler had stepped onto the dock and crept toward Louie. Wade was in the yard a little further back, moving in their direction. Louie obviously hadn't seen either of them.

His attention was on her.

He leveled the weapon, and she gasped. But before she could duck beneath the surface, Tyler called out and broke into a full run. Louie spun, pulling the trigger as he turned, and Wade fell to his knees on the grass.

Dear God, no, not Wade. They should never have involved him.

The next second, Tyler plowed into Louie, knocking

him to the dock. The gun hit the boards and tumbled to a stop a few feet from the end.

Louie roared, then threw Tyler off him. Tyler hit the boards with a thud and an audible grunt. When Louie rose and lunged for his weapon, Tyler grabbed his ankles and jerked his legs from under him. Louie landed facedown and released a string of curses.

For a brief moment, Tyler looked past Louie. His eyes locked with hers, and she knew what she had to do. She stumbled through the waist-deep water, making her way toward the dock. Tyler would fight with everything in him to protect her. But Louie was a formidable foe. And if Tyler couldn't keep him from getting his hands on that weapon, he'd gun her down in the water without a moment's hesitation.

Louie pushed himself to his feet and faced his opponent. He wore the same attire she remembered, cutoff jean shorts and a wifebeater shirt. He stood with clenched fists, muscles rippling beneath the tattoos covering his arms and chest. Although he'd lost some of his girth, everything left was solid steel.

He let out a bellow of rage and swung one meaty fist at Tyler's face. Tyler twisted to avoid it, then countered with his own punch. It connected with Louie's nose. Tyler wasn't as big as Louie, but all those years of military physical training showed. Louie released another bellow, then shook his head. Blood and sweat sprayed from his face in an arc.

Nicki crept closer, moving silently through the water. She approached at an angle, with Tyler facing her more fully than Louie. Unless Louie turned, she might be able to approach the dock undetected.

And get the gun.

Once she got it, she wasn't sure what she'd do with it. Other than one target practice session with a long-ago ex-boyfriend, she'd never held a gun.

On the dock, Tyler aimed a volley of punches at Louie's face. Louie managed to block half of them. The other half didn't have nearly the effect they should have had. A lesser man would have been facedown on the deck boards.

When Louie's next punch connected with Tyler's jaw, she had to clamp a hand over her mouth to keep from crying out. The two men exchanged several more punches, until both of their faces were battered and bleeding.

Suddenly Louie slammed into Tyler, knocking him to the dock and landing on top of him. Several moments passed.

Come on, Tyler. Get up.

Instead, he rolled his head side to side as if trying to clear it. With no chance to break his fall, he'd hit it hard.

Fight, Tyler, just a little longer. She reached the end of the dock, then moved along its side. Louie rose to his knees, made a fist and slammed it into Tyler's temple.

What hitting his head on the dock hadn't done, that final punch had. Tyler's eyes closed and his body went limp.

Nicki released a strangled cry. Louie turned, his gaze settling on her, then shifting to the gun. He rose and lunged for it at the same time she grabbed it.

It was heavier than it looked—cold and hard and lethal. And it felt foreign in her hands. She clutched the handle in her right hand, then wrapped her left around it, palm up. If she could at least *look* like she knew what she was doing, Louie would be less likely to attack her.

She backed away, putting some distance between them. Louie stepped to the edge of the dock.

"You won't shoot me."

Confidence oozed from him, the same cockiness she'd observed as a child. He lowered himself to the dock, letting his legs dangle in the water. "You're not a killer. You don't have it in you."

She continued to back up. Louie was right. She wasn't a killer.

But what if the only choices were to kill or be killed? Could she do it then? Tyler had killed. Numerous times.

Louie slid into the water and moved toward her. Her pulse jumped to double-time, her heart threatening to beat out of her chest. Her hands shook, betraying her fear.

Louie's eyes dipped to the barrel of the gun, which seemed to have developed a mind of its own. It waved up and down and side to side.

The edges of his mouth curled up in a wicked grin. "See? You can't do it. Give me the gun, Nicki, and everything will be all right. I won't hurt you."

It was the same promise he'd made that night after killing her mother. Unlock the door and everything would be all right. She didn't believe it then, and she didn't believe it now.

She gripped the gun more tightly.

"One more step, and I'll shoot." The strength in her tone surprised her.

Louie's brows shot up, and for several moments he stood motionless. Then he laughed, an evil, menacing sound. "No, you won't."

She rested her finger on the trigger, poised and waiting. Louie had said she wasn't a killer. She wasn't. But she wasn't a victim, either. Not anymore.

Louie took a step. A deafening *pow* reverberated through the air, and the gun kicked, throwing her arms upward. A scream shot up her throat, and her hands opened. The weapon fell into the water with a splash.

Louie stood about ten feet in front of her, mouth agape, hands clutching his stomach. Blood seeped between his fingers. He dropped to his knees, then fell forward, face in the water.

Nicki gasped and took a step toward him. If she didn't do something, he was going to drown.

And the world would be a better place.

No, she couldn't do it. Pulling the trigger in self-defense was one thing. Letting him drown when she was standing ten feet away was another. She closed the distance between them.

Movement in her peripheral vision drew her attention. Four figures were running toward the shoreline—two officers in uniform and Hunter and Amber in plain clothes.

Another siren split the silence, increased in volume, then stopped. When she reached Louie, she grasped his shoulders and lifted his face out of the water. The next moment, his hand came up and clamped around her throat. Panic shot through her, and she struggled to take in a breath through her constricted windpipe. When she tried to pry his fingers from her neck, he squeezed harder. Her head pounded and her ears began to ring. Blackness encroached from all sides.

Suddenly Louie's hand relaxed, and he fell forward. Her knees buckled as Hunter reached her.

He looped an arm around her waist. "Whoa, steady. Are you all right?"

"I'm fine." Her voice was little more than a croak. "Wade needs help. He's been shot."

"They're already attending to him."

She looked toward the shore, where two paramedics knelt on either side of him. She breathed a sigh of relief. *Lord, please let him be all right.*

"And Tyler's hurt."

As if in response, a moan came from the dock. She waded over and climbed onto the wooden structure. Tyler still lay on his back with his eyes closed. His lower lip was swollen and split open, and caked blood had dried in several places on his face.

She put a hand on his chest. "Tyler?"

He moaned again, and one eye fluttered open. The other was too badly swollen.

"It's over. Louie is—" What, injured? Dead? Someone had dragged him from the water and laid him on the beach. Two more paramedics had arrived and were working on him.

Conflicting emotions tumbled through her. If Louie survived, she'd live with the knowledge that someone out there wanted her dead. If he died, it would be at her hand. Neither was a good option.

Tyler's good eye closed. "Louie is what?"

On the shore, one of the paramedics shook his head and they both rose. In that moment, all she felt was relief.

She took Tyler's hand and squeezed it. "He'll never be a threat to anyone again."

THIRTEEN

Tyler clawed his way to consciousness, the sounds of explosions still ringing in his ears. It was only a nightmare. He was no longer in Afghanistan. But where was he?

Near his head, something emitted rhythmic beeps. Like medical equipment in a hospital. That was it. He'd been injured and they'd flown him to Landstuhl, Germany.

There was more, but remembering required too much effort. He tried to open his eyes. They refused to cooperate. He was drifting, floating.

The telltale whistle of a mortar round blazed a path through his mind, jarring him back to semiconsciousness.

Burns. He'd been burned. His right shoulder and the upper part of his back. He remembered now. There would be weeks of skin grafts. The doctor had already warned him.

The doctor at Brooke Army Medical Center. He wasn't in Germany. He was back stateside, Fort Sam Houston, Texas.

The grafts were going to be painful. Burns were always painful. He'd deal with it.

But the pain he'd prepared himself for wasn't there. At least, it wasn't in his shoulder and back. Instead, he had the granddaddy of all headaches. And he felt as if he'd tried to dive face-first through a slab of concrete. What was going on?

He tried again to open his eyes. This time he was successful. With one eye, anyway. The other was glued shut. His mouth didn't feel right, either. His jaw was stiff, his lips dry. When he ran his tongue over them, the lower one seemed huge.

He rolled his head to the side. Someone sat in the corner, curled up in the chair, sleeping. A woman. Her head rested on the arm of the chair, and her knees were drawn up to her chest. Bright auburn hair had fallen over her face, hiding most of it from view.

Nicki.

The fogginess cleared in an instant, and memories of the past days' events flooded his mind. He reached for the control to raise the top part of his bed. The gentle hum joined the other sounds of the room.

Nicki sat up, sweeping her hair out of her face and tucking it behind her ear. Her eyes widened. They held relief tinged with concern. A slow smile climbed up her cheeks.

"You're awake." She swung both feet to the floor and stood to approach him. "How do you feel?"

"Like I've been used as a punching bag."

"I think you have." The smile faded and she took his hand. "You saved my life. If you hadn't tackled Louie when you did, he'd have shot me."

"When I saw him take aim, I almost had a heart attack. All I could think about was that I was going to lose you." And for the first time in twelve years, he'd prayed. No bargains or promises this time. Just heartfelt pleas for protection for Nicki and strength and success for himself. And God had answered.

He pressed his free hand to the side of his head and winced. "How's Wade?"

"The bullet lodged in his right lung. He was in surgery a couple of hours, but he's going to be all right."

She lowered her head. "I feel terrible. We should never have involved him. All I wanted to do was borrow his phone. Instead, I ended up getting him shot."

"It wasn't your fault. All the blame is with Louie." He shifted position and winced again. His head and face weren't the only places that hurt. He was probably going to be finding muscles he didn't know he had for the next three weeks.

"Speaking of Louie, what happened to him?"

"Dead."

He raised his brows. "How did that happen? The last thing I remember is having my head slammed into the dock and everything going black. I think there might have been another punch in there, too."

"There was." She gave him a sympathetic smile. "After you were knocked out, I grabbed the gun. I warned him, but he came after me anyway."

Pride swelled inside him, but he didn't congratulate her. Too often, victory didn't feel so good. "Are you all right?"

She nodded a little too quickly.

"Having killed someone isn't an easy thing to live with. Trust me, I know." It was likely to haunt her for years to come. "If you ever need to talk about it, you know where to find me."

"Thanks."

He closed his eyes. "My head feels like it's stuffed full of cotton. I think my brain is firing on only two cylinders."

"You have a concussion and lots of bruises, but fortunately, nothing's broken."

"You couldn't prove it by me." He shifted to get more comfortable, then gave up. "It looks like Andy might be finishing the renovations on his own. We were only a few days from having it complete."

She nodded. Sadness seemed to emanate from her. "What are your plans once you've mended?"

He searched her face. Did she want him to stay? He couldn't tell. Her eyes were shielded, fixed on their joined hands.

No, she'd already answered all his silent questions at the park. Whatever she felt for him, and he was sure it had deepened over the past few weeks, she wasn't willing to sacrifice their friendship to explore it.

And if that was all she wanted, that was what he'd take. But it would have to be long-distance. Being with her every day, hearing her sparkling laughter as she played with Callie, seeing her crooked half smile when she teased him, all her little quirks—it would be pure torture. And he'd had enough of that in his life.

"I guess I'll be heading out again." He pivoted his head to stare at the darkened TV screen on the opposite wall. *Please say you want me to stay.*

But she was silent, except for the small sigh that escaped her mouth. Was it disappointment?

No, it was likely relief. She probably didn't want to deal with his problems. And he couldn't blame her. The nightmares and flashbacks, never knowing when he might get violent or lose it in public—no one deserved to be saddled with all that.

She gave him a slow nod, the movement drawing his gaze back to her face.

"Where will you go?"

"I'm thinking about Montana this time." At least, as of two seconds ago. Until that moment, he'd avoided all thoughts of leaving her. He gave her a half-hearted smile. "Big Sky Country."

"Montana is awfully cold."

He shrugged. "Maybe I'll leave again before the snow sets in."

Before answering, she swallowed hard. "This time we need to do a better job of staying in touch."

"I agree. I'm not sure what happened last time."

One side of her mouth lifted. "I think you dropped the ball."

"I think it was you."

"Maybe it wasn't either of us. That final letter might be trapped in some crevice in the back corner of the Atlanta post office, covered in dust."

He smiled, then let it fade. "No excuses this time."

She nodded. "Not with texting."

"And Facebook. We need to be friends." He squeezed her hand. "I don't want to lose you again, Nicki."

She nodded again, but this time the motion was jerky. "I'm going to let you get some rest." She pulled her hand from his grasp. "I promised I'd try to come in to work this afternoon."

He watched her walk from the room, then lay his head back against the pillow and closed his eyes.

Leaving was the right thing to do. It just wasn't easy. But often the right thing wasn't.

Footsteps sounded outside his door, and he opened his eyes in time to see Andy walk into the room.

"It's good to see you awake. How do you feel?"

Tyler stifled a moan. "Ask me in a few days."

"Pretty bad, huh? You don't look so hot, either."

He started to lift a brow, then stopped. Even that small motion hurt.

Andy moved the chair closer to the hospital bed and sank into it. "I met Nicki getting off the elevator. What did you say to her?"

"Nothing."

"Don't give me that. She was crying. What did you do?"

Annoyance surged through him. He didn't need his big brother meddling in his affairs.

"I told her we were almost done with the renovations, and once I got out of here I'd be leaving." He glared at Andy. "Nothing that's any concern of yours."

Andy shook his head. "When are you going to stop running? You've found a good woman who's crazy about you, and you're ready to throw it all away. For what?"

"I'm not throwing anything away. We're friends. That's all. And wherever I go, we'll still be friends."

"You're an idiot."

"Thanks, bro. I love you, too."

Andy heaved a sigh. "Maybe you and Nicki *are* just friends. But you're not satisfied with that. I recognized it almost from your first day here."

"It doesn't matter what I want."

"What about what Nicki wants? Aren't her wishes

important enough for you to get your act together and settle down?"

Tyler crossed his arms over his chest. "Look, if you came here to beat me up, you can go back home."

"Okay, I'll drop it for now. But this isn't over."

Yeah, it was over, whether Andy wanted it to be or not. Before Tyler could say as much, a nurse entered the room.

"I see you decided to join the land of the living. How do you feel?"

"Like I've been run over by a truck."

She checked his vitals, made a few notes on the clipboard she carried, then added something to his IV.

"There. That should have you feeling better soon."

He closed his eyes and let the medicine do its work. Already the edge of his pain seemed a little duller.

He drew in a deep breath and let it out slowly. Nicki had so much to overcome—the memories of her mother's murder, the fact that her own sister tried to kill her, the terror of being pursued by Louie, his death at her hands. Whatever she needed, he'd always be there for her. As a friend. Asking to be anything more wouldn't be fair to Nicki.

She'd had her share of users and losers. But someday, someone would come along who would value her uniqueness. Who would be awed by her beauty, both inside and out. Who would appreciate her toughness but be sensitive to her vulnerability.

Who would love her the way he did.

The pain that pierced his heart almost took his breath away. He clenched one fist and put it over his chest.

The monitor beeped and the IV dripped fluids into his veins, but the pain refused to abate.

Unfortunately, this was the type for which the doctors had no cure.

Nicki jammed the spade into the dirt and grasped a weed with her left hand. After a couple of gentle tugs, the roots slid free of the ground holding them, and she tossed the plant onto the growing pile next to her.

They were Joan and Andy's weeds, not hers. Her own flower beds were in pretty bad shape, between neglect and too much foot traffic over recent weeks.

She cast a glance in that direction. The carport side of her house was still a burned-out shell, but renovations would be starting soon. She'd settled on a contractor, and the insurance company had approved his quote. Once all the work was done, she'd tackle beautifying the yard.

But today, she was focused on repaying Joan and Andy for some of their kindness. And avoiding Tyler.

He was inside packing, getting ready to head for parts unknown. She had no choice in letting him go, but she didn't have to watch him make the preparations.

She focused her attention on the task in front of her and attacked the weeds with renewed vigor. The doctor had discharged Tyler yesterday. She'd visited him several times over the past few days. There'd been no talk of future plans for either of them. He'd kept his conversation casual and so had she. But an undercurrent of tension had run between them.

What happened to the easy camaraderie they'd shared all those years ago? It almost felt as if they were strangers. Or former friends with too many hurts between them to move past.

At some point over the prior weeks, their friendship had morphed into something else. And now she was kicking herself. She'd done it again. Four months out of one failed relationship and she was running headlong toward another dead end. But unlike several of her exes, Tyler wasn't a user *or* a loser. He was just afraid to commit. Of course, she'd had more than her fair share of those, too.

She moved over a couple of feet, then sat back on her heels, ready to tackle the next section. Letting herself feel anything deeper for Tyler than friendship had been stupid. But what she felt wasn't one-sided. The kiss at Fanning Springs had proved it.

And she'd stopped it. She'd been too afraid to explore this new spark between them, scared that if it didn't work out, their relationship would be ruined.

But the damage was already done. They'd crossed that line from friend to something else, then tried to step back over it again. What they were left with was neither.

Now Tyler was leaving.

The front door opened, then shut, and she stopped her work long enough to watch him load his bags into the passenger side of his pickup. He circled back around to the driver's side, then stopped to face her.

"I guess that's it. We'll stay in touch, right?" His tone was hesitant.

"Sure." She pushed herself to her feet, spade still in her hand. Should she go hug him? Not unless he initiated it. After all, he was the one leaving, not her.

He shifted his weight to the other foot but made no

move to open the door. He seemed troubled. Lost. And her heart broke.

She wasn't the only one with fears. Tyler, who'd faced down the enemy, boldly served his country and survived three tours of duty, never knowing whether each minute would be his last, had fears, too. And when everything got to be too much, he pulled up roots and ran.

The first time he'd left her, he hadn't had a choice. Now he did. When faced with the thought of settling down and letting someone close enough to share his traumas, he was choosing the easy way out.

Well, not without a fight.

She dropped the spade and stalked toward him, then stopped with her back against his closed driver's side door. She crossed her arms and glared up at him.

He raised his brows. "What are you doing?"

"When are you going to stop running?"

His jaw tightened. "What, have you been talking to my brother?"

"I haven't needed to. Do you think I don't know what you're doing? Just when you get settled in somewhere and start getting close to the people around you, you take off again. You're so afraid someone's going to see past that tough exterior of yours. Well, too late. I already have."

He matched her stance, arms crossed, legs shoulder-width apart. "I'd planned to stay only until the work on the inn was finished. You knew that from the start. Nothing's changed."

No, nothing had changed, yet everything had. They'd spent almost every spare moment together since he arrived. They'd shared their fears and fought for their lives. Now she was in love with him.

But she wasn't going to beg him to stay. She uncrossed her arms and let them fall to her sides. "All right, then. Go." She stepped away from the truck and opened the door. "Keep on running. What you're hiding from is always going to find you."

He made no move to get into truck, just stood there watching her. Indecision flashed in his eyes, and a muscle twitched in the side of his jaw.

"Well?" she prodded him.

"You're asking me to stay."

"I want to be there for you, Tyler, as a friend and more, if you'll let me."

He closed his eyes and clenched his fists. His jaw was still tight, further evidence of the struggle going on inside him.

He sighed and once again met her gaze. "I have nightmares."

"So do I."

"Mine are dangerous. You've experienced that firsthand."

"I think I can handle it."

"You've been through so much—your mother's murder, foster care, the death of your adoptive parents. Your sister, then Louie." He shook his head. "You need someone stable."

Her heart fell. "So I'm good enough for friendship, but not anything more."

"That's not what I mean." He slipped his keys into his jeans pocket, then took both of her hands. "I care for you too much to saddle you with my issues."

His touch was reassuring, his hands calloused, strong

but gentle. Like the man. "Sometimes the best way to take your mind off your own problems is to help someone else with theirs."

Without releasing her hands, he stepped closer, until she had to tilt her head backward to look at him. His face was inches from hers.

"Do you know what you're getting yourself into?" His voice was the softest whisper, his breath warm against her lips.

"I think I have a pretty good idea." Her tone matched his, low and smooth, belying the turmoil inside her. If they hadn't passed the point of no return before, they were getting ready to now.

He leaned closer, and her eyes drifted closed. His lips met hers, gentle at first, tentative, testing. She didn't pull away. He deepened the kiss, and she still didn't pull away.

All her fears and past mistakes faded into the background, and a whole world of new possibilities opened before her. There was no cause for concern, no reason to hold back.

Because this was Tyler. Her best friend. The one who was there through those troubled early teenage years and would be there for whatever lay ahead.

The one who knew her better than anyone in the world.

And he loved her anyway.

EPILOGUE

Nicki walked along the raised dirt trail, Tyler's hand in hers. A gentle breeze rustled the trees around them, but otherwise, the late August morning was silent.

She drew in a clean breath. The air was hot and humid. Maybe it would help warm some of the chill that had settled inside her the moment she stepped out of Tyler's truck.

Though she loved the old Railroad Trestle Nature Trail, she hadn't walked it since that day with Jenny. She'd tried. Several times she'd parked her truck at the trailhead, then turned around and gone home without even stepping out. Once she'd gotten as far as the large sign at the entrance. She'd stood there and read every word. She'd learned the history of the Cedar Key Railroad but hadn't been able to bring herself to step through the open gate.

Today she was going to walk it. The whole thing. She couldn't preach to Tyler the importance of facing his fears if she wasn't willing to do it herself. But she didn't have to do it alone.

She smiled up at Tyler. Behind the mangroves to her right, sunlight glistened on the surface of the water.

On her other side, marsh grasses filled a small clearing. Callie and Sasha trotted ahead of them.

Almost three weeks had passed since Louie had pursued them through the woods. She was still living with Joan and Andy, but the work on her house was progressing nicely.

And the inn was completed, furnished and scheduled to open next weekend. They were going to open with a bang—every room was booked. Of course, it was Labor Day weekend. But according to Andy, the coming weeks didn't look too shabby, either.

Tyler smiled down at her. "I'm enjoying my last weekend off for a while."

"Me, too." Saturdays together were going to come to a screeching halt.

Although the renovation work was done, Paradise Inn was going to be a true family venture. Andy was the owner and manager, Joan would handle housekeeping, and Tyler would be in charge of maintenance and whatever else needed to be done to keep things running smoothly.

Up ahead, the branches of a red cedar arched over the trail. Nicki recognized the spot immediately. Strength drained from her limbs, leaving behind a watery weakness. Tyler, always sensitive to her moods, squeezed her hand.

"Right there under that tree is where Jenny attacked me."

She shuddered, and Tyler released her hand to wrap his arm around her. Her life had almost ended that day. As she'd lain bleeding on the sandy trail, her knife-wielding sister on top of her, she'd been sure she was going to die the same way her mother had.

"I'm ready to go home now." She'd revisited this place too often in her dreams over the past few weeks. Why go there now, when she was fully awake and had a choice? "Callie, come." The dog walked toward her, enthusiasm dampened.

Tyler turned her to face him, resting both hands on her shoulders. "You love this place. Are you going to let Jenny take that away from you?"

She drew in a shaky breath. Tyler was right. Several times she had walked the trail with her sketch pad and a fold-up camp chair, then sat at its end, overlooking the water and mangroves. There was no reason to not go back to those peaceful outings. Jenny was in jail, where she'd maybe get the help she needed. And Louie was dead.

"All right." She put her hand in his. She could do this with Tyler next to her.

He flashed her an encouraging smile. "That's my girl." He began walking, leading her down the trail. "You're a fighter. Always have been."

As they passed under the cedar, she scanned the ground. There was no sign of what had happened there four weeks earlier. Not that she'd expected there to be. Any scuff marks in the dirt would have long since been washed away by the summertime rains. So would any bloodstains.

When they reached the end of the trail, the breeze that had rustled the trees around them blew wisps of hair into her face. She tucked them behind her ear and looked out over the water to the mangrove-lined shore beyond. Sasha and Callie occupied themselves with sniffing their surroundings, and Tyler stepped up beside her. There wasn't another soul in any direction. A blanket of tranquility lay over the landscape, wrapping her in a soothing embrace.

She smiled up at him. "Thank you."

"For what?"

"For making me come out here. Sometimes the best way to banish bad memories is to make new ones. Happy ones."

He took both of her hands in his. "I'm planning to make lots of happy memories with you."

She cocked a brow at him. "That sounds kind of permanent." Though he hadn't talked of leaving since that day in Andy's driveway, he hadn't talked long-term, either. They'd spent every spare moment together. He'd gone to church with her, listened to her stories and shared his own. But she still sensed he was taking life one day at a time.

"It does sound permanent. But that's my intention." He drew her into his arms. "When I was a scrawny fifteen-year-old, angry at the world, you reached out to me. You listened to all my ranting and were always there for me. I loved you back then, and I love you now more than ever."

Nicki swallowed hard. This wasn't the first time he'd said he loved her. Over the past two weeks, he'd told her several times. And she'd told him. But something was different this time. There was a solemnness in his gaze as if he was preparing for an important announcement.

Her stomach turned several flips, and her heart started to pound. She waited for him to continue.

"A life with me won't be easy, but I'm pretty sure you know what you're in for. Do you think you can put up with me?" He gave her a crooked smile.

Her heart pounded harder. "If you can put up with me."

"I don't think that will be a problem." He squeezed her hands. "I know you've had a lot of bad experiences with men, and they've made you apprehensive. I'm not perfect. I've got a lot of faults. But I love you with all my heart, and I'd never intentionally do anything to hurt you." He squeezed her hands. "Nicki, will you marry me?"

Her mouth went dry and her heart skipped a beat. It was her second marriage proposal in a year. She'd accepted the first one, and look where it had gotten her.

When Tyler showed up, she hadn't been looking for a relationship. In fact, she'd sworn off men unless God plopped one in her lap.

Tyler didn't exactly land in her lap, but his appearance was just as sudden and unexpected.

"Nicki?"

Concern had crept into his eyes. She'd waited too long.

She pulled her hands from his grasp to wrap her arms around his neck. Committing to marrying Tyler wouldn't be repeating past mistakes. There were no secrets between them. And there would be no surprises.

"Yes, I'll marry you."

Relief flooded his face, then pure joy. His arms went around her waist, and he pulled her to him. Then he kissed her long and deep, proving anew his love and devotion.

And all her hesitation, each concern, every doubt floated away on the salt-scented breeze.

* * * * *

If you enjoyed this exciting story of
suspense and intrigue, pick up
these other stories from Carol J. Post:

MIDNIGHT SHADOWS
MOTIVE FOR MURDER
OUT FOR JUSTICE
SHATTERED HAVEN
HIDDEN IDENTITY
MISTLETOE JUSTICE

Available now from Love Inspired Suspense!

Find more great reads at www.LoveInspired.com.

Dear Reader,

Thank you for joining me for another trip back to Cedar Key. It's one of our favorite vacation spots, with its quaint, artsy atmosphere and friendly people. Doing research on this series has been a pleasure.

Nicki and Tyler were fun characters for me to write. After a traumatic early childhood and two years in foster care, Nicki had developed a toughness that often kept her from connecting with others. And Tyler had his own issues to overcome. Like so many of our servicemen who see combat, he brought many of the traumas of war home with him, both physically and emotionally. Neither Tyler nor Nicki was able to begin the path of healing until they decided to open their hearts to love—each other's and God's.

I hope you'll drop me a line. I love to connect with my readers. You can find me on Facebook (facebook .com/caroljpost.author), Twitter (@caroljpost), my website (caroljpost.com) and email (caroljpost@gmail.com). For news and fun contests, join my newsletter mailing list. The link is on my website. I promise I won't sell your info or spam you!

God bless you!
Carol

REQUEST YOUR FREE BOOKS!

2 FREE RIVETING INSPIRATIONAL NOVELS
PLUS 2 FREE MYSTERY GIFTS

Love Inspired
SUSPENSE
RIVETING INSPIRATIONAL ROMANCE

YES! Please send me 2 FREE Love Inspired® Suspense novels and my 2 FREE mystery gifts (gifts are worth about $10). After receiving them, if I don't wish to receive any more books, I can return the shipping statement marked "cancel." If I don't cancel, I will receive 4 brand-new novels every month and be billed just $4.99 per book in the U.S. or $5.49 per book in Canada. That's a savings of at least 17% off the cover price. It's quite a bargain! Shipping and handling is just 50¢ per book in the U.S. and 75¢ per book in Canada.* I understand that accepting the 2 free books and gifts places me under no obligation to buy anything. I can always return a shipment and cancel at any time. Even if I never buy another book, the two free books and gifts are mine to keep forever.

123/323 IDN GH5Z

Name	(PLEASE PRINT)	
Address		Apt. #
City	State/Prov.	Zip/Postal Code

Signature (if under 18, a parent or guardian must sign)

Mail to the **Reader Service:**
IN U.S.A.: P.O. Box 1867, Buffalo, NY 14240-1867
IN CANADA: P.O. Box 609, Fort Erie, Ontario L2A 5X3

**Are you a current subscriber to Love Inspired® Suspense books
and want to receive the larger-print edition?
Call 1-800-873-8635 or visit www.ReaderService.com.**

* Terms and prices subject to change without notice. Prices do not include applicable taxes. Sales tax applicable in N.Y. Canadian residents will be charged applicable taxes. Offer not valid in Quebec. This offer is limited to one order per household. Not valid for current subscribers to Love Inspired Suspense books. All orders subject to credit approval. Credit or debit balances in a customer's account(s) may be offset by any other outstanding balance owed by or to the customer. Please allow 4 to 6 weeks for delivery. Offer available while quantities last.

Your Privacy—The Reader Service is committed to protecting your privacy. Our Privacy Policy is available online at www.ReaderService.com or upon request from the Reader Service.
We make a portion of our mailing list available to reputable third parties that offer products we believe may interest you. If you prefer that we not exchange your name with third parties, or if you wish to clarify or modify your communication preferences, please visit us at www.ReaderService.com/consumerschoice or write to us at Reader Service Preference Service, P.O. Box 9062, Buffalo, NY 14240-9062. Include your complete name and address.

LIS15

"I looked up the license plate of the black sedan from the restaurant," Miles said, his expression grim. "The sedan is registered to Sci-Tech."

"They sent gunmen after us?" Paige asked in a strained whisper.

"Yeah, that's what it looks like."

"They're after me because of my ex-husband, aren't they?"

"I think so, yes." Miles reached over and cradled her icy hands in his. "I'm sorry."

Paige gripped his hands tightly. "You have to find Travis before it's too late."

He didn't want to point out that it might already be too late. Whatever Abby had seen on the tablet had frightened her to the point she wouldn't speak. Had Travis told her to keep quiet? Or had she seen something horrible? He found himself hoping for the first option, but feared the latter.

"I'm not sure where to look for Travis," he admitted. "There's no way to know where he'd go to hide if he thought he was in danger."

"Did you give the police the list of names I gave you?" Paige asked. "I know they're only a few names, but…"

"I've been searching on their names, but I haven't found anything yet. At least we have another link to Sci-Tech. No wonder they were stonewalling me."

"I might be able to get inside the building," Paige offered.

"No." His knee-jerk reaction surprised him, and he tried to backpedal. "I mean, if they're the ones behind this, then it's not safe for you to go there. Besides, how would you get in?"

She lifted her uncertain gaze to his. "I know a couple of the security guards pretty well. If I waited until after-hours, when there's only one security guard manning the desk, I might be able to convince them to let me in."

"I know you want to help, but it's not worth the risk." He couldn't stand the idea of Paige walking into the equivalent of the lion's den. "You don't know for sure which security guard would be on duty. And besides, if anything happened—Abby would be lost without you."

She blinked, and he thought he saw the glint of tears. "Logically, I know you're right, but it's hard to sit back and do nothing, not even trying."

"I'll find a way to do something while keeping you and Abby safe." He couldn't stand the thought of her worrying about things she couldn't change. He'd protect her, no matter what.

Don't miss
THE ONLY WITNESS
by Laura Scott, available February 2017 wherever
Love Inspired® Suspense books and ebooks are sold.

www.LoveInspired.com

*Discovering he has a two-year-old son is a huge
surprise for veterinarian Wyatt Harrow. But so are his
lingering feelings for the boy's pretty mom…*

Read on for a sneak preview
of the fifth book in the
LONE STAR COWBOY LEAGUE: BOYS RANCH
miniseries, *THE DOCTOR'S TEXAS BABY*
by *Deb Kastner*.

Wyatt glanced at Carolina, but she wouldn't meet his
eyes.

Was she feeling guilty over all Matty's firsts that she'd
denied Wyatt? First breath, first word, the first step Matty
took?

He couldn't say he felt sorry for her. She should be
feeling guilty. She'd made the decision to walk away.
She'd created these consequences for herself, and for
Wyatt, and most of all, for Matty.

But today wasn't a day for anger. Today was about
spending time with his son.

"What do you say, little man?" he asked, scooping
Matty into his arms and leading Carolina to his truck.
"Do you want to play ball?"

Not knowing what Matty would like, he'd pretty
much loaded up every kind of sports ball imaginable—a
football, a baseball, a soccer ball and a basketball.

Carolina flashed him half a smile and shrugged
apologetically. "I'm afraid I don't know much about

these games beyond being able to identify which ball goes with which sport."

"That's what Matty's got a dad for."

He didn't really think about what he was saying until the words had already left his lips.

Their gazes met and locked. She was silently challenging him, but he didn't know about what. Still, he kept his gaze firmly on hers. His words might not have been premeditated, but that didn't make them any less true. He was sorry if he'd hurt her feelings, though. He wanted to keep things friendly between them.

"There's plenty of room on the green for three. What do you say? Do you want to play soccer with us?"

Shock registered in her face, but it was no more than what he was feeling. This was all so new. Untested waters.

Somehow, they had to work things out, but kicking a ball around together at the park?

Why, that almost felt as if they were a family.

And although in a sense that was technically true, Wyatt didn't even want to go down that road.

He had every intention of being the best father he could to Matty. And in so doing, he would establish some sort of a working relationship with Carolina, some way they could both be comfortable without it getting awkward. He just couldn't bring himself to think about that right now.

Or maybe he just didn't want to.

Don't miss
THE DOCTOR'S TEXAS BABY
by Deb Kastner, available February 2017
wherever Love Inspired® books and ebooks are sold.

www.LoveInspired.com

LIEXP0117

Turn your love of reading into rewards you'll love with
Harlequin My Rewards

**Join for FREE today at
www.HarlequinMyRewards.com**

Earn **FREE BOOKS** of your choice.

Experience **EXCLUSIVE OFFERS** and contests.

Enjoy **BOOK RECOMMENDATIONS**
selected just for you.

PLUS! Sign up now
and get **500** points
right away!

Earn
FREE
REWARDS
Join
Today!
HarlequinMyRewards.com

MYR16R